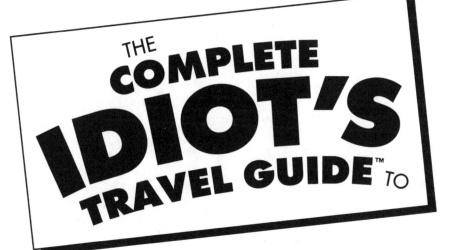

Boston

by Marie Morris

Macmillan Travel USA
A Pearson Education Macmillan Company
1633 Broadway,
New York NY 10019

MACMILLAN is a registered trademark of Macmillan, Inc.
FROMMER'S is a registered trademark of Arthur Frommer. Used under license.
THE COMPLETE IDIOT'S TRAVEL GUIDE name and design are trademarks of Macmillan, Inc.

ISBN 0-02-862912-4
ISSN 1520-5622

Editor: Bob O'Sullivan
Production Editor: Michael Thomas
Design by designLab
Page Layout: Carrie Allen, Melissa Auciello-Brogan, Laura Goetz, David Pruett, Linda Quigley
Staff Cartographers: John DeCamillas, Roberta Stockwell
Additional Cartography: Raffaele Degennaro, Ortelius Design
Illustrations by Kevin Spear

Special Sales

Bulk purchases (10+ copies) of Frommer's and selected Macmillan travel guides are available to corporations, organizations, mail-order catalogs, institutions, and charities at special discounts, and can be customized to suit individual needs. For more information write to Special Sales, Macmillan General Reference, 1633 Broadway, New York, NY 10019.

Manufactured in the United States of America

Contents

v

Maps

About the Author
Marie Morris is a native New Yorker, and a graduate of Harvard College, where she studied history. She has worked for the *New York Times, Boston* magazine, and the *Boston Herald*, and she covers Boston for a number of *Frommer's* travel guides. She lives in Boston, not far from Paul Revere.

An Invitation to the Reader
In researching this book, we discovered many wonderful places—hotels, restaurants, shops, and more. We're sure you'll find others. Please tell us about them, so we can share the information with your fellow travelers in upcoming editions. If you were disappointed with a recommendation, we'd love to know that, too. Please write to

The Complete Idiot's Travel Guide to Boston
Macmillan Travel
1633 Broadway
New York, NY 10019

An Additional Note
Please be advised that travel information is subject to change at any time—and this is especially true of prices. We therefore suggest that you write or call ahead for confirmation when making your travel plans. The authors, editors, and publisher cannot be held responsible for the experiences of readers while traveling. Your safety is important to us, however, so we encourage you to stay alert and be aware of your surroundings. Keep a close eye on cameras, purses, and wallets, all favorite targets of thieves and pickpockets.

The following abbreviations are used for credit cards:

AE	American Express	EURO	Eurocard
CB	Carte Blanche	JCB	Japan Credit Bank
DC	Diners Club	MC	MasterCard
DISC	Discover	V	Visa

Introduction

Even for experienced travelers, few words hold the same terror as "surprise." The last thing you want when you're far from home is disturbing news disguised as a cheap thrill ("Guess what, honey—all the hotels are full, but the Bates Motel is running a special!"). This book will, I hope, remove that element from your visit to Boston. Armed with pointers about everything from how to find a hotel in your price range to how to get back from a club in the wee hours, you can relax and experience the city. Confident in your ability to handle the unanticipated, you can think of unexpected events as opportunities rather than emergencies. Explore the historic sights, admire the autumn foliage, elevate yourself with cultural events, and even uncover one of the city's dirty little secrets: Lots of people come here just to shop and watch sports.

Whether you've never even been to sleep-away camp or you've lost count of your frequent-flier miles, *The Complete Idiot's Travel Guide to Boston* will help you design the best trip for you. The book consists of seven sections that cover everything from booking a ticket to getting around, where to stay, where to play, and where to head when you've had your fill of the city proper. And we'll give you the lowdown on selected destinations in the suburbs and on Cape Cod.

Part 1 describes what you need to know before you go. Every minute you spend planning at home spares you at least a few minutes of worrying once you arrive, so devote some quality time to this section. It addresses such questions as when and how to travel, whether to join a tour, and how much it's all going to cost. Part 1 includes telephone numbers, addresses, and Web sites for organizations that can provide more information, as well as budgeting tips and worksheets to help you manage your time and money.

Part 2 is all about hotels. It includes descriptions (with pluses and minuses) of neighborhoods in Boston and nearby Cambridge, tips on making reservations and getting a good deal, and guidance to help point you toward lodgings that suit your needs. To save you the work of listing the hotels in a certain neighborhood, in your price range, and so on, this section includes several indexes.

Part 3 explains the area's geography. It begins with the trip to your hotel from the airport, train or bus station, or highway. Then you'll learn about the neighborhoods in terms of attractions and how to get around and between them on foot, by public transportation, or (if you absolutely must) by car.

Part 4 covers food, from pizza joints to top-flight gourmet destinations, from cups of New England clam chowder to lobsters the size of your Yorkie. Here, too, plenty of indexes will help point you in the right direction.

In **Part 5,** you'll learn all about the local sights, from museums and historic buildings to sports arenas and great shopping destinations. Finally, I'll suggest some of my favorite itineraries and help you design your own.

Part 6 concentrates on the city's cultural offerings and nightlife. You'll learn how to find out what's happening, how much it's likely to cost, and where to get discount tickets. Besides being a hot spot for high culture, Boston offers plenty of ways to let your hair down, from comedy clubs to neighborhood bars (remember "Cheers"?).

Part 7 gives you the lowdown on Boston-area day trips (and overnight stays, if you're so inclined). It's a "greatest hits" treatment of the attractions in Lexington and Concord, Plymouth, Salem and its North Shore neighbors, and three of Cape Cod's most enjoyable destinations—Sandwich, Chatham, and Provincetown.

Extras

Several unique features will help you make the most efficient use of the information in this book.

Indexes cross-reference the listings, letting you see at a glance your options in a particular category—kid-friendly restaurants, hotels near Harvard Square, and so on.

Throughout the book, mostly at the end of chapters, you'll find **worksheets** that help you plan and keep track of your trip using your own tastes and preferences. Go ahead and underline, highlight, or check off as you read—you'll be a step ahead when the serious planning starts.

The **kid-friendly icon** appears throughout the book to identify activities, attractions, and establishments that are particularly suited to people traveling with children.

In Chapter 13, this icon appears beside the attractions that are featured stops on Boston's Freedom Trail.

Appendices at the back of the book list important phone numbers, addresses, and Web sites covering every aspect of your trip, from reservations to emergencies.

Finally, the book includes a variety of **sidebar boxes** that highlight tidbits of useful information. They come in five varieties:

Time-Savers

Here you'll find ways to cut down on down-time, avoid lines and hassles, and streamline the business of traveling.

Extra! Extra!

Check these boxes for handy facts, hints, and insider advice.

Dollars & Sense

Here you'll find tips on saving money and cutting corners to make your trip affordable as well as enjoyable.

Tourist Traps

These boxes steer you away from rip-offs, activities that aren't worth the trouble, shady dealings, and other potential pitfalls.

History 101

Turn to these boxes for interesting historical facts about the city.

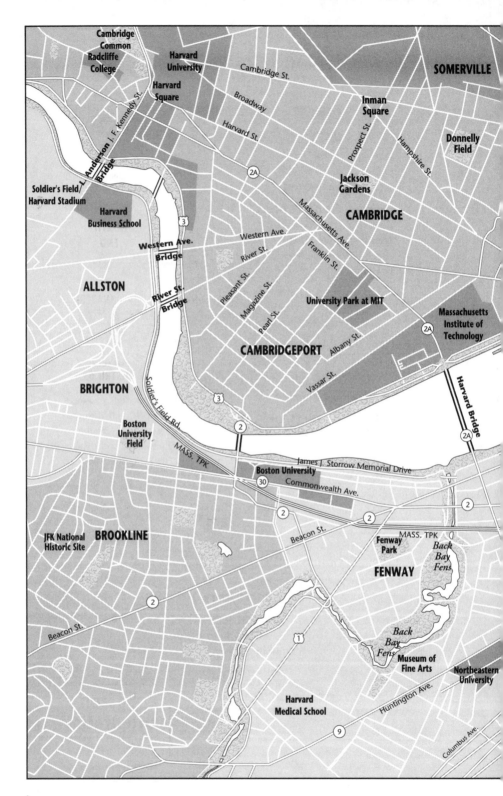

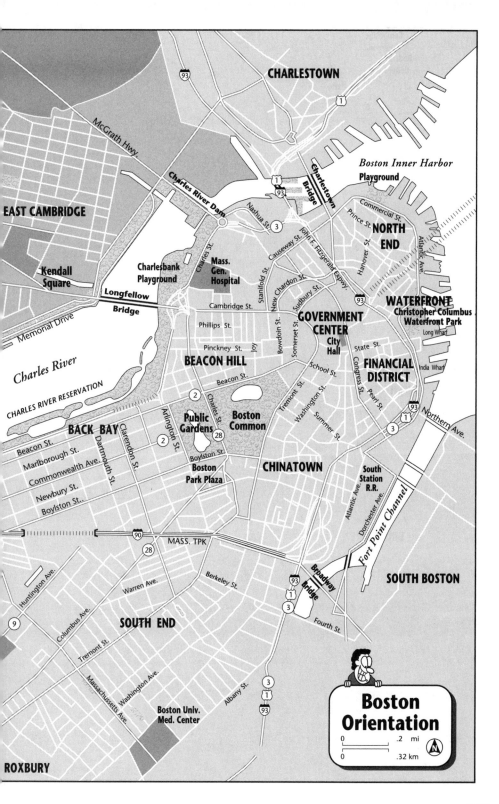

Boston Orientation

CHARLESTOWN

Boston Inner Harbor

EAST CAMBRIDGE

Kendall Square

Charlesbank Playground

Mass. Gen. Hospital

NORTH END

WATERFRONT
Christopher Columbus
Waterfront Park
Long Wharf

Longfellow Bridge

Memorial Drive

Charles River

CHARLES RIVER RESERVATION

Cambridge St.

Phillips St.

Pinckney St. Joy

BEACON HILL

GOVERNMENT CENTER
City Hall

State St.

FINANCIAL DISTRICT

India Wharf

Beacon St.

Public Gardens

Boston Common

School St.

Tremont St.

Washington St.

Summer St.

Pearl St.

BACK BAY

Beacon St.

Marlborough St.

Commonwealth Ave.

Newbury St.

Boylston St..

Arlington St.

Clarendon St.

Dartmouth St.

Charles St.

Boylston St.

Boston Park Plaza

CHINATOWN

South Station R.R.

Fort Point Channel

SOUTH BOSTON

MASS. TPK

Huntington Ave.

Columbus Ave.

Warren Ave.

Berkeley St.

Broadway Bridge

Fourth St.

SOUTH END

Tremont St.

Massachussetts Ave.

Washington Ave.

Albany St.

Boston Univ. Med. Center

ROXBURY

McGrath Hwy.

Charles River Dam

Nashua St.

Charlestown Bridge

Playground

Commercial St.

Prince St.

Hanover St.

Atlantic Ave.

Causeway St.

John F. Fitzgerald Expwy.

Staniford St.

New Chardon St.

Sudbury St.

Bowdoin St.

Somerset St.

Congress St.

Northern Ave.

Dorchester Ave.

Atlantic Ave.

Boston Orientation

0   .2 mi

0   .32 km

Part 1

What You Need to Do Before You Go

Congratulations on your wise decision to visit Boston—and to use this book as you prepare for your trip. The city's unique blend of historic and cultural attractions, entertaining diversions, and manageable size makes it a wildly popular business, convention, and tourist destination. That means you certainly won't be alone on your trip to the "Hub of the solar system," but it doesn't mean that you can't have a singularly enjoyable time. You just need to do some planning.

This section aims to take the stress out of the planning process—or at least reduce it as much as possible. The time you invest at this stage can mean the difference between plunging confidently into a new city or being immobilized by the choices you didn't take the time to make beforehand. I'll walk you through the process of deciding when to go, booking your tickets, not paying too much for them, and packing up. In other words, even if you've never left the house before, here's what you need to get out the door. What are you waiting for?

THINGS YOU MAY WANT TO TAKE
1) UNDERWEAR
2) AIRLINE TICKETS
3) WALLET

Chapter 1

How to Get Started

In This Chapter

➤ What you need to know beforehand

➤ Where to get information

➤ When to go, with a month-by-month list of events

➤ Tips for travelers with special needs

Information, Please

Remember when you first said to yourself (or your spouse, significant other, or trusty pet), "Boston sounds like fun"? That was when you started planning your trip. Becoming an expert on the city can take a lifetime, but organizing a great visit requires just a few hours and a telephone, a computer, or a pen and some stamps. Before you know it, you'll be swimming in brochures and materials from tourist offices, chambers of commerce, and travel Web sites.

As you sort through the information, bear in mind that it comes from sources that are anything but unbiased. If a business is paying for a listing, chances are the listing won't say, "We'll take your money and run!" Compare what you turn up with the info in this book (and in an in-depth guidebook like *Frommer's Boston,* if you want to learn more). And always remember that if something sounds too good to be true, it probably is.

Get It in Writing: Tourist Offices

The organizations listed here will give you a wide-screen view; as you proceed through the planning process and this book, I'll point you toward more specialized sources, too.

➤ The **Greater Boston Convention & Visitors Bureau,** 2 Copley Place, Suite 105, Boston, MA 02116-6501 (☎ **888/SEE-BOSTON** or 617/536-4100; fax 617/424-7664; www.bostonusa.com; e-mail visitor@ bostonusa.com).

The bureau offers a comprehensive visitor information kit and a "Kids Love Boston" kit; each costs $5.25 and includes a travel planner, guidebook, map, and coupon book with shopping, dining, attractions, and nightlife discounts. Call the main number to gain access to the "Boston by Phone" service, which provides information on attractions, dining, performing arts and nightlife, shopping, and travel services.

➤ The **Massachusetts Office of Travel and Tourism,** 100 Cambridge St., 13th floor, Boston, MA 02202 (☎ **800/227-6277** or 617/727-3201; fax 617/727-6525; www.mass-vacation.com; e-mail vacationinfo@ state.ma.us).

This organization publishes a free "Getaway Guide" magazine that includes information about attractions and lodgings, a map, and a seasonal calendar. Because it covers the whole state, the office has less Boston-specific material than the Convention & Visitors Bureau, but it's still useful (and free!).

➤ The **Cambridge Office for Tourism**, 18 Brattle St., Cambridge, MA 02138 (☎ **800/862-5678** or 617/441-2884; fax 617/441-7736; e-mail cambtour@us1.channel1.com).

Surf City: Using the Internet

If you don't have a home computer, by all means head to a public library, school, or cyber-cafe to check out the wealth of online sources of information about Boston.

➤ **www.bostonusa.com**

The Greater Boston Convention & Visitors Bureau site (see above).

➤ **www.mass-vacation.com**

The on-line face of the Massachusetts Office of Travel and Tourism (see above). Includes an entertaining, informative "lobster tutorial."

➤ **www.Boston.com**

Boston Globe's complete on-line city guide, featuring current events, other publications (among them *Boston* magazine), museums and other arts resources, including the Museum of Fine Arts. You can take an interactive tour of the Freedom Trail, too.

➤ **www.frommers.com**

The Frommer's Web site has a Boston section.

➤ **www.city.net/countries/united_states/massachusetts/boston** and
www.city.net/countries/united_states/massachusetts/cambridge

These Excite! sites are packed with information and useful links.

➤ **www.bostonphoenix.com**

The on-line version of the arts-oriented weekly, with extensive entertainment listings.

➤ **www.massport.com**

The Massachusetts Port Authority (which runs the airport, among other things) has an excellent site with many links for visitors.

➤ **www.boston.sidewalk.com**

Microsoft's Boston lifestyle and entertainment listings.

➤ **www.pinkweb.com/boston.index.html**

A guide to gay- and lesbian-owned and gay-friendly businesses.

➤ **www.ci.boston.ma.us and www.ci.cambridge.ma.us**

The municipal sites of Boston and Cambridge.

Time-Savers

There are two main approaches to travel research using the Internet: exploring before you leave, and bringing along a computer (or otherwise arranging access) and downloading the most up-to-date possible information. I'm solidly in the first camp, because most sites aren't updated often enough to justify lugging a laptop. If you can't or don't want to complete your homework at home, at least start there. Bookmark a handful of sites you want to check at the last minute, and don't waste time typing URLs.

Season to Taste: When Should I Go?

There's no bad time to visit Beantown, but here are some peaks and valleys to be aware of. Also check the events in the calendar below for busy periods; you'll need to plan well in advance for Harborfest or the Boston Marathon, for example, but they're worth it.

The Name Game

Why "Beantown"? Like so many other things about Boston, the explanation dates from colonial times. In Puritan New England, Sunday was the day of rest—even lighting a fire violated the Sabbath. But putting a crock of beans to bake in the oven section of a brick fireplace on Saturday was okay. The retained heat cooked the beans in time for Sunday dinner at noon, and "Boston baked beans" got their name.

Between **April and November,** there are few slow periods. Conventions take place all year, clustering in the spring and fall. The Convention & Visitors Bureau can tip you off to especially large gatherings. Snow can linger into April, and full-blown spring usually doesn't arrive until early May—but that makes the first run of truly balmy weather all the more enjoyable.

Regardless of the weather, the **college graduation season** (May and early June) is especially busy, and as a bonus, you get to contend with hordes of out-of-state drivers. In **July and August,** vacationing families flock to Boston, creating long lines and lots of opportunities to witness tantrums. June, July, and August are about the only months when you might encounter consecutive days of 90°-plus temperatures, usually accompanied by debilitating humidity.

During **foliage season,** from late September to mid-November, many leaf-peepers stay in town or pass through on the way to northern New England. Again, this is convention time, and those meeting planners know their stuff—this is when you're most likely to hit a run of intoxicating weather, with comfortably warm, sun-soaked days and cool nights.

In **December,** the leaves are gone but the meetings linger; you might be able to nab a good deal on a weekend. The "slow" season is **January through March,** when many hotels offer great deals, especially on weekends. If bitter cold and biting winds get you down, concentrate on indoor activities. This is the season when the city is most likely to be socked in by snow, and when some suburban attractions are closed for the winter.

Timing Is Everything

Letting New England's capricious weather dictate when you travel is never a great idea—"If you don't like it, wait 10 minutes" is a cliché for good reason. Not visiting in, say, March because you don't like cold weather practically guarantees that you'll miss the first 70° day of the year.

Rhyme & Reason

This is the second-best Boston poem to know (after "Paul Revere's Ride," of course). The short column of lights on top of the old John Hancock building in the Back Bay (next to the distinctive 60-story glass tower) comes with a weather-forecasting verse:

Steady blue, clear view;
flashing blue, clouds due;
steady red, rain ahead;
flashing red, snow instead.

During the summer, flashing red means the Red Sox game is canceled. Neat, huh?

Boston's Average Temperatures & Rainfall

	Jan	Feb	Mar	Apr	May	June	July	Aug	Sept	Oct	Nov	Dec
Temp. (°F)	30	31	38	49	59	68	74	72	65	55	45	34
Rainfall (in.)	4.0	3.7	4.1	3.7	3.5	2.9	2.7	3.7	3.4	3.4	4.2	4.9

Save the Date: Big Events & Festivals

Here's a chronological roundup of Boston's most popular annual festivities. Listing every event would easily take up another entire book, but that wouldn't be particularly helpful. Help yourself by getting information from the sources listed above and checking Web sites as your departure time approaches.

The Boston **Mayor's Office of Special Events & Tourism** (☎ **617/635-3911**) can provide information about specific happenings. And if something falls through or you're planning on the fly, the "Calendar" section of the Thursday *Boston Globe* and the "Scene" section of the Friday *Boston Herald* are always packed with ideas.

January

➤ **Martin Luther King Jr. Birthday Celebration,** various locations. Events include speeches, musical tributes, gospel celebrations, and panel discussions. Check the Thursday *Globe* "Calendar" section for specifics. Third Monday of the month.

➤ **Chinese New Year,** Chinatown. The dragon parade draws a crowd no matter how cold it is, and the Children's Museum puts on special programs. Depending on the Chinese lunar calendar, the holiday falls between January 21 and February 19.

February

➤ **Black History Month,** various locations. Activities include lectures, discussions, special museum exhibits, and tours of the Black Heritage Trail led by National Park Service rangers (☎ **617/742-5415**). All month.

Kidding Around

Just about every school in the state closes during the third week in February (the week that starts with Presidents' Day). School vacation week activities include kid-oriented exhibitions, plays, programs, and tours. Expect large crowds at family friendly destinations—something to bear in mind if you're taking a break from your own little angels. Contact individual attractions for information on special programs and extended hours.

March

➤ **New England Spring Flower Show,** Bayside Expo Center, Dorchester. Even (especially!) if there's still snow on the ground, this show draws huge crowds. Presented by the Massachusetts Horticultural Society (☎ **617/536-9280**). Second or third week of the month.

➤ **Big Apple Circus,** near Museum Wharf. The New York–based "one-ring wonder" performs in a heated tent for about a month every spring to support the Children's Museum. Visit the museum box office or contact Ticketmaster (☎ **617/931-ARTS**). Late March through early May.

April

➤ **Patriots Day,** North End, Lexington, and Concord. A state holiday commemorating the events of April 18 and 19, 1775—the start of the Revolutionary War. Lanterns are hung in the steeple of the Old North Church, and riders dressed as Paul Revere and William Dawes travel from Boston's North End to Lexington and Concord to warn the Minutemen that royal troops are on the march. Battles are reenacted on the town green in Lexington and then at the Old North Bridge in Concord. Third Monday of the month. For more info, contact the Paul Revere House, ☎ **617/523-2338;** the Old North Church, ☎ **617/523-6676;** the Lexington Chamber of Commerce Visitor Center, ☎ **781/862-1450;** or the Concord Chamber of Commerce, ☎ **508/369-3120.**

History 101

Be the only one in your group to know that Paul Revere and William Dawes roused the countryside by shouting, "The regulars are out!" Most colonists considered themselves British, so it wouldn't have made much sense to yell "The British are coming," would it?

➤ **Boston Marathon,** Hopkinton, Massachusetts, to Boston. The world's most famous marathon starts at noon on Patriots Day (see above), and the first finishers cross the line, on Boylston Street in front of the Boston Public Library, starting a little after 2pm. Good vantage points include Commonwealth Avenue and Kenmore Square. Third Monday of the month. ☎ **617/236-1652.**

May

➤ **Boston Kite Festival,** Franklin Park. Kites of all shapes and sizes take to the air above a celebration that includes kite-making clinics, music, and other entertainment. Middle of the month. ☎ **617/635-4505.**

➤ **Lilac Sunday,** Arnold Arboretum, Jamaica Plain. The only day of the year that picnicking is permitted at the Arboretum. The sensational spring flowers include more than 400 varieties of lilacs in bloom. Usually held on the third Sunday of the month. ☎ **617/524-1717.**

➤ **Street Performers Festival,** Faneuil Hall Marketplace. Everyone but the pigeons gets into the act as musicians, magicians, jugglers, sword-swallowers, and artists strut their stuff. End of the month. ☎ **617/338-2323.**

June

➤ **Dragon Boat Festival,** Charles River near Harvard Square, Cambridge. Teams of paddlers synchronized by a drummer race in boats with dragon heads and tails. The winners go to the national championships; the spectators go to a celebration of Chinese culture and food on the shore. Second Sunday of the month.

➤ ***Boston Globe* Jazz & Blues Festival,** various locations, indoors and outdoors. Big names and rising stars of the music world appear at lunchtime, after-work, evening, and weekend events. Some events require advance tickets; some are free. Third week of the month. ☎ **617/267-4301.**

➤ **Art Newbury Street,** Newbury Street. More than 30 galleries attract art lovers with special exhibits and outdoor entertainment. End of the month. ☎ 617/267-7961.

July

➤ **Boston Harborfest,** downtown, the waterfront, and the Harbor Islands. In Boston, Fourth of July is a week long and loads of fun. Events include concerts, guided tours, talks, cruises, fireworks, the Boston Chowderfest, and the annual turnaround of the USS *Constitution.* First week of the month (June 29 to July 4, 1999; June 28 to July 4, 2000). ☎ 617/227-1528.

➤ **Boston Pops Concert & Fireworks Display,** Hatch Memorial Shell on the Esplanade. Overnight camping is no longer permitted, but people wait from dawn till dark for the music to start. The program includes the *1812 Overture,* with actual cannon fire. July 4. ☎ 617/266-1492.

Time-Savers

So spending July 4 on the Esplanade baking in the sun in a sea of humanity isn't your idea of a party. (Can you guess where I stand on this?) In that case, don't set out for the fireworks until the sky starts to grow dark. Bring a radio, take the Red Line to Kendall Square, and watch the pyrotechnics from the Cambridge side of the river.

August

➤ **Italian-American Feasts, North End.** These weekend street fairs begin in July, and the last two are the biggest—the Fishermen's Feast, also known as the feast of the Madonna del Soccorso, and the Feast of St. Anthony. There's food, carnival games, live music, and dancing in the streets (really). Middle to end of the month.

September

➤ **Cambridge River Festival,** Memorial Drive from John F. Kennedy Street to Western Avenue. A salute to the arts, with music, dancing, children's activities, and international food on the banks of the Charles. Beginning of the month. ☎ 617/349-4380.

➤ **Boston Film Festival,** various locations. So it's not Sundance, but the lack of wall-to-wall glitz means you might actually get to see a movie and meet an actor or filmmaker you've heard of. Most screenings are open to the public without advance tickets. Middle of the month. ☎ 617/266-2533.

October

➤ **Head of the Charles Regatta,** Boston and Cambridge. More than 4,000 rowers of all ages race in front of hordes of fans along the banks of the Charles River and on the bridges spanning it. It's a big party, but alcohol consumption is strictly forbidden. Third or fourth weekend of the month. ☎ 617/864-8415.

➤ **Ringling Brothers and Barnum & Bailey Circus,** FleetCenter. The Greatest Show on Earth makes its annual 2-week visit. Middle of the month. ☎ 617/624-1000.

➤ **Salem Haunted Happenings,** various locations. Parades, parties, a special MBTA train ride from Boston, fortune-telling, cruises, and tours lead up to a ceremony on Halloween. Final 2 weeks of the month. For specifics, contact the Salem Office of Tourism & Cultural Affairs, ☎ 800/777-6848.

November

➤ **An Evening with Champions,** Harvard's Bright Athletic Center, Allston. World-class ice skaters and local students (who've been known to grow into Olympians) stage three performances to benefit the Jimmy Fund, the children's fund-raising arm of the Dana-Farber Cancer Institute. First weekend of the month. ☎ 617/493-8172.

➤ **Thanksgiving Celebration,** Plymouth. Luckily, you don't have to eat what the Pilgrims ate. There's a "stroll through the ages," showcasing 17th- and 19th-century Thanksgiving preparations in historic homes. Plimoth Plantation (☎ 508/746-1622), where the colony's first years are re-created, offers a Victorian Thanksgiving feast, for which reservations are required. Thanksgiving Day. ☎ 800/USA-1620.

December

➤ *The Nutcracker,* Wang Center for the Performing Arts. Boston Ballet's annual holiday extravaganza is one of the country's biggest and best, with spectacular sets. All month. Call Ticketmaster (☎ 617/931-ARTS) as soon as you plan your trip, ask whether your hotel offers a *Nutcracker* package, or cross your fingers and visit the box office at 270 Tremont St. when you arrive.

➤ **Christmas Tree Lighting,** Prudential Center. Carol singing precedes the lighting of a magnificent tree from Nova Scotia—an annual expression of thanks from the people of Halifax for Bostonians' help in fighting a devastating fire there in 1917. First Saturday of the month. ☎ 800/SHOP-PRU or 617/267-1002.

➤ **Boston Tea Party Reenactment,** Tea Party Ship & Museum, Congress Street Bridge. The pre-Revolutionary uprising comes to life in a dramatization of the events of December 16, 1773. Middle of the month. ☎ 617/338-1773.

➤ **First Night,** Back Bay and the waterfront. An arts-oriented, no-alcohol, city-wide New Year's Eve celebration, from early afternoon to midnight. Includes a parade, ice sculptures, art exhibitions, theatrical performances, and indoor and outdoor entertainment. There's a spectacular midnight fireworks display over the harbor. Some attractions are free and some require tickets, but for most you just need a First Night button, available for about $15 at visitor centers and stores around the city. December 31. For details, contact First Night (☎ **617/542-1399**) or check the newspapers when you arrive.

Extra! Extra!

In 1999, Boston will play host to three big sporting events. Start calling around right this red-hot minute if you *have* to visit during the first round of the NCAA men's basketball tournament (March 12 and 14), the baseball All-Star Game (July 9 to 13; game on the 13th), or golf's Ryder Cup (September 21 to 26). Hotel occupancy rates will be sky-high, and bargains on anything will be hard to find. If you can, seriously consider traveling at another time—or sucking up to your friends who live in the area.

We Are Family: Traveling with Your Children

Boston is a top-notch family destination, with tons of activities that appeal to children, and relatively few that don't. (Plus, getting the most out of the city usually involves a fair amount of walking. You will best be able to appreciate this when bedtime rolls around.)

Kids This icon appears throughout this book to identify hotels, restaurants, and attractions that are especially family friendly.

On Your Mark, Get Set . . .

If your children are old enough to enjoy traveling, they're old enough to help with planning (and even with budgeting, if you're comfortable with that). They might surprise you—a fourth-grader who just finished *Johnny Tremain* may know as much about the Revolutionary War period as you do (or more), and a middle-schooler who aced a unit on Egypt may be eager to visit the Museum of Fine Arts. Even a reluctant teenager who can't conceive of anything less cool than a family trip can find something that's not too objectionable.

Time-Savers

Okay, it isn't strictly a time-saver, but you can spare yourself a lot of aggravation (and, aha!, a lot of time cajoling) by drawing your unenthusiastic teenager into the planning process as early as possible. The promise of a college tour or an IMAX movie won't tip the scales, but it might be a good place to start.

Turn the kids loose with this book and any brochures you want them to see (if there's no time to visit Salem, for instance, there's no sense in tempting them). After the children have marked things that interest them in order of preference, and the adults in the party have had a chance to do the same, you're ready to formulate an itinerary that incorporates everyone's suggestions. If there isn't as much overlap as you'd like, consider this an opportunity to teach them about compromise and negotiation. See chapter 16 for pointers.

Youth Is Served: Keeping the Kids Entertained

No matter how much input they had, at some point your young traveling companions will probably get tired and cranky. (So might their adult traveling companions, but that's another story.) Whatever you plan, remember to pack materials and toys that can help your offspring not get too fidgety—paper and pencils or crayons, a hand-held computer game, a personal stereo or radio (with headphones, please), or a favorite book.

Many details that apply to traveling with adults go double when kids are along: Don't try to do too much, don't forget to schedule some playtime, and don't assume that more expensive is better. An hour or two of feeding the ducks and admiring the flowers in the Public Garden is cheaper and more relaxing than dragging a howling 6-year-old through the Museum of Science.

Pump Up the Volumes

Your kids may have started their research already. Classic children's books set in Boston include *Make Way for Ducklings,* by Robert McCloskey, and *Johnny Tremain,* by Esther Forbes. The hero of E. B. White's *The Trumpet of the Swan* winds up at the lagoon in the Public Garden—a stone's throw from where Mrs. Mallard and her eight ducklings have been immortalized in bronze.

Adventures in Baby-Sitting

A family vacation doesn't have to mean nonstop togetherness (unless that's what you want). The front-desk staff or concierge at your hotel should be able to recommend a reliable sitter. If you're organized enough to know when you make reservations that you'll need child care, you might be able to make arrangements then.

The agency **Parents in a Pinch (☎ 617/739-KIDS)** will line up a carefully screened child-care provider, and will share references with parents who request them. I'd consider this an emergency option for the budget-conscious, though. The referral fee is $30 for an evening or half day, $40 for a full day; it goes on your credit card (AE, MC, V). Then you pay the sitter (cash or check) $8 per hour for one child, plus 50¢ an hour for each additional child (with a 4-hour minimum), plus reimbursement for transportation and authorized expenses.

A Touch of Gray: Advice for Seniors

As baby boomers move into their second half-century, the image of Granny and Grandpa lounging on the porch becomes even more hilarious. Turning 50 entitles you to join the **AARP** (American Association of Retired Persons), 601 E St. NW, Washington, DC 20049 (☎ **800/424-3410;** www.aarp.org), which offers discounts on car rentals, accommodations, airfares, and sightseeing. It's open to anyone 50 or older, retired or not, and makes a good introduction to the world of travel bargains available to seniors.

Mature Outlook, P.O. Box 9390, Des Moines, IA 50306-9519 (☎ **800/336-6330;** fax 847/286-5024; www.sears.com), is a similar organization, offering discounts on lodging, dining, and car rentals. The $20 annual membership fee also gets you $100 in Sears coupons and a bimonthly magazine. Membership is open to all Sears customers 18 and over, but the primary focus is on the 50-and-over market.

Dollars & Sense

Most of the major domestic airlines, including American, Continental, TWA, United, and US Airways, offer discount programs for senior travelers—be sure to ask whenever you book a flight.

Many Boston-area businesses, including hotels, restaurants, museums, and movie theaters, offer discounts to seniors with identification. Discounts are usually available in restaurants and theaters only during off-peak hours, but museums and other attractions offer reduced rates at all times.

Seniors can ride the MBTA **subways** for 20¢ (a 65¢ savings), and **local buses** for 15¢ (a 45¢ savings). On **zoned and express buses** and on the **commuter rail,** the senior fare is half the regular fare. On the commuter rail, proof of age is a valid driver's license or passport, but for the subway and buses you need a special pass. It's available for a nominal fee weekdays from 8:30am to 5pm at the Back Bay MBTA station, or by mail (Senior and Access Pass Program, 145 Dartmouth St., Boston, MA 02116-5162; ☎ **617/222-5438** or 617/222-5976).

A **Golden Age Passport** ($10) gives you free lifetime admission to all recreation areas run by the federal government, including parks and monuments. It's available at any National Park Service site that charges admission.

Mature Traveler Newsletter, which covers senior citizen travel, is a valuable resource. It is available by subscription ($30 a year) from GEM Publishing Group, Box 50400, Reno, NV 89513-0400 (☎ **800/460-6676**). GEM also publishes *The Mature Traveler's Book of Deals,* a collection of more than 1,000 senior discounts on airlines, lodging, tours, and attractions around the country; it costs $9.95.

Another helpful publication is *101 Tips for the Mature Traveler,* available from Grand Circle Travel, 347 Congress St., Suite 3A, Boston, MA 02210 (☎ **800/221-2610** or 617/350-7500; fax 617/350-6206; www.gct.com).

Although these three companies have Boston addresses, they run programs all over the country: **Grand Circle Travel** (see above) organizes educational and adventure vacations for people 50 and up. **Elderhostel, Inc.,** 75 Federal St., Boston, MA 02110 (☎ **617/426-8056;** www.elderhostel.org), organizes programs for those 60 and older. Participants generally live in a college dorm, take courses at the college in the morning, and explore the city in the afternoon. **SAGA International Holidays,** 222 Berkeley St., Boston, MA 02116 (☎ **800/343-0273;** www.sagaholidays.com), offers inclusive tours and cruises for those 50 and older.

Hundreds of other travel agencies specialize in vacations for seniors. But beware: Many of them are of the tour bus variety, with free trips thrown in for those who organize groups of 20 or more. Seniors seeking more independent travel should probably consult a regular travel agent.

Advice for Travelers with Disabilities

People with disabilities have more travel choices and resources than ever before. A good place to start is *A World of Options,* a 658-page book of resources for disabled travelers that covers everything from biking trips to scuba outfitters. It costs $45 and is available from Mobility International USA, P.O. Box 10767, Eugene, OR 97440 (☎ **541/343-1284,** voice and TDD; www.miusa.org). For more personal assistance, call the Travel Information Service at ☎ **215/456-9603** or 215/456-9602 (for TTY).

Boston, like all other U.S. cities, has taken steps to provide access for people with disabilities. Hotels must provide accessible rooms; museums and street curbs have ramps for wheelchairs. Many smaller accommodations, including most B&Bs, have not been retrofitted. Be aware that you'll find a lot of narrow streets, cobbled thoroughfares, and brick sidewalks in older neighborhoods (notably Beacon Hill and the North End).

Newer stations on the Red, Blue, and Orange lines of the MBTA subway are wheelchair accessible; the Green Line (which uses trolleys rather than subway cars) is in the process of being converted. Call ☎ **617/222-3200** to see if the stations you need are accessible. All MBTA buses have lifts or kneelers; call ☎ **800/LIFT-BUS** for more information. Some bus routes are wheelchair accessible at all times; you might have to make a reservation as much as a day in advance for others. One taxicab company with wheelchair-accessible vehicles is **Boston Cab** (☎ **617/536-5010**); advance notice is recommended. In addition, there is an Airport Handicap Van (☎ **617/561-1769**).

For reduced **public transportation** fares, persons with disabilities can apply to purchase a Transportation Access Pass (TAP) from the MBTA Access Pass Office, 10 Boylston Place, Boston, MA 02116 (☎ **617/222-5976**). The application must be completed by a licensed health care professional.

An excellent source of information is **Very Special Arts Massachusetts,** 2 Boylston St., Boston, MA 02116 (☎ **617/350-7713;** fax 617/482-4298; TTY 617/350-6836; www.vsamass.org; e-mail vsamass@aol.com). It has a comprehensive Web site and publishes *Access Expressed! Massachusetts:*

A Cultural Resource Directory ($5), which includes general access information and specifics about more than 200 arts and entertainment facilities in the state.

Other useful information outlets:

➤ The **Massachusetts Coalition for Citizens with Disabilities,** 20 Park Plaza, Suite 603, Boston, MA 02116 (☎ **800/55-VOTER** or 617/482-1336, voice or TDD).

➤ **Access-Able Travel Source,** P.O. Box 1796, Wheat Ridge, CO 80034 (☎ **303/232-2979;** www.access-able.com).

➤ **Society for the Advancement of Travel for the Handicapped,** 347 Fifth Ave., Suite 610, New York, NY 10016 (☎ **212/447-0027;** fax 212/725-8253; www.sath.org).

Many of the major car-rental companies offer hand-controlled cars for disabled drivers. **Avis** can provide a vehicle at any of its locations in the United States with 48-hour advance notice; **Hertz** requires between 24 and 72 hours' notice at most of its locations. **Wheelchair Getaways (☎ 800/ 873-4973;** www.blvd.com/wg.htm) rents specialized vans with wheelchair lifts and other features for the disabled in more than 100 cities across the United States. The Boston-area franchise is **Wheelchair Getaways of Massachusetts and Rhode Island,** 81 Pond St., Norfolk, MA 02056 (☎ **800/727-1656**).

Travelers with disabilities may also want to consider joining a tour that caters specifically to them. One of the best operators is **Flying Wheels Travel,** 143 West Bridge, P.O. Box 382, Owatonna, MN 55060 (☎ **800/535-6790;** www. flyingwheels.com). It offers escorted tours and cruises, as well as private tours in minivans with lifts. Another good company is **FEDCAP Rehabilitation Services,** 211 W. 14th St., New York, NY 10011. Call ☎ **212/727-4200** or fax 212/721-4374 for information about membership and summer tours.

Vision-impaired travelers can contact the **American Foundation for the Blind,** 11 Penn Plaza, Suite 300, New York, NY 10001 (☎ **800/232-5463**), for information on traveling with Seeing Eye dogs.

Advice for Gay & Lesbian Travelers

Boston is a gay- and lesbian-friendly destination, with a live-and-let-live attitude that long ago replaced the city's legendary puritanism. Boston's South End has a large gay population, and the Porter Square area of Cambridge is home to many lesbians. A number of nightclubs cater to a gay clientele at least one night a week.

Bay Windows (☎ 617/266-6670) and *In Publications* (☎ 617/ 426-8246) publish weekly newspapers that concentrate on upcoming gay-related events, news, and features. The weekly *Boston Phoenix* publishes a monthly supplement, "One in 10," and has a gay-interest area in its Web site (www.bostonphoenix.com).

History 101

In 19th–century New England, the term *Boston marriage* referred to two women who had set up housekeeping together, sometimes so that they could pursue careers, but more often because they were romantically involved.

The **Pink Pages**, 66 Charles St., Boston, MA 02114 (☎ **800/338-6550**), is a guide to gay- and lesbian-owned and gay-friendly businesses that's available for $10.95; it also has a comprehensive Web site (www.pinkweb.com/boston. index.html).

Resources for Gay & Lesbian Travelers

➤ The **Gay and Lesbian Helpline** (☎ **617/267-9001**) offers information Monday through Friday 4 to 11pm, Saturday 6 to 8:30pm, and Sunday 6 to 10pm.

➤ The **Boston Alliance of Gay and Lesbian Youth** (BAGLY) (☎ **800/ 422-2459**; www.bagly.org).

Money Matters

When money isn't busy making the world go around or personifying the root of all evil, it's often pouring out of travelers' wallets. This chapter discusses ways of carrying money, offers budgeting tips, and suggests ways to keep from blowing the budget you've calculated so carefully.

Should I Carry Traveler's Checks or the Green Stuff?

Traveler's checks are something of an anachronism from the days when people wrote checks rather than going to the ATM. In those days, travelers could not be sure that they'd be able to cash a check, and because traveler's checks could be replaced if lost or stolen, they were a sound alternative to setting out with wads of cash.

These days, traveler's checks are less necessary because most cities (including Boston) have plenty of 24-hour ATMs linked to a national network that most likely includes your bank at home. Even if you opt for traveler's checks, you'll want to keep some cash handy for things like vending machines, parking meters, and cab fare. Call your bank before leaving home, or check the back of your ATM card to see what network or networks accept your bank's cards. **Cirrus** (☎ 800/424-7787) and **PLUS** (☎ 800/843-7587) are the most popular networks. Their 800 numbers will give you specific locations of ATMs.

Tourist Traps

Try to strike a balance between running to the ATM every time you need 20 bucks and walking around with a fat roll of bills. You'll most likely rack up service charges with each ATM transaction, and those fees can add up. Especially costly are the privately operated nonbank ATMs (most commonly found in convenience stores).

Many banks impose a fee every time you use a card from a "foreign" bank. At banks in Massachusetts, a message should appear on the screen to warn you that you're about to be charged and offer you the chance to cancel the transaction. Bear in mind that even if the bank doesn't charge you, that won't stop your out-of-state bank from tacking on its own fee (usually between 50¢ and $3).

Dollars & Sense

AAA members can purchase American Express traveler's checks at most offices without paying the usual service charge (1% to 4%).

Check It Out

If you need the security of traveler's checks and don't mind the hassle of showing identification every time you want to cash a check, you can get them at almost any bank. Be sure to keep a list of serial numbers (*not* in the same place as the checks) in case your wallet is lost or stolen.

American Express offers checks in denominations of $10, $20, $50, $100, $500, and $1,000. You'll pay a service charge ranging from 1% to 4%, though AAA members can obtain checks without a fee at most AAA offices. You can also order American Express traveler's checks over the phone by calling ☎ **800/221-7282**; Amex gold and platinum cardholders who call this number are exempt from the 1% fee.

Visa also offers traveler's checks, available at Citibank locations across the country and at several other banks. The service charge ranges between 1.5% and 2%; checks come in denominations of $20, $50, $100, $500, and $1,000. **MasterCard** also offers traveler's checks.

All Charged Up: Plastic Money

Credit cards are invaluable when traveling. They are a safe way to carry money and provide a convenient record of all your travel expenses when you arrive home.

You can also get **cash advances** off your credit cards at any bank, but consider that a last resort. Most companies impose a service fee (a percentage of the advance amount) and start charging interest on the advance the moment you receive the cash. On airline credit cards, you won't receive frequent-flyer miles. At most banks, you don't need to go to a teller; you can get a cash advance at the ATM if you know your personal identification number (PIN). If you've forgotten your PIN (or didn't even know you had one), call the phone number on the back of your credit card *before you leave home* and ask the bank to send it. It usually takes 5 to 7 business days. Some banks will tell you your PIN over the phone if you tell them your mother's maiden name or some other security clearance, but the middle of a long trip far from home is not the time to find out that your bank has tough security.

Debit Minus *I* Equals *Debt*

If your ATM card is also a debit card, consider bringing along at least one conventional credit card. Debit cards deduct money directly from your checking account and save you the trouble of having a check approved. They are convenient, but they can also lead you into temptation. Using a credit card look-alike, you may forget that you're spending the equivalent of cash (and depleting your checking account), not running up a credit card balance.

What Do I Do if My Money Gets Stolen?

Almost every credit card company has an emergency 800 number to call if your wallet or purse is stolen. The company may be able to wire you a cash advance immediately, and in many places, it can get you an emergency card in a day or two. The issuing bank's toll-free number is usually on the back of the credit card. (But that doesn't help you much if the card was stolen, does it? So just call information at ☎ **800/555-1212** for the number.) **American Express** cardholders and traveler's check holders should call ☎ **800/221-7282** for all money emergencies. Visa and MasterCard both strongly suggest that you contact the issuing bank, but both also have global service numbers: **Visa** customers can call ☎ **800/847-2911; MasterCard** holders should call ☎ **800/307-7309.**

If you opt to carry traveler's checks, be sure to keep a record of their serial numbers so you can handle just such an emergency. It's not a bad idea to keep a similar record of your credit card numbers and the companies' emergency numbers, either (and through some bizarre corollary of Murphy's Law, going to all that trouble practically guarantees that you'll never even misplace them).

Odds are that if your wallet is gone, you've seen the last of it, and the police aren't likely to recover it. However, after you realize that it's gone and you cancel your credit cards, it is still worth a call to inform the police. You may need the police report number for credit card or insurance purposes later.

How Much Will This Trip Set Me Back?

Budgeting is the eat-your-vegetables part of planning any trip, and Boston is more palatable than many other destinations. Although it regularly lands on the list of the 10 most expensive business destinations in the United States, it also has a huge student population. You'll find options to suit every budget, from unlimited expense account to "Dear Mom and Dad, Please send money." Bear in mind, though, that the typical impoverished student isn't paying for two museum admissions, four souvenirs, and three sit-down meals every day—you may need to do some prioritizing. The **worksheet** at the end of this chapter will help you figure it all out.

Making a budget is easy; sticking to it is hard (unless Mom and Dad always send money when you ask). On an out-of-town trip, you need to allow for transportation to and from your destination, lodging, food, admission to attractions, local transportation, shopping, entertainment, and incidentals such as tips and phone calls. A good rule of thumb is to make your best estimate of your expenditures, then add 10%.

What Things Cost in Boston

Taxi from airport to downtown	$18–$24
Water shuttle from airport to downtown	$10
Bus from airport to downtown	$8
MBTA subway token	85¢
MBTA bus fare	60¢
Pay phone call	35¢
Glass of beer	$2.50–$4.50
Can of soda	75¢–$1
Cup of coffee	$1 and up
Roll of ASA 100 Kodacolor film, 36 exposures	$6.75–$8
Adult admission to the Museum of Fine Arts	$10
Child (under 18) admission to the MFA	Free
Movie ticket	$4.75–$7.75
Theater ticket	$30–$90

Lodging

This is the least elastic part of your budget. The average price of a hotel room in Boston recently topped $170—and before you swoon, remember that that means plenty of rooms go for less than that. Boston and Cambridge offer many options, from bare bones to insanely luxurious. If you can't find a room at a B&B (which aren't all that cheap, anyway) and don't want to cope with a hostel, expect to spend at least $100 a night, not including the 12.45% hotel tax. If the price of a centrally located chain hotel seems high, don't forget that the tariff at a suburban lodging doesn't include the time and expense of commuting to the downtown attractions—or the Grecian Formula you might need after contending with Boston traffic.

Transportation
We've said it once, but it bears saying again: You absolutely don't need to rent a car to get around Boston and Cambridge. Many attractions don't offer free parking, on-street spaces are almost nonexistent, and garages are pricey. If you drive to Boston, leave the car in a garage and use it for day trips. Do the math first, though, because you may find that the cost of driving plus parking isn't all that much less than a supercheap airfare. If you're not motoring and you decide to take a day trip (see part 7), you'll probably want to rent a car (see chapter 4).

Taxis are fairly expensive and sometimes tough to come by, but sometimes indispensable—and the money you save by not renting a car for a day can pay for several days' worth of taxi rides. **Public transit** in and around the city is dirt cheap (85¢ for a subway token, 60¢ for the local bus), and 1-, 3-, and 7-day visitor passports good for unlimited local rides can make it an even better deal.

One great transportation option is looking right at you (move the book out of the way)—in "America's Walking City," many popular destinations are most easily reached **on foot.**

Dining
In an area with so many student-friendly restaurants, you won't have to break the bank, and you might even want to think about splurging. You can always have pizza at home, but can you get fresh lobster? If you don't go wild, you can have breakfast for $5 or less, lunch for the same amount or a bit more, and a more than adequate dinner for as little as $15. Or start the day with a bagel and coffee or juice ($2 to $3), pause at midday for a sandwich or salad ($5), and go seriously upscale at dinner, by which time you should be starving.

Dollars & Sense
You have a water bottle at home. Attractions and visitor centers have water fountains. Your hotel has an ice machine. Bottled water (not to mention soda and juice) isn't cheap—at least $1 a pop. Bring the bottle, fill it with ice in the morning, and refill with water throughout the day. It might sound silly, but those dollars add up.

Attractions
Everyone's definition of "must" is a little bit different, so turn to chapter 13, make a list, and start adding. But first check out the available discounts, which range from the deals that come with the MBTA's visitor passport to coupon books to hours when admission is by donation or free.

Shopping
For a lot of people, shopping falls (or should fall) under "entertainment." You don't *need* to go to Filene's Basement, but if 2 hours there sounds more uplifting than 2 days at museums or historic attractions, include shopping in your budget. A designer jacket that costs a fraction of its retail price makes a better souvenir (and anecdote) than a T-shirt ever could.

Entertainment
A day spent walking all over the city may leave you too wiped out for anything more strenuous than an hour in front of the TV. Be realistic, but also be aware that Boston offers lots of relatively inexpensive cultural opportunities, such as half-price theater tickets and cheap or free student performances. And if you've been waiting all your life to see the Boston Symphony Orchestra, start there. Then worry about incidentals (you know, airfare, lodging, that sort of thing).

Tipping
For most service providers, including **waiters** and **cab drivers,** the standard tip is 15%, rising to 20% for particularly good service. The math is easy enough at restaurants, where the meal tax is 5%—triple (or quadruple) the tax to calculate the tip. If you're with a large group (six to eight or more), the restaurant may already have added a service charge, so be sure to check. If you're just drinking at a **bar,** 10% to 15% is typical. **Bellhops** get $1 or $2 a bag, **chambermaids** $1 per person per day, and **valet-parking** and **coat-check attendants** $1 to $2.

What if I'm Worried I Can't Afford It?
You are about to venture into a part of the world where Yankee thrift was invented and refined into an art form. There's nothing smart about spending more than you need to anywhere, and in these parts it's practically unheard of. Relax and fill out the worksheet at the end of this chapter. If the grand total seems too high, think about where you can and are willing to economize. Check out the "Dollars & Sense" boxes scattered throughout this book. If you're still worried about your finances, here are some more tips:

1. **Go in the off-season.** If you can travel at nonpeak times (especially January through March), you'll find hotel prices that are as much as half what they are during peak months.

2. **Travel on off days of the week.** If you can travel on a Tuesday, Wednesday, or Thursday, you may find cheaper airfares. When you

inquire about airfares, ask if you can obtain a lower rate by flying on a different day.

3. **Reserve your flight well in advance.** Advance Purchase Excursion (APEX) fares can be a great deal.

4. **Reserve your flight a couple of days in advance.** Last-minute Internet fares (released Wednesday for the weekend that starts 2 days later) aren't a sure thing, but they sure are a bargain. See "Procrastination Pays (Sometimes)" in chapter 3.

5. **Research Alternate Gateways.** Flying to Warwick, Rhode Island, or Manchester, New Hampshire, can be *much* cheaper than flying to Logan, so if you have more time than money, it's worth checking out. See the Dollars & Sense box on page 32 for details.

6. **Try a package tour.** For many destinations, including Boston, you can book airfare, hotel, ground transportation, and even some sightseeing just by making one call to a travel agent or packager, for a lot less than if you tried to put the trip together yourself. See the section on package tours in chapter 3 for specific suggestions.

7. **Pack light.** You'll save on tips *and* on the cabs that you won't need to take to and from the airport.

8. **Reserve a hotel room with a kitchen.** It may not feel like as much of a vacation if you still have to do your own cooking and dishes, but you'll save a lot of money by not eating in restaurants three times a day. Even if you only make breakfast and an occasional bag lunch in the kitchen, you'll still save in the long run. And you'll never be shocked by a hefty room service bill.

9. **Always ask for discount rates.** Membership in AAA, frequent flyer plans, trade unions, AARP, or other groups may qualify you for discounted rates on car rentals, plane tickets, hotel rooms, even meals. Ask about everything; you could be pleasantly surprised.

10. **Ask if your kids can stay in your room with you.** A room with two double beds usually doesn't cost more than one with one queen-size bed. And many hotels won't charge you the additional person rate if the additional person is pint-sized and related to you. Even if you have to pay $15 or $20 for a rollaway bed, you'll save hundreds by not taking two rooms.

11. **Don't rent a car to get around town.** Yes, again. If you're planning an out-of-town day trip, go wild. Otherwise, save the expense of renting and parking.

12. **Buy an MBTA visitor passport.** And use it—it can be a great deal, especially if you take advantage of the accompanying discounts.

13. **Buy an ArtsBoston coupon book or a Boston CityPass.** See chapter 13 for details.

Dollars & Sense

The following attractions offer reduced admission prices at the following times: **Children's Museum,** $1 for all Friday 5 to 9pm; **Computer Museum,** half price Sunday 3 to 5pm; **Museum of Fine Arts,** voluntary contribution ($5 suggested for adults) Wednesday 4 to 9:45pm; **New England Aquarium,** $1 off all fees summer Wednesday and Thursday 4 to 8pm.

The following museums are free at the following times: the **Institute of Contemporary Art,** Thursday 5 to 9pm; **Harvard University museums,** Saturday morning.

14. **Hit the museums when admission is discounted or free.** See box above for details.

15. **Try expensive restaurants at lunch instead of dinner.** Lunch tabs are usually a fraction of what dinner would cost at most top restaurants, and the menu often boasts many of the same specialties.

16. **Skip the souvenirs.** Your photographs and your memories should be the best mementos of your trip. If you're worried about money, you can do without the T-shirts, refrigerator magnets, and key chains.

Budget Worksheet: You Can Afford This Trip

Expense	Amount
Airfare (x no. of people traveling)	
Car Rental (if applicable)	
Lodging (x no. of nights)	
Parking (x no. of nights)	
Breakfast *may be included in your room rate* (x no. of nights)	
Lunch (x no. of nights)	
Dinner (x no. of nights)	
Baby-sitting	
Attractions and entertainment (admission charges to museums, tours, theaters, nightclubs, etc.)	
Transportation (cabs, subway, buses, etc.)	
Shopping (if you write down a figure, maybe you'll actually stick to it)	
Souvenirs (T-shirts, postcards, tricornered hats)	
Tips (think 15% to 20% of your meal total plus $1 to $2 a bag every time a bellhop moves your luggage)	
Don't forget the cost of getting to and from the airport in your hometown, plus long-term parking (x no. of nights)	
Grand Total	

How Will I Get There?

The answer to this question depends on several variables. How much time, money, and patience do you have? Where are you coming from? Where else do you plan to go? Once you arrive, will you be comfortable exploring on your own or do you want the structure of a group tour? Finally, do you want to work out all these details yourself (using the **worksheet** at the end of this chapter, of course), or get a travel agent to help you? Here goes—last things first.

Travel Agent: Friend or Foe?

A good travel agent is like a good mechanic or plumber or doctor: hard to find, but invaluable once you have the right person. And the best way to find a good travel agent is the same way you find a good plumber or mechanic or doctor—word of mouth.

Any travel agent can help you find a bargain airfare, hotel, or rental car. A good travel agent will stop you from ruining your vacation by trying to save a few bucks. The best travel agents can tell you how much time to budget in a destination, find a cheap flight that doesn't require you to change planes three times, get you a better hotel room than you can find on your own, arrange for a competitively priced rental car, and even recommend restaurants.

Travel agents work on commission. The good news is that you don't pay the commission; the airlines, accommodations, and tour companies do. The bad news is that unscrupulous travel agents will try to persuade you to book the vacations that generate the most money in commissions.

To make sure you get the most out of your travel agent, do a little homework. Read about your destination (you've already made a sound decision by buying this book) and pick out some accommodations and attractions you think you like. If necessary, get a more comprehensive travel guide like *Frommer's Boston.* If you have access to the Internet, check prices on the Web (see "Winning the Airfare Wars" later in this chapter for more information on how to do that) so you can do a little prodding. Then take your guidebook and Web information to the travel agent and ask him or her to make the arrangements for you. Because they have access to more resources than even the most complete Web travel site, travel agents should be able to get you a better price than you could get by yourself. And they can issue your tickets and vouchers on the spot. If they can't get you into the hotel of your choice, they can recommend an alternative, and you can immediately look for an objective review in your guidebook.

Time-Savers

If your trip coincides (intentionally or not) with a major cultural event, such as Boston Ballet's *Nutcracker* or a big show at a major museum, ask about packages that include lodging and tickets. You won't have to deal with long lines, and you might get a break on the price, too.

In the past few years, some airlines and resorts have begun limiting or eliminating travel agent commissions altogether. The immediate result has been that travel agents don't bother booking those services unless the customer specifically requests them. But some travel industry analysts predict that if other airlines and accommodations throughout the industry follow suit, travel agents may have to start charging customers for their services. When that day arrives, the best agents should prove even harder to find.

Not That Kind of Hub

One of Boston's many nicknames, "the Hub of the solar system" (often mistakenly rendered "the Hub of the universe," and shortened in newspaper headlines to just "Hub"), comes from Oliver Wendell Holmes's *The Autocrat of the Breakfast-Table* (1858): "Boston State-House is the hub of the solar system. You couldn't pry that out of a Boston man, if you had the tire of all creation straightened out for a crowbar."

Should I Join an Escorted Tour or Travel on My Own?

Do you like to let your bus driver worry about traffic while you sit in comfort and listen to a tour guide explain everything you see? Or do you prefer following the guidebook and your nose, even if you don't catch all the highlights? Do you like to have lots of events planned for each day, or would you rather improvise as you go along? The answers to these questions will determine whether you should choose the guided tour or travel on your own.

Sign Me Up!

Some people love escorted tours. They free travelers from spending lots of time behind the wheel; they take care of all the details; and they tell you what to expect at each attraction. You know your costs up front, and there aren't many surprises. Escorted tours can take you to the maximum number of sights in the minimum amount of time.

Sign Me Out!

Other people need more freedom and spontaneity—they can't stand guided tours. They prefer to discover a destination by themselves, making their own timetable and not feeling like part of a herd of sheep. They don't mind getting caught in a thunderstorm without an umbrella or finding that a recommended restaurant is no longer in business. That's just the adventure of travel.

Trolley Tours: Declarations of Independence?

One unusual thing about Boston tourism is the prominent role played by trolley tour companies (see chapter 12). In fact, you'll often find that the sightseeing portion of a package (see below) is a free or discounted 1-day trolley tour. Escorted tours certainly are available, but a typical multiple-day bus tour spends only a day or two in Boston on the way to or from other New England destinations and activities—historic attractions, outlet shopping, skiing, and especially foliage watching.

Evidence suggests that there are almost as many companies running foliage tours as there are leaves on the trees. If you want the if-it's-Friday-this-must-be-Salem approach, plenty of companies offer escorted tours of New England; if you want a less superficial and more custom-tailored approach to Boston, you might want to stay put and do some planning on your own.

The largest of the tour companies is **Gray Line;** its New England incarnation is **Brush Hill Tours,** 435 High St., Randolph, MA 02368 (☎ **800/ 343-1328** or 781/986-6100; fax 781/986-0167; www.grayline.com). It operates Beantown Trolley (see chapter 12) and offers a variety of half- and full-day escorted tours to destinations such as Plymouth, Salem, Cape Cod, and Newport, Rhode Island. The 3-night "Boston Package" includes lodging, airport or train station transfers, a trolley tour, and a 1-day excursion to another local destination. At press time, prices started at $413 in the summer and fell to $294 in the winter, per person, double occupancy at the Midtown Hotel; for the Radisson Hotel Boston, $469 and $321, respectively.

Another possibility is *Yankee Magazine*'s **Best of New England Vacations** (☎ **800/996-2463;** www.bnevacations.com). At press time, prices for 2 nights at the Cambridge Inn Ramada, a tour of Boston, and a copy of the magazine's travel guide started at $174 per person, double occupancy; for the Regal Bostonian Hotel, prices started at $359 per person, double occupancy.

Tourist Traps

If you plan to join a guided tour because you don't want to do a lot of walking, think again. Boston's 17th-century street patterns mean that many attractions on Beacon Hill and in the North End (that is, most of the Freedom Trail) are on streets that are closed to buses. If you're visiting the older parts of the city, there's pavement-pounding in your future—be very suspicious if a tour operator tries to tell you otherwise.

Check the Small Print

If you do choose an escorted tour, ask some questions before you buy:

1. What is the cancellation policy? Do you have to put a deposit down? Can the company cancel the trip if it doesn't get enough people? How late can you cancel if you are unable to go? When do you pay? Do you get a refund if you cancel? If *they* cancel?

2. How jam-packed is the schedule? Do they try to fit 25 hours into a 24-hour day, or is there ample time for relaxing by the pool or shopping? If you don't enjoy getting up at 7am every day and not returning to your hotel until 6 or 7pm, certain escorted tours may not be for you.

3. How big is the group? The smaller the group, the more flexible it will be, and the less time you'll spend waiting for people to get on and off the bus. Tour operators may be evasive about this, because they may not know the exact size of the group until everybody has made reservations, but they should be able to give you a rough estimate. Some tours have a minimum group size, and may be canceled if they don't attract enough people.

4. What is included? Don't assume *anything*. You may have to pay to get yourself to and from the airport. Or a box lunch may be included in an excursion, but drinks might cost extra. Or beer might be included but wine might not.

5. How much choice do you have? Can you opt out of certain activities, or does the bus leave once a day, with no exceptions? Are all your meals planned in advance? Can you choose your entree at dinner, or does everybody get the same chicken cutlet?

If you choose an escorted tour, think strongly about purchasing trip-cancellation insurance, especially if the tour operator asks to you pay up front. But don't buy insurance from the tour operator! If the operator doesn't fulfill its obligation to provide you with the vacation you've paid for, there's no reason to think it will fulfill its insurance obligations, either. Get travel insurance through an independent agency. (See the section on travel insurance in chapter 4.)

The Pros & Cons of Package Tours

Package tours are not the same thing as escorted tours. They are simply a way of buying your airfare and accommodations at the same time. For popular destinations like Boston, they can be the smart way to go, because they save you a ton of money. In many cases, a package that includes airfare, hotel, and transportation to and from the airport will cost you less than the hotel alone would if you booked it yourself. That's because packages are sold in bulk to tour operators, who resell them to the public. It's kind of like buying your vacation at Sam's Club, except that it's the tour operator who buys the box of 1,000 garbage bags and resells them 10 at a time at a cost that undercuts what you'd pay at the supermarket.

Packages vary as much as garbage bags, too. Some offer a better class of hotels than others. Some offer the same hotels for lower prices. Some offer flights on scheduled airlines; others book charters. In some packages, your choices of accommodations and travel days may be limited. Some packages let you choose between escorted vacations and independent vacations; others allow you to add on just a few excursions or escorted day trips (also at prices lower than if you booked them yourself) without booking an entirely escorted tour.

Each destination usually has one or two packagers that are better than the rest because they buy in even bigger bulk. The time you or your travel agent spend shopping around will be well rewarded.

Extra! Extra!

The **www.vacationpackager. com** Web site allows you to enter your preferences, link up with many different tour operators, and design your own package.

Wrap Up That Package!

The best place to start looking is the travel section of your local Sunday newspaper. Also check the ads in national travel magazines like *Arthur Frommer's Budget Travel, Travel & Leisure, National Geographic Traveler,* and *Condé Nast Traveler.* **Liberty Travel** (☎ **888/271-1584;** www.libertytravel.com) is one of the biggest packagers in the Northeast, and usually boasts a full-page ad in Sunday papers. You won't get much in the way of service, but you will get a good deal. **American Express Vacations** (☎ **800/241-1700**) is another option.

Another good resource is the airlines themselves, which often package their flights together with accommodations. When you pick the airline, you can choose one that has frequent service to your hometown and on which you accumulate frequent flyer miles. Although disreputable packagers are uncommon, they do exist. By buying your package through the airline, you can be pretty sure that the company will still be in business when your departure date arrives.

Among the airline packages, your options include **American Airlines Vacations** (☎ **800/321-2121**), **Delta Vacations** (☎ **800/872-7786**), and **Northwest WorldVacations** (**800/800-1504**). Prices depend on such variables as departure city, time of year, day of the week, class of hotel, and whether you include such extras as tours (often available at discounted rates) and a rental car. For purposes of comparison only—they'll almost certainly change—here are a few prices. All are **per person, double occupancy.** At press time, American was offering 2 nights at the Boston Park Plaza Hotel for $153 to $252, plus airfare, or 2 nights at the Swissôtel Boston for $183 to $218, plus airfare. Northwest offered 2 nights at the Swissôtel Boston and a trolley tour for $198 to $242 per person, plus airfare. Delta Vacations offered airfare from Los Angeles, 3 nights at the Copley Square Hotel, a rental car for 3 days, and trolley tour discounts for $825. Airfare from St. Louis, 5 nights at the Boston Marriott Copley Place, a trolley tour, and a rental car for 5 days was $962.

The biggest hotel chains, casinos, and resorts also offer packages. If you already know where you want to stay, call the chain and ask if it offers land/air packages.

Dollars & Sense

One often-overlooked resource, if you live close enough to take advantage of it, is **Amtrak Vacations** (☎ **800/250-4989;** www.amtrak-northeast.com). At press time, its Best Buys Boston package included 2 nights at the Midtown Hotel, a trolley tour, and round-trip coach transportation from New York for $279 per person or from Washington, D.C., for $315. From more distant cities, sleepers may be available for an extra charge.

Winning the Airfare Wars

Airfares are capitalism at its purest. Passengers on the same airplane—often seated in the same row—rarely pay the same fare. Rather, they pay what the market will bear.

Business travelers who need the flexibility to purchase their tickets at the last minute, change their itinerary at a moment's notice, or want to get home before the weekend pay the premium rate, known as the full fare. Passengers who can book their ticket far in advance, don't mind staying over Saturday night, or are willing to travel on a Tuesday, Wednesday, or Thursday pay the least—usually a fraction of the full fare. On most flights, even the shortest hops, the full fare is close to $1,000 or more, but a 7-day or 14-day advance purchase ticket is closer to $200 to $300. Obviously, it pays to plan ahead.

Let's Make a Deal

The airlines also periodically hold sales, in which they lower the prices on their most popular routes. These fares have advance purchase requirements and date of travel restrictions, but you can't beat the price: usually no more than $400 for a cross-country flight. (If you're scoring at home, that's cheaper than the walk-up shuttle fare from Boston to New York, a 218-mile route.) Keep your eyes open for these sales as you plan your vacation, then pounce on them. The sales tend to take place in seasons of low travel volume—for Boston, January through March. You'll almost never see a sale around the peak summer vacation months of July and August, or around Thanksgiving or Christmas, when people have to fly, regardless of the fare.

Dollars & Sense

If you're willing to spend time to save money, consider flying into Warwick, Rhode Island (outside Providence), or Manchester, New Hampshire. Sound crazy? I've flown out of Providence for about one-third the price of flying out of Boston on the same day at the same time.

   T.F. Green Airport (☎ 888/268-7222; www.pvd-ri.com) is in Warwick, Rhode Island, about 60 miles south of Boston. It's served by American, Continental, Delta, Southwest, United, and US Airways. **Bonanza** (☎ 800/556-3815) offers bus service between the airport and Boston's South Station daily 9am to 9pm; the fare is $15 one way, $27 round-trip. Allow at least 90 minutes.

   Manchester International Airport (☎ 603/624-6556; www.flymanchester.com) is about 51 miles north of Boston. It's served by Continental, Delta Connection, Northwest, Southwest, United, and US Airways. There's no public bus service to Boston, but you can arrange to be picked up and dropped off by **Flight Line** (☎ 800/245-2525). The one-way fare is $28, and 24 hours' notice is required.

Consolidators, also known as bucket shops, are a good place to check for the lowest fares. Their prices are much better than the fares you could get yourself, and are often even lower than those your travel agent can get. You see their ads in the small boxes at the bottom of the page in your Sunday travel section. Some of the most reliable consolidators include **1-800-FLY-4-LESS** or **1-800-FLY-CHEAP.** Another good choice, **Council Travel** (☎ 800/226-8624), caters especially to young travelers, but its prices are available to people of all ages.

Surfing the Web to Fly the Skies

Another way to find the cheapest fare is by using the Internet to do your searching for you. After all, that's what computers do best—search through millions of pieces of data and return information. The number of virtual travel agents on the Internet has increased exponentially in recent years. There are too many companies to mention, but a few of the better-respected ones are **Travelocity** (www.travelocity.com), **Microsoft Expedia** (www.expedia.com), and **Yahoo!** (http://travel.yahoo.com/travel/). Each has its own quirks, but they all provide variations of the same service. Just enter the dates you want to fly and the cities you want to visit, and the computer looks for the lowest fares. Expedia's site will e-mail you the best airfare deal once a week if you choose. Travelocity uses the SABRE computer reservations system that most travel agents use, and has a "Last Minute Deals" database that advertises really cheap fares for those who can get away at a moment's notice.

Remember that you don't *have* to book through the online travel agency; you can ask your flesh-and-blood travel agent to match or beat the best price you've managed to turn up on the Internet.

The Last-Minute Lowdown

Great last-minute deals are available directly from the airlines through a free e-mail service called **E-savers.** Each week, usually on Wednesday, the airline sends you a list of discounted flights, generally leaving that Friday or Saturday, and returning the following Monday or Tuesday.

There are three ways to sign up for all the major airlines at once. You can go to each individual airline's Web site (see box "Airlines on the Web"), which you might want to do anyway to familiarize yourself with their routes and policies. A new service, **Smarter Living** (www.smarterliving.com) sorts through the offerings and e-mails you information only for flights from airports you select. **Epicurious Travel (http://travel.epicurious.com/travel/c_planning/ 02_airfares/email/signup.html**) e-mails your information directly to each airline once you fill out the individual forms.

Airlines on the Web

American Airlines: www.americanair.com
Continental Airlines: www.flycontinental.com
Delta Airlines: www.delta-air.com
Northwest Airlines: www.nwa.com
Southwest Airlines: www.southwest.com
TWA: www.twa.com
United Airlines: www.ual.com
US Airways: www.usairways.com

The Comfort Zone: Making Yourself at Home in the Air

Ordinarily, you'll get your seat assignment when your ticket is issued, and there's a bit more to it than just "window or aisle?" The seats in the front row of each airplane cabin, called the **bulkhead seats,** usually have the most leg room. They have some drawbacks, however. Because there's no seat in front of you, there's no place to put your carry-on luggage, except in the overhead bin. The front row also may not be the best place to see the in-flight movie. And lately, airlines have started putting passengers with young children in the bulkhead row so the kids can sleep on the floor. This is terrific if you have kids, but a nightmare if you have a headache.

Emergency-exit row seats also have extra leg room. They are assigned at the airport, usually on a first-come, first-served basis. Ask when you check in whether you can be seated in one of these rows. You must be at least 15 years old. In the unlikely event of an emergency, you'll be expected to open the emergency exit door and help direct traffic.

You might want to ask for **a seat toward the front** of the plane. The minute the captain turns off the "Fasten Seat Belts" sign after landing, people jump up out of their seats like wedding guests when the bride appears. They then stand around for 5 to 10 minutes while the ground crew puts the gangway in place. The closer to the front of the plane you are, the less hurry-up-and-waiting you'll have to do. Why do you think they put first class in the front?

If you're not in a great hurry, ask for **a seat over the wing or at the back.** When the plane lands, stay where you are, finish your magazine article, primp a little, wait for the congestion to clear, and saunter off like a runway model. The baggage carousel will just be starting when you get there.

If you have special dietary needs, be sure to **order a special meal.** Most airlines offer vegetarian meals, macrobiotic meals, kosher meals, meals for the lactose intolerant, and other special preparations. Ask when you make your reservation if the airline can accommodate your dietary restrictions. Some people without special needs order special meals anyway, because they are made to order, unlike the mass-produced chow served to the rest of the passengers.

Wear comfortable clothes. The days of getting dressed up in a coat and tie to ride an airplane went out with Nehru jackets and poodle skirts. And **dress in layers;** the supposedly controlled climate in airplane cabins is anything but predictable. You'll be glad to have a sweater or jacket that you can put on or take off as the temperature on board dictates.

Bring some toiletries aboard on long flights. Take a travel-size bottle of moisturizer or lotion to refresh your face and hands at the end of the flight. If you're taking an overnight flight (aka the red-eye), don't forget to pack a toothbrush. If you wear contact lenses, take them out before you board, or at least bring eye drops. Also bring a **bottle of water** as an antidote to the Sahara-like cabin conditions.

And if you're flying with **kids,** don't forget chewing gum (for ear pressure problems), a deck of cards or favorite toys to keep them entertained, extra bottles or pacifiers, and a stocked diaper bag.

Jet Lag? I Don't Get Jet Lzzzzz . . .

Jet lag is not usually a problem for flights within the United States, but some people are affected by 3-hour time zone changes. Try this: Start to get acclimated to local time at home, by getting up earlier than usual for 2 or 3 days before you leave. This should tire you out on your first day in Boston, and make it easier to handle waking up when your body's telling you it's still dark at home. And always drink plenty of water when you travel, to avoid dehydration.

Driving to Boston: Don't Say I Didn't Warn You . . .

It looks easy enough—on paper. Major highways approach Boston from the north, west, and south (the Atlantic Ocean approaches from the east), plenty of secondary roads parallel them, and it all appears quite simple. Wrong! Downtown Boston is ground zero for an $11 billion (and counting) highway project that's not scheduled to be completed until 2004. While the downtown or Central Artery portion of I-93 (the north-south interstate) is being moved underground, expect delays at all hours. See chapter 5 for a discussion of staying in the suburbs.

It's Big. Dig?

The "Big Dig," otherwise known as the Central Artery/Third Harbor Tunnel project, is a public-works undertaking with an 11-figure price tag. That's not a typo—the projected cost is currently about $11 billion, and the dig is so big it even has its own Web site (www.bigdig.com). It involves rerouting the elevated highway that cuts through downtown Boston—the Central Artery, or John F. Fitzgerald Expressway—so it runs underground. Planners compare it to performing open-heart surgery on a marathoner while the marathon is going on. Driving on it is only slightly less painful, so try not to.

If You Insist

Getting within striking distance of Boston actually is pretty easy. The Massachusetts Turnpike (I-90), usually called the Mass Pike, is a toll road that runs east-west from the New York border to downtown Boston. The next-to-last exit leaves you in Cambridge. The main north-south route through Boston is I-93, which extends north well into New Hampshire. The main north-south route on the East Coast is I-95, which splits off and runs around Boston as a sort of beltway about 11 miles from downtown, where it's better known as State Route 128.

> ➤ From **New York City, points south, and southwestern Connecticut,** you have several options. My favorite is to take the Hutchinson River Parkway into Connecticut, where it becomes the Merritt Parkway. About 20 miles south of Hartford, follow signs to I-91 north, which leads to I-84 east. At Sturbridge, Massachusetts, pick up the Mass. Pike. (You can also take I-95 from New York City, but it's a heavily traveled truck route and not exactly relaxing or scenic.)

> ➤ From **Vermont and western New Hampshire,** take I-89 to Concord, New Hampshire, then I-93 south.

> ➤ From **Maine and southeastern New Hampshire,** take I-95 south to Route 1 or I-93 south.

> ➤ From **Rhode Island and eastern Connecticut,** you're stuck with I-95. Where it intersects with I-93/Mass. Route 128, follow signs to Braintree, which for some reason outnumber signs pointing to Boston.

> ➤ From **everywhere,** try not to approach downtown Boston on weekdays from 7 to 9am and 3:30 to 6:30pm. The Friday afternoon rush hour is especially brutal—make sure the car has plenty of gas and antifreeze.

All Aboard! Riding the Rails

Amtrak (☎ 800/USA-RAIL or 617/482-3660; www.amtrak.com) runs to **Back Bay Station** and **South Station** from New York and points south and in between. Use Back Bay, on Dartmouth Street across from the Copley Place mall, if you're staying in the Back Bay or South End. Go to South Station, on Atlantic Avenue near the waterfront, if you're staying downtown or in Cambridge (South Station is also a Red Line subway stop). Bring a sweater or sweatshirt (to wear or use as a pillow) and a snack (the on-board offerings are pricey).

Express trains make the trip from New York in a little over 4 hours; others take 4½ to 5 hours or longer. All-reserved Northeast Direct service predominates; fares range from $95 to $128 round-trip. The round-trip unreserved fare is about $90.

For longer trips, it might be easier than you think to find an airfare that's cheaper than the train. From Washington, D.C., count on 8½ hours; Northeast Direct fares run from $132 to $172 round-trip. Unreserved fares range from $122 to $156. Traveling time from Chicago is 22 hours (sleepers are available), and fares range from $128 to $198 round-trip. All fares are subject to change and may fluctuate depending on the time of year. During slow times, excursion fares may be available. Discounts are not available Friday and Sunday afternoon. Always ask for the discounted rate.

Getting There by Bus

Yes, it's cheap. Yes, you can indulge your fantasies about seeing the country-side, swapping stories with soldiers on leave, and playing peekaboo with lit-tle kids (how old are those movies you've been watching?) But with one exception, consider long-distance bus travel a last resort. That exception is New York. The fare is about half that of the train, the Port Authority Bus Terminal is convenient, the bus is fairly comfortable, and the trip sometimes takes less than its scheduled 4½ to 5 hours.

The Boston bus terminal, formally named the **South Station Transportation Center,** is at 700 Atlantic Ave., next to the train station. It's served by the following bus lines: **Greyhound** (☎ 800/231-2222 or 617/526-1801; www.greyhound.com), **American Eagle** (☎ 800/453-5040 or 508/993-5040), **Bonanza** (☎ 800/556-3815 or 617/720-4110), **Brush Hill** (☎ 781/986-6100), **Concord Trailways** (☎ 800/639-3317 or 617/426-8080), **Peter Pan** (☎ 800/237-8747 or 617/426-8554), **Plymouth & Brockton** (☎ 617/773-9401 or 508/746-0378; www.p-b.com), and **Vermont Transit** (☎ 800/451-3292).

All's Fare: Choosing an Airline

Arranging and booking flights is a complicated business—that's why a whole industry has developed to handle it for you. If you're searching around for a deal (or just trying to keep it all straight), it helps to draw yourself a map. The following worksheets will do just that.

You may not be able to get a direct flight, especially if you're trying to save money, so we've included space for you to map out connections you might have to make. If the fare you're quoted involves a connecting flight, make sure you ask how long the layover (time between flights) will be. You cer-tainly don't want to be hanging around an airport for 6 or 8 hours, but you also don't want to be jogging through a terminal with seconds to spare while gate attendants yell, "We've got a runner!" into their walkie-talkies. (Never mind how I know.) Mark layover times in the designated spot on the work-sheet, so you can easily compare them when you're reviewing everything.

1   Schedule & Flight Information Worksheets

Travel Agency: _____ **Phone #:** _____

Agent's Name: _____ **Quoted Fare:** _____

Departure Schedule & Flight Information

Airline: _____ Airport: _____

Flight #: _____ Date: _____ Time: _____am/pm

Arrives in _____ Time: _____ am/pm

Connecting Flight (if any)

Amount of time between flights: _____ hours/mins.

Airline:_____ Flight #:_____ Time: _____am/pm

Arrives in _____ Time: _____ am/pm

Return Trip Schedule & Flight Information

Airline:_____ Airport: _____

Flight #: _____ Date: _____ Time: _____am/pm

Arrives in _____ Time: _____ am/pm

Connecting Flight (if any)

Amount of time between flights: _____ hours/mins.

Airline:_____ Flight #:_____ Time: _____am/pm

Arrives in _____ Time: _____ am/pm

2   Schedule & Flight Information Worksheets

Travel Agency: _____ Phone #: _____

Agent's Name: _____ Quoted Fare: _____

Departure Schedule & Flight Information

Airline: _____ Airport: _____

Flight #: _____ Date: _____ Time: _____am/pm

Arrives in _____ Time: _____ am/pm

Connecting Flight (if any)

Amount of time between flights: _____ hours/mins.

Airline:_____ Flight #:_____ Time: _____am/pm

Arrives in _____ Time: _____ am/pm

Return Trip Schedule & Flight Information

Airline:_____ Airport: _____

Flight #: _____ Date: _____ Time: _____am/pm

Arrives in _____ Time: _____ am/pm

Connecting Flight (if any)

Amount of time between flights: _____ hours/mins.

Airline:_____ Flight #:_____ Time: _____am/pm

Arrives in _____ Time: _____ am/pm

3 Schedule & Flight Information Worksheets

Travel Agency: _____ **Phone #:** _____

Agent's Name: _____ **Quoted Fare:** _____

Departure Schedule & Flight Information

Airline: _____ Airport: _____

Flight #: _____ Date: _____ Time: _____am/pm

Arrives in _____ Time: _____ am/pm

Connecting Flight (if any)

Amount of time between flights: _____ hours/mins.

Airline:_____ Flight #:_____ Time: _____am/pm

Arrives in _____ Time: _____ am/pm

Return Trip Schedule & Flight Information

Airline:_____ Airport: _____

Flight #: _____ Date: _____ Time: _____am/pm

Arrives in _____ Time: _____ am/pm

Connecting Flight (if any)

Amount of time between flights: _____ hours/mins.

Airline:_____ Flight #:_____ Time: _____am/pm

Arrives in _____ Time: _____ am/pm

4   Schedule & Flight Information Worksheets

Travel Agency: _____   **Phone #:** _____

Agent's Name: _____   **Quoted Fare:** _____

Departure Schedule & Flight Information

Airline: _____   Airport: _____

Flight #: _____ Date: _____ Time: _____am/pm

Arrives in _____ Time: _____ am/pm

Connecting Flight (if any)

Amount of time between flights: _____ hours/mins.

Airline:_____ Flight #:_____ Time: _____am/pm

Arrives in _____ Time: _____ am/pm

Return Trip Schedule & Flight Information

Airline:_____   Airport: _____

Flight #: _____ Date: _____ Time: _____am/pm

Arrives in _____ Time: _____ am/pm

Connecting Flight (if any)

Amount of time between flights: _____ hours/mins.

Airline:_____ Flight #:_____ Time: _____am/pm

Arrives in _____ Time: _____ am/pm

Chapter 4

Tying Up the Loose Ends

> ### In This Chapter
>
> ➤ More on cars in and around Boston
>
> ➤ Tips on buying (or not buying) travel insurance
>
> ➤ What to do in case of illness
>
> ➤ Making entertainment reservations
>
> ➤ What to pack

Now you know how you're getting to Boston, and that wasn't so bad, was it? Unless you're planning to hang around the airport for a while and then head home, however, you have some more decisions to make—little things like where to stay and what to do. We'll get to those soon. First we have to get you out the door, secure in the knowledge that you're as well prepared as you can be. Here's a roundup of the stuff that takes 2 minutes when you're at home and keeps you up nights when you're not.

Do I Need to Rent a Car in Boston?

Simply put, no. For getting around Boston and Cambridge, a car is far more trouble than it's worth. You'll be up against horrific traffic, deranged drivers, impossible parking, and a little thing called the "Big Dig," that enormous highway construction site downtown.

Okay, Smarty, Do I Need to Rent a Car in the Boston Area?

If you're off to the suburbs or Cape Cod, and you don't want to be tethered to a public transportation schedule or tour group, you have my blessing. And don't forget that you don't have to be saddled with a car (and the accompanying parking hassles) for the length of your stay if you're only using it for a day or two. The major car-rental agencies have downtown Boston offices, and most operate in Cambridge as well. Some companies, including **Enterprise** (☎ **800/736-8222**), offer pick-up and drop-off service.

Tourist Traps

Boston levies a $10 surcharge on car rentals that's earmarked for construction of a new convention center. Yes, that does seem a bit sneaky. Get around it by renting in Cambridge, Brookline, or another suburb.

Let's Make a Deal: Getting the Best Rate

And you thought airfares were complicated! Auto-rental rates depend on the size of the car, how long you keep it, where and when you pick it up, how far you drive it (sometimes), and a number of other factors, including the time of year.

Asking the right questions can save you a ton of money. Weekend rates usually are less than weekday rates, and they sometimes start as early as noon Thursday; be sure to find out. If you're keeping the car for 5 or more days, the weekly rate may be cheaper than the daily rate. If you're renting in Boston (see "Tourist Traps" box), ask if the rate is different at the airport and in town. If you'd like to drop off the car at a different location than the one where you picked it up, most companies charge a steep fee; others, notably National, do not.

Dollars & Sense

Many companies offer promotional rates or other deals that are available only if you know the right code. You might see codes in newspaper and magazine ads, or on those slips of paper that flutter out of your credit card and frequent flyer statements. Even if you're not taking advantage of a special deal, don't forget to ask about deals for members of AAA, AARP, frequent flyer programs, trade unions, and other organizations to which you belong. You might be entitled to a discount of 5% to 30%.

Catching a Deal on the Web

Spare yourself the annoying chore of comparing rates on each company's Web site by using a search engine. One useful resource, **Yahoo Travel** (http://travel.yahoo.com/travel/; choose "Reserve car"), allows you to look up rental prices for any size car at more than a dozen companies in hundreds of cities. You enter the size car you want, the rental and return dates and times, and the city where you want to rent, and the server returns a price. It will even make your reservation for you. (If you're taking advantage of a promotional rate, you'll probably have to do some calling, but you'll at least have a sense of the undiscounted price.)

What Are All These Other Charges?

On top of the standard rental prices, optional charges apply to most car rentals. You might not need to concern yourself with these—check with your auto insurance agent at home and read the fine print on your credit card agreement to see if you already have coverage.

The **collision damage waiver** (CDW), which requires you to pay for damage to the car in a collision, is illegal in some states, but is covered by many credit card companies. It can be as much as $10 a day, so be sure to check beforehand.

The car-rental companies also offer additional **liability** insurance (if you harm others in an accident), **personal accident** insurance (if you harm yourself or your passengers), and **personal effects** insurance (if your luggage is stolen from your car). If you have insurance on your car at home, you are probably covered for most of these unlikelihoods. If your policy doesn't cover you for rentals, or if you don't have auto insurance, you should consider the additional coverage (the car-rental companies are liable for certain base amounts, depending on the state). But weigh the likelihood of getting into an accident or losing your luggage against the cost of this coverage (as much as $20 a day combined), which can significantly add to the price of your rental.

Some companies also offer **refueling** packages, in which you pay for an entire tank of gas up front. The price is usually fairly competitive with local gas prices, but you don't get credit for any gas remaining in the tank. If you reject this option, you pay only for the gas you use, but you have to return it with a full tank or face sky-high charges (as much as $4 a gallon) for any shortfall. If time is short and a stop at a gas station will make you miss your plane, then take advantage of the fuel purchase option. Otherwise, skip it.

Use this worksheet to help you keep track of rates. Before you start, know the date and time you expect to pick up and return the car, the applicable discounts, and whether you'll need insurance. Be sure the reservations agent knows you're willing to be flexible (if you are), and be sure you ask for the **grand total**, including taxes, fees, and surcharges, not just the daily rate.

Car Rental Comparison Worksheet

Company	Type of car	No. of Days	Rate
Alamo (☎ 800/327-9633)			
Avis (☎ 800/831-2847)			
Budget (☎ 800/527-0700)			
Dollar (☎ 800/800-4000)			
Enterprise (☎ 800/325-8007)			
Hertz (☎ 800/654-3131)			
National (☎ 800/227-7368)			
Thrifty (☎ 800/367-2277)			
Other			
Other			
Other			

What About Travel Insurance?

There are three kinds of travel insurance: **trip cancellation, medical,** and **lost luggage.** Trip cancellation insurance is a good idea if you have paid a large portion of your vacation expenses up front. It's also critical if you or a family member gets sick or dies, and you can't travel.

The other two types of insurance don't make sense for most travelers. Your existing health insurance should cover you if you get sick while on vacation. *Before you leave home,* call your insurer to see whether you are fully covered away from home, and what procedures you need to follow. This is especially important if you belong to an HMO (like mine) that strictly defines "life-threatening emergency." You may need advance authorization for treatment of ailments—such as broken bones—that you would swear are emergencies but that aren't considered life-threatening.

History 101

Doctors at Boston's Massachusetts General Hospital performed the world's first operation under general anesthesia (the removal of a jaw tumor) in 1846.

45

Your homeowner's insurance should cover stolen luggage if you have off-premises theft. Check your existing policies before you buy any additional coverage. The airlines are responsible for $1,250 on domestic flights if they lose your luggage; if you plan to carry anything more valuable than that, keep it in your carry-on bag.

Some credit cards (American Express and certain gold and platinum Visa and MasterCards, for example) offer automatic flight insurance against death or dismemberment in case of an airplane crash. If you feel you need more insurance, try one of the companies listed below. But don't pay for more insurance than you need. For example, if you only need trip cancellation insurance, don't purchase coverage for lost or stolen property. Trip cancellation insurance costs approximately 6% to 8% of the total value of your vacation. Among the reputable issuers of travel insurance are:

➤ **Access America,** 6600 W. Broad St., Richmond, VA 23230 (☎ **800/284-8300**)

➤ **Mutual of Omaha,** Mutual of Omaha Plaza, Omaha, NE 68175 (☎ **800/228-9792**)

➤ **Travel Guard International,** 1145 Clark St., Stevens Point, WI 54481 (☎ **800/826-1300**)

➤ **Travel Insured International, Inc.,** P.O. Box 280568, East Hartford, CT 06128 (☎ **800/243-3174**)

What if I Get Sick Away from Home?

It can sometimes be hard to find a doctor you trust when you're away from home. (In Boston, if it's any consolation, you'll at least have a lot of choices.) Bring all your medications with you, as well as a prescription for more if you might run out. If you have health insurance, be sure to carry your identification card in your wallet. Bring an extra pair of contact lenses in case you lose one. And don't forget the Pepto-Bismol for common travelers' ailments like upset stomach or diarrhea.

Medic!

If you suffer from a chronic illness, talk to your doctor before traveling. For such conditions as epilepsy, diabetes, or a heart ailment, wear a **Medic Alert Identification Tag.** It immediately alerts any doctor to your condition and gives him or her access to your medical records through Medic Alert's 24-hour hot line. Membership is $35, plus a $15 annual fee. Contact the Medic Alert Foundation, P.O. Box 1009, Turlock, CA 95381-1009 (☎ **800/825-3785;** www.medicalert.org).

If you're really worried about getting sick away from home, consider buying medical insurance (see the section on travel insurance, above). It will cover you more completely than your existing health insurance, but again, weigh the expense against the likelihood that something catastrophic will happen.

If you do get sick, ask the concierge at your hotel to recommend a local doctor—even his or her own doctor if necessary. Most large hotels can recommend someone at any hour. Boston being the medical mecca that it is, there are several reliable referral services. Try **Beth Israel Deaconess Health Information Line** (☎ 617/667-5356), **Brigham and Women's Hospital Physician Referral Service** (☎ 800/294-9999), **Massachusetts General Hospital Physician Referral Service** (☎ 800/711-4-MGH), or **New England Medical Center Physician Referral Service** (☎ 617/636-9700).

If you can't get a doctor to help you right away, try an emergency room. Many have walk-in clinics for emergency cases that are not life-threatening. You may not get immediate attention, but you won't pay the high price of an emergency room visit (usually a minimum of $300 just for signing your name, on top of whatever treatment you receive). See appendix A for listings of local hospitals.

Making Reservations & Getting Tickets Ahead of Time

You'll never have trouble finding something to do in Boston, but don't count on waltzing up to a ticket window half an hour before a sporting event, symphony or ballet performance, or road production of a hot Broadway show and coming away with anything but a laugh and a brochure. If you have something specific in mind, you'll need to plan ahead.

The major ticket agencies that serve Boston are **Ticketmaster** (☎ 617/931-2000; www.ticketmaster.com), **Next Ticketing** (☎ 617/423-NEXT; www.boston.com/next), and **Tele-Charge** (☎ 800/447-7400).

Boston Entertainment: What's Up?

The general outlets listed in chapter 1 can give you an idea of what to expect during your visit. Tourist information offices often know about big shows (stage as well as museum) many months in advance. The front desk staff at your hotel might be able to tip you off, too. To find out more before you leave home, you might check at your local newsstand for a copy of the monthly *Boston* magazine, or call ☎ **617/262-9700** to order a single copy.

The *Boston Globe* "Calendar" section (Thursday) and *Boston Herald* "Scene" section (Friday) generally list upcoming events only a week in advance; if you're traveling on short notice, ask if it's possible for the staff at your hotel to save you a copy. There are two other excellent sources of entertainment and nightlife listings: The *Boston Phoenix* (Thursday) stays on newsstands all week, and the biweekly *Improper Bostonian* (Tuesday) is available free at newspaper boxes around the city.

Time-Savers

The concierge or desk staff at your hotel may be able to help you get tickets to events and shows. It doesn't hurt to ask, especially if something's on that you're particularly eager to see. If you do wind up taking advantage of this service, a tip is in order.

Entertainment on the Web

➤ **www.boston.com** includes the *Globe* "Calendar" section and *Boston* magazine's listings.

➤ **www.bostonphoenix.com** has all the nonvirtual edition's listings.

➤ **www.boston.sidewalk.com** includes Microsoft's cultural and restaurant coverage.

➤ **www.fleetcenter.com** lists upcoming sports events, ice shows, and concerts.

Sports on the Web

➤ **Bruins** (hockey): www.bostonbruins.com

➤ **Celtics** (basketball): www.bostonceltics.com

➤ **Patriots** (football): www.patriots.com

➤ **Red Sox** (baseball): www.redsox.com

➤ **Boston Athletic Association:** www.bostonmarathon.org

➤ **Suffolk Downs** (horse racing): www.suffolkdowns.com

Performing Arts on the Web

➤ **Boston Symphony Orchestra** and **Boston Pops:** www.bso.org

➤ **Boston Ballet:** www.boston.com/bostonballet

➤ **Wang Center** (includes Wang Theatre and Shubert Theater): www.boston.com/wangcenter

➤ **American Repertory Theatre:** www.amrep.org

➤ **Huntington Theatre Company:** www.bu.edu/huntington

Museums on the Web

➤ **Computer Museum:** www.tcm.org

➤ **Harvard University Museum of Cultural and Natural History:** www.peabody.harvard.edu

➤ **Institute of Contemporary Art:** www.primalpub.com/ica

➤ **Isabella Stuart Gardner Museum:** www.boston.com/gardner

➤ **Museum of Fine Arts:** www.mfa.org

➤ **Museum of Science:** www.mos.org

➤ **New England Aquarium:** www.neaq.org

➤ **Society for the Preservation of New England Antiquities:** www.spnea.org

Dinner at Eight?

At popular restaurants, tables for Friday and Saturday night sometimes are booked a couple of months in advance. If you have your heart set on eating at a place you've read or heard about, remember that lots of other people know about it, too, and make your reservation as soon as possible. This is another area where your concierge may be able to lend a hand. It doesn't always work, but it's worth a try. And if you're able to be flexible, weeknights sometimes are considerably less busy.

Baggage Compartment: What to Pack & How Much

Assemble everything you think you'll need, then get rid of half of it. I say this not because the airlines won't let you take it all—they will, with some limits—but because you don't want to get a hernia from lugging around everything in your bottom three dresser drawers.

Start by picking out a pair of comfortable **walking shoes** (not sandals). Sore feet make everything less enjoyable, and you're going to be doing a lot of walking. Dressing in layers is always a good idea. You never know when the wind will start coming out of the east, or when you'll find yourself in a store, museum, or theater where refrigeration substitutes for air-conditioning. At the height of summer, something as skimpy as a **long-sleeved T-shirt** may be enough; the rest of the year, take a **sweater, light jacket,** or **fleece top.**

Other essentials: a **camera, toiletries and medications** (packed in your carry-on bag so you'll have them if the airline loses your luggage), a **sun hat** and **sunscreen,** and **sleepwear.** During the day, **jeans or khakis** are suitable almost everywhere. See the list below for more fashion advice.

Carry On, Carry Off

When choosing your **suitcase,** think about the kind of traveling you'll be doing. If you'll be walking with your luggage on hard floors, a bag with wheels makes sense. If you'll be negotiating uneven roads or lots of stairs, wheels won't help much. A fold-over **garment bag** will help keep dressy clothes wrinkle-free, but can be a nuisance if you'll be packing and unpacking a lot. Hard-sided luggage protects breakable items better, but weighs more than soft-sided bags.

49

Best Foot Forward

The footwear that traditionally screams "tourist" is sandals with socks—never an attractive look anyway, and in fin de siècle Boston, possibly hazardous. Because of the Big Dig, there's gravel everywhere, just waiting to insinuate itself into your arches. Wear closed shoes when you go sightseeing.

Pack the biggest, hardest items (usually **shoes**) at the bottom of your bag, then fit smaller items in and around them. Pack **breakable items** between or rolled up in several layers of clothes, or keep them in your carry-on bag. Put **things that could leak**—shampoo, sunscreen, moisturizer—in plastic zipper bags, and throw in a few **extra plastic bags** for dirty laundry. Lock your suitcase with a small **padlock** (available at most luggage stores, if your bag doesn't already have one), and put **identification tags** on the inside and outside.

You're allowed **two pieces of carry-on luggage,** a limit most airlines have begun enforcing strictly, especially on crowded flights. Ask the reservations clerk or travel agent for the exact dimensions allowed, and expect to be forced to check a bag at the gate if you try to sneak on an extralarge piece. A laptop computer counts as a piece of luggage, and can't be checked unless it's in the original, unopened factory packaging.

In a bag that you know won't have to be checked (and possibly delayed or lost), pack **anything irreplaceable,** such as your return ticket, passport, expensive jewelry, and prescription medication. Also bring along anything **breakable,** a **book** or **magazines,** a personal **stereo** with headphones, and a **snack** in case you don't like the airline food. Leave a little space for the **sweater or jacket** that you won't want to be wearing while you're waiting for your luggage in an overheated terminal.

It's Called the Red-Eye for a Reason

If you're **flying overnight,** don't forget to pack a **toothbrush** and **toothpaste.** If you wear contact lenses, you'll want **glasses and solutions** or at least **eyedrops.** And after tumbling off an all-night flight, I'm always glad to have a **clean shirt** to change into.

Winter Wonderland

From late November through at least March, you'll need a **warm jacket** or **heavy coat, hat and gloves,** and **sturdy boots.** If there's snow on the ground, don't worry about packing your party shoes unless you're planning an elegant dinner at a restaurant in your hotel.

Strappy sandals and slush just don't mix. That's not to say your neon-green après-ski boots won't be frowned on, but my plain snow boots have fit right in at some of the fanciest restaurants in the city.

Top Hat, White Tie & Tails?

Boston is a generally casual city—all those students lowering the bar, don't-cha know. During the day, especially in the summer, just about anything goes. In the evening, you won't feel overdressed in a coat and tie or dressy outfit at the theater, symphony, ballet, or better restaurants. A few restaurants require jackets for men, but most have no dress code, so I'll appeal to your conscience: If you were paying through the nose for a dinner that included a marriage proposal or anniversary celebration, would you want to be two tables over from someone in an I'M WITH STUPID T-shirt?

Packing Checklist—Don't Forget Your Toothbrush

- [ ] Socks (one pair for each day)
- [ ] Underwear (one pair for each day)
- [ ] Shoes (try to keep this to two or three pair; don't forget a good pair of walking shoes)
- [ ] Pants and/or skirts
- [ ] Shirts or blouses
- [ ] Sweaters and/or jackets
- [ ] Umbrella (you never know when you'll need one)
- [ ] A sun hat and sunscreen
- [ ] A belt
- [ ] A coat and tie or a dress (if you plan to go someplace fancy in the evening)
- [ ] Shorts
- [ ] Coat or jacket, hat and gloves, boots
- [ ] Bathing suit (and maybe a towel, if you're going to the beach)
- [ ] Workout clothes
- [ ] Toiletries (don't forget a razor, shaving cream, toothbrush, toothpaste, comb, deodorant, makeup, contact lens solutions, hair-care products, hair dryer if necessary, extra pair of glasses, sewing kit)
- [ ] Camera (with film; it can be very expensive when you're traveling)
- [ ] Medications (pack these in a carry-on bag so that you'll have them even if you lose your luggage)

Part 2

Finding the Hotel That's Good for You

A hotel is like a job: You might not appreciate it when all's well, but if things start to go wrong, boy, do you know it. Whether you consider your hotel room a home away from home or a storage locker that happens to contain a bed, you need a suitable place to rest up.

Boston and its immediate suburbs offer the full range of accommodations, from simple to splendid. This section will help you figure out where you fit on that scale. We'll discuss location, with the pluses and minuses of each neighborhood. We'll discuss price, "rack rates," how to avoid paying them, and how to get a deal. We'll discuss amenities and the compromises you might be willing to make—there's no point in paying for a pool or a business center that you won't be using. And we'll guide you through the process of deciding how important each of those elements is to you, and help you find a hotel that fits your profile.

Chapter 5

Pillow Talk: The Lowdown on the Boston Hotel Scene

In This Chapter

➤ How to choose a neighborhood

➤ Should I get out of town?

➤ How to get the most for your money

➤ How to choose a hotel

➤ How to choose a room

With business and tourism booming, Boston's lodging market is one of the hottest in the country. The average occupancy rate is well over 80%, and a number of new hotels are under construction. That doesn't mean you have to pay a fortune to stay in a convenient location, or take your life in your hands to stay within budget. It does mean (you knew this was coming, right?) you have to do some planning. The information here and the reviews and worksheet in chapter 6 will help you through it.

Location! Location! Location!

Open to a map and you'll see: Central Boston is tiny, and the parts of the city where you'll be spending most of your time make up a compact, manageable area. You can get just about everywhere you might want to go on foot, by public transit, or in a cab. Cambridge is across the Charles River; Harvard Square is 15 to 20 minutes from downtown Boston by Red Line subway. Here's a rundown of the most popular neighborhoods in both cities, along with some advice about staying in the suburbs.

Downtown Boston

This small neighborhood—the territory east and northeast of Boston Common—consists of four even smaller areas. I'll describe them separately, but bear in mind that geographically they're almost indistinguishable. One quality they share is a lack of abundant open space, but this is where you'll find many of the stops on the Freedom Trail. It's a predominantly commercial area, especially compared to nearby Beacon Hill and the North End, which are more residential. If you plan to spend a lot of time in the Back Bay or Cambridge, downtown isn't the most convenient place to stay—weigh the positives against the time and expense of getting back and forth. And in case you're wondering, there is no midtown or uptown.

The **Waterfront** is the narrow area east of I-93. It's lively all day, especially in the summer, and convenient to public transportation and the airport. Its main drawback is the Big Dig. Despite the efforts of everyone involved, the construction site is always confusing, often dusty, and sometimes noisy.

The area around **Faneuil Hall Marketplace** is almost always busy, day and night—lively, but not relaxing. It's centrally located, there's plenty to do at the marketplace and nearby, and public transportation is convenient. A minus, and it can be a big one: The Big Dig borders on this area, too.

The **Financial District,** west of the Waterfront and south of Faneuil Hall, is great if you're in town for business, not so great if you're not. The downtown attractions and shopping are nearby, but public transportation isn't right next door (as it is elsewhere downtown). The Financial District is frantic on weekdays and slows down considerably at night and on weekends.

Downtown Crossing lies between the Financial District, State Street and Court Street, Tremont Street, and Kneeland Street. It's a busy shopping area, not quite as upscale as the Back Bay, with lots of offices. This is another convenient section that's fairly quiet at night.

In a nutshell:

➤ It's close to many attractions, including most of the Freedom Trail.

➤ Public transportation is generally convenient.

➤ The beautiful harbor is close by.

But:

➤ Most nightlife is either overwhelming or underwhelming.

➤ You'll be commuting to the Back Bay and Cambridge.

➤ The Big Dig.

Beacon Hill

If you have a picture of Boston in your mind's eye, it probably looks like Beacon Hill, with beautiful town houses and lots of red brick and cobblestones. This plush area in the shadow of the State House is mostly residential, with shops on

Charles Street and stores on Cambridge Street. Bounded by Government Center, Boston Common, and the river, it's convenient to Massachusetts General Hospital, Cambridge's Kendall Square, and three T stops.

In a nutshell:

➤ It's close to downtown.

➤ It's gorgeous.

➤ Public transportation access is good.

But:

➤ There aren't many hotels.

➤ Boston Common isn't as pleasant as the Public Garden.

➤ That hill is *steep*.

Back Bay

The largest neighborhood in central Boston, the Back Bay is bounded by the Public Garden, the Charles River, Kenmore Square, and to the south by either Huntington Avenue or St. Botolph Street, depending on whom you ask. From Commonwealth Avenue to the river, it's mostly residential; on Newbury Street and points south, there's excellent shopping, in tons of boutiques and two large malls. The downtown attractions aren't far, but they're not next door, either. The main transportation option (besides walking) is the anti-quated Green Line, with the Orange Line close enough to be an option. The bus to Cambridge runs along Massachusetts Avenue (known as "Mass. Ave."), and Back Bay Station serves Amtrak as well as the Orange Line.

To make the area a bit easier to describe, I'll use an artificial demarcation line. The part of the Back Bay **east of Copley Square** includes the lovely Public Garden, its adjacent luxury hotels (the Four Seasons and the Ritz-Carlton), and some of the most city's most fashionable shops. Although it's not technically part of the Back Bay, the **Theater District** is within shouting dis-tance, centered around the intersection of Tremont and Stuart streets.

From Copley Square west, the Back Bay gets funkier, with more college stu-dents, shoppers, and tourists. The Prudential Center and Copley Place form a megamall, with three huge hotels, dozens of stores, and access to the Hynes Convention Center. The **South End** is a separate neighborhood whose most prominent lodging (the Chandler Inn Hotel) is almost in the Back Bay.

History 101

The Back Bay gets its name from the body of water that was filled in to create it. That undertaking started in 1835 and wasn't completed until 1882. Thanks to this and other large landfill projects, the city tripled in area in the 19th century.

In a nutshell:

➤ There are plenty of hotel rooms.

➤ Public transportation is good.

➤ You can shop till you drop.

But:

➤ You'll be commuting to the downtown attractions.

➤ Cambridge isn't all that convenient (the bus is sometimes maddeningly slow).

➤ You can shop till you drop.

The Outskirts, Including Brookline

Visitors to Boston can grow spoiled by the fact that downtown is so small—what I'm describing as "outskirts" would be centrally located in many other large cities. If being smack in the middle of everything isn't for you, consider staying a little farther from downtown, around **Kenmore Square** or in **Brookline.** In exchange for generally lower prices and a slower pace, you commit to commuting, usually on the Green Line. (One hotel in this area, the Doubletree Guest Suites, isn't on a public transit line.) You'll be close to Fenway Park, and in somewhat more residential surroundings (the Doubletree is an exception here, too). Although Harvard Square is not far geographically, it's not that easy to get to unless you feel like driving or taking a long walk.

In a nutshell:

➤ Prices are generally lower.

➤ The atmosphere is more residential and less frantic.

➤ Fenway Park is nearby.

But:

➤ Most attractions are some distance away.

➤ You're tethered to the Green Line.

➤ Harvard Square is inconvenient unless you have a car.

Harvard Square

Thousands of students contribute to the lively atmosphere in Harvard Square, which offers a good mix of sightseeing and shopping. If you've visited before but haven't been back in a while, don't expect the bohemian atmosphere of years past—this is an upscale area, with prices to match. The neighborhood radiates out from the intersection of John F. Kennedy and Brattle streets and Massachusetts Avenue. It's always busy, but it's not far from quieter areas, notably the banks of the river and the posh residential area to the west. Subway access to downtown Boston is good, and the Mass. Ave. bus runs to the

Back Bay. (Because I'm concentrating on areas with easy access, I've omitted the many fine lodgings elsewhere in Cambridge. For a more complete selection, consult *Frommer's Boston*.)

In a nutshell:

➤ It's bustling and lively.

➤ Public transportation is good.

➤ Shopping is excellent.

But:

➤ It's expensive.

➤ It can get very crowded.

➤ You'll be commuting to the downtown attractions.

Should I Just Stay at a Suburban Motel?

First, let's define "suburban motel"—a moderately priced place, usually part of a chain, that's not connected to downtown Boston *by subway*. This is an excellent question, and off the top of my head, I'd say no. Still, the answer depends on a number of variables, including the time of year, your tolerance for commuting, the length of your stay, whether you're traveling by car, whether children are along, and the state of your budget. You may learn about a suburban motel through your travel agent, by picking it out of a guidebook (AAA is my choice for this sort of thing), or by calling your favorite chain and asking for a room in the Boston area. A discussion of the variables follows.

➤ **What time of year is it?:** If it's foliage or graduation season and you're traveling at the last minute, you may not have a choice.

➤ **Do you like commuting?:** You'll likely drive or take the commuter rail (or both) to get downtown.

Tourist Traps

If you can't or don't want to use our accommodations suggestions—what's your problem? Seriously, one thing to watch out for is lodgings with "Boston" in their names that are closer to New Hampshire or Rhode Island than to downtown. If the reservations clerk is vague about just how inconvenient a hotel is, ask *very* specific questions, such as "How long is the walk to the Museum of Science?"

➤ **How long is your stay?:** Life is too short to spend 2 days sweating the train schedule or searching for parking. If you're in town for a week, you'll probably feel less pressure to pack in a lot of activities, and the time spent in transit won't be as bothersome.

➤ **Are you driving?:** If you must travel by car, you might welcome the chance to use a free parking space and venture into town. Often this goes along with:

➤ **Are the children along?:** My siblings and I didn't care if we were in a castle or a barn, as long as it had a pool, a candy machine, and maybe some video games. Assume *nothing*—talk to your kids about what they want out of this vacation. If they're not fired up about everything you hope to see and do, easy access to activities isn't as important. You can balance a few manageable sojourns into town with some quality time on the water slide.

➤ **The state of your budget:** A less convenient location sounds a lot better if you get a great deal. Just make sure it is a *great* deal—if the savings goes right into carfare and parking fees, it isn't.

What Kind of Place Is Right for You?

You're probably tired of being told this, but it's true: The answer to this question depends on you. Boston has lodgings of every description, from one step above a holding cell (you're on your own there) to one step below Buckingham Palace. What says "vacation" to you? If you live in a Victorian house in a little town, a downtown tower may look like Oz to you. If this is a once-in-a-lifetime trip—your honeymoon, a milestone anniversary—extravagant pampering may be just the thing. If you travel a lot for business, the homey atmosphere of a B&B might be a good choice. If you can only spend $100 a night but you're dying to stay at the Four Seasons, join the club.

Giant hotels that are part of the huge chains tend to be well appointed, centrally located, and dull, dull, dull. We list a few of these because they're particularly agreeable or the only choice in a certain neighborhood, but there are plenty of other reliable options in the area. See Appendix B for a list of the major chains' toll-free numbers and Web sites.

Independent hotels might offer almost the same level of appointments (and prices) but generally are smaller and more distinctive, with more personal service. Their business and fitness facilities might not be as extensive as those at the chain hotels, so be sure to ask about your own make-or-break features.

We also list some motels, inns, and guest houses. When you book a room at one of these smaller properties, you're choosing affordability over opulence, and I can't say I blame you. The establishments listed in chapter 6 all have at least 12 rooms (most have a lot more), which leaves out a whole parallel universe of great, small places. Most of them are B&Bs; read on for more information.

Where There's Smoke

Accommodations reserved for nonsmokers—often in blocks as large as several floors—are increasingly common, but nonsmokers should not assume they'll get a smoke-free room without specifically requesting one. As smokers are squeezed into fewer rooms, the ones they use become saturated with the smell of smoke, even in hotels that are otherwise antiseptic. To avoid this disagreeable situation, be sure that everyone who handles your reservation knows you need a smoke-free room. And if you want to say you're allergic, we'll never tell.

Make Yourself at Home: The Scoop on B&Bs

As hotel prices head for the stratosphere, bed-and-breakfasts grow ever more popular. In Boston and Cambridge, they range from spare rooms with shared bathrooms to antique-filled honeymoon suites. Most B&Bs are so small that it's not worth your time to call around to a whole bunch. One of the following agencies will do the work for you, but be sure to make arrangements *well in advance,* especially during busy periods. With enough notice, an agency can make a good match—and intervene before an innkeeper who makes a gourmet breakfast to order meets a guest who just wants directions to the nearest McDonald's.

Expect to pay at least $60 a night, and sometimes much more, for a double in the summer; many places have a 2-night minimum stay, and some offer winter discounts.

➤ **Bed and Breakfast Associates Bay Colony Ltd.,** P.O. Box 57166, Babson Park Branch, Boston, MA 02157-0166 (☎ **888/486-6018** or 781/449-5302; fax 781/449-5958; www.bnbboston.com; e-mail info@bnbboston.com).

➤ **Bed and Breakfast Agency of Boston,** 47 Commercial Wharf, Boston, MA 02110 (☎ **800/CITY-BNB** or 617/720-3540; fax 617/523-5761).

➤ **Host Homes of Boston,** P.O. Box 117, Waban Branch, Boston, MA 02168-0001 (☎ **617/244-1308**; fax 617/244-5156).

➤ **Bed & Breakfast Reservations North Shore/Greater Boston/Cape Cod,** P.O. Box 35, Newtonville, MA 02460 (☎ **800/832-2632** outside Massachusetts or 617/964-1606; fax 617/332-8572; www.bbreserve.com; e-mail bnbinc@ix.netcom.com).

➤ **New England Bed and Breakfast,** P.O. Box 1426, Waltham, MA 02154 (☎ **617/244-2112**).

The Price Is Right: How to Get a Deal

The **rack rate** is the maximum amount that a hotel charges for a room. It's the rate you'd get if you walked in off the street and asked for a room for the night. You sometimes see the rate printed on the fire/emergency exit diagrams posted on the back of your door.

Hotels are happy to charge you the rack rate, but you should *never* have to pay it! Hardly anybody does. Perhaps the best way to avoid paying the rack rate is surprisingly simple: Just ask for a cheaper or discounted rate. You may be pleasantly surprised.

In all but the smallest accommodations, the price depends on many factors, not the least of which is how you make your reservation. A travel agent may be able to negotiate a better deal with certain hotels than you could get by yourself. (That's because the hotel gives the agent a discount in exchange for steering his or her business toward that hotel.) Reserving a room through the hotel's toll-free number may result in a lower rate than if you called the hotel directly. On the other hand, the central reservations number may not know about discounts at specific locations. For example, local franchises may offer a special group rate for a wedding or family reunion, but they may neglect to tell the central booking line. Your best bet is to call both the local number and the central number and see which one gives you a better deal.

Ask a lot of questions. Room rates change with the season and as occupancy rates rise and fall. If a hotel is close to full, it is less likely to offer discounts; if it's close to empty, it may be willing to negotiate. This can change from day to day, so if you're willing to be flexible, say so. Downtown business hotels are most crowded on weekdays, and many offer discounted rates for weekend stays. Room prices are subject to change without notice, so even the rates quoted in this book may not be the actual rates when you make your reservation. Be sure to mention membership in AAA, AARP, frequent flyer programs, and any other corporate rewards program when you make your reservation. You never know when it might be worth a few dollars off your room rate.

Dollars & Sense

The unpredictable weather makes January through March the only slow season in the Boston hotel business. You may have to put up with some snow, and you'll almost definitely encounter bitter cold and howling winds, but you might also snag a great deal.

Here are a few ways to save money on your room:

➤ **Weekend packages:** The most commonly offered package is for a weekend, and sometimes it includes breakfast or parking, too. Business-oriented hotels in particular offer discounts to keep volume up. If your first-choice hotel doesn't, try another. Many deals are advertised in the travel section of major newspapers.

➤ **Corporate discounts:** Many hotels, especially branches of the large chains, offer corporate rates; be sure to ask if you qualify.

➤ **Senior and AARP rates:** If you're over 64 (or over 49 and an AARP member), there's a good chance you're eligible for a senior discount.

➤ **AAA rates:** Many budget and moderate chains, and lots of smaller accommodations, give a break to AAA members.

➤ **All-in-one/inclusive packages:** Packages often include lodging, meals, transportation, sightseeing, or some combination thereof. See chapter 3 for more information.

➤ **Family rates or packages:** Deals for families vary from hotel to hotel and from weekday to weekend. Ask what's available, and be sure to find out *exactly* how many kids of what age can stay free. For more pointers, see the section on traveling with kids, below.

➤ **Holiday rates:** If you have to travel on a holiday, ask if the hotel offers a special rate.

You Do the Math: Taxes & Other Charges

As you calculate the price of your room, don't forget to include the **room tax.** In Boston and Cambridge, it's 12.45%, which includes 2.75% that goes toward a new convention center. When you make your reservation, be sure to ask whether the quoted rate includes taxes. Package rates generally do, but it never hurts to be sure.

Brookline is not subject to the convention center tax, but don't choose a hotel based on that—the savings is negligible, and probably balanced out by subway fare. Not all suburbs have a local tax, so some towns charge only the 5.7% state tax.

Dollars & Sense

Minibar and **telephone** charges can seriously inflate your bottom line. The markup on food and drinks is astronomical, so stop the kids before they spend their college tuition on macadamia nuts and guava juice. If you have to have snacks around, bring your own. And don't call all over town for a restaurant reservation until you know your hotel's telephone policy. Many offer free local calls, but if yours doesn't, you might be on the hook for $1 a call or more. Bring some change and a calling card for the public phones in the lobby.

The Price Categories: What You Get for Your Money

The hotel reviews in chapter 6 begin with dollar signs, ranging from one to four. Here's a breakdown of the categories. Prices are for 1 night in the least expensive double room (the most expensive may be considerably pricier) and do not include taxes. And remember that off-season rates and package deals can knock the price down a category or two.

➤ **$ (inexpensive)** lodgings cost less than $100 a night. I think of this as the "**serious penny-pincher/impoverished student**" category. Don't expect lots of services or amenities, such as room service and a health club. These places are not a lot of things: not huge, not glamorous, not all that conveniently located, and sometimes not equipped with a private bathroom, air-conditioning, or TV. They are, essentially, comfortable spots to crash after a day of sightseeing.

If the establishments we list don't suit you, you might have better luck with a bed-and-breakfast agency (see "Make Yourself at Home," above).

➤ **$$ (moderate)** hotels cost $100 to $175 a night. In my book, this is the "**family on vacation**" category. You'll find slightly larger rooms with private bathrooms, TV, and air-conditioning. There's no room service, but some hotels include continental breakfast in the room rate. These places are more centrally located, and some offer access to a pool or fitness room (ask if there's an extra charge). In a saner part of the world, most of them would be inns and family run motels. In tourism-mad Boston, many are links in moderately priced chains.

➤ **$$$ (expensive)** hotels cost $175 to $250 a night. By me, this is the "**splurging family/modest corporate**" division. Rooms are good-sized and nicely appointed, often with great views. Expect room service, business amenities (including in-room data ports), cable TV, an on-premises restaurant, valet parking, function space, and probably a pool or health club or both. Most rooms will have two phones with modem access, and many will have minibars, hair dryers, coffeemakers, irons, and ironing boards. Staff members will be numerous, pleasant, and helpful, if not necessarily bending over backward.

Extra! Extra!

In hotels that offer room service, it's not always available 24 hours a day. If a midnight snack is important to you, make sure you ask when you make your reservation. Boston is definitely not the kind of place where you can count on running out at 2am for a meal—or even a pizza.

This is the most confusing category, because every hotel, like every traveler, has a different definition of what's essential. Ask a lot of questions, and if you don't like the answers, keep trying until you're satisfied that you have the right place. Even if it's not your money, this is too much to pay for even 1 night of thinking, "If only I'd made one more call." In Boston's competitive market, there's almost certainly another hotel that will meet your specific needs, be they veggie pizza at 3am, an on-call masseuse, the presidential suite for your golden retriever, or something really weird.

➤ **$$$$ (very expensive)** hotels cost more (sometimes a *lot* more) than $250 a night. On my scale, this is "**and at these prices**" territory, populated by magnates, honeymooners, and other pampered travelers for whom money is no object. Expect everything the $$$ hotels offer, and perhaps such extras as courtesy cars, VCRs, and people you've never seen before greeting you by name—last name, with a title, of course. Rooms are huge and lavishly appointed, and no request is really weird. Your every want, need, and whim will be met. (And at these prices, they should be.)

There's just one caveat—a big one: Boston has a shortage of rooms, and some hotels that definitely belong in this category based on service and (oh, boy) price may not have every single amenity you'd expect. The feature that's most likely to be missing is an on-premises health club with a pool, but if another item is a deal-breaker for you, be sure to ask about it.

Getting the Best Room (And What to Do if You Don't)

Somebody has to get the best room in the house, and it might as well be you. Here are some recommendations:

➤ **Always ask for a corner room.** They're usually larger, quieter, and closer to the elevator, and have more windows and light than standard rooms. They may cost a bit more.

Speak Up!

In a perfect world, front-desk clerks would be like waiters, showing up 10 minutes after you check into your room to ask if everything's all right. In the real world, you are one of thousands of guests, and nobody is a mind-reader. If *anything* about your room is not what you requested, it's up to you to do something about it. Your "no-smoking" room reeks of tobacco, paint fumes fill the hall, the rollaway won't open all the way because the room is so small—these things shouldn't happen, but sometimes they do. Be polite but firm, and return to the front desk if you have to. If the staff can't resolve the situation, ask to see a manager. Stay calm, be civil (yes, it's hard when you're tired and frustrated), and you should get what you want.

➤ **Ask for a room on a high floor.** At some places, this is the "club" level or some other designation that costs extra. If you don't want to pay for the extra amenities (usually business features), ask for the highest standard floor.

➤ When you make your reservation, ask if the hotel is renovating; if it is, **request a room away from the renovation work,** and ask again when you check in.

➤ Nonsmokers will want to **ask for a room that's reserved for non-smokers;** if you don't express a preference, you may be unpleasantly surprised (see box "Speak Up!").

➤ Inquire, too, about the location of the **restaurants, bars, and discos** in the hotel—they can be a source of irritating noise.

➤ If you aren't happy with your room when you arrive, **talk to the front desk right away.** If another room is available, the staff should be happy to accommodate you, within reason. (See box "Speak Up!")

Family Ties: Strategies for Families Staying with Their Kids

Before you go any further, make sure you and the kids are on the same page (see "Should I Just Stay at a Suburban Motel?" above). If you're blowing big bucks on a downtown hotel with a business center and all they care about is an outdoor pool, there's frustration in your family's future.

Kids This icon designates establishments that are especially child-friendly. Remember, though, that Boston is a world-class family destination, and every hotel in town is accustomed to dealing with families.

Here are some money-saving strategies:

➤ Select a hotel that lets **children stay free.** Some draw the line at 12, others at 17, 18, or even 19. Almost everywhere, a room with two double beds costs the same as a room with one queen- or king-size bed. Even if a crib or rollaway (or 15-year-old) costs extra, it's still cheaper than taking two rooms. Yes, the adults will sacrifice some privacy, but if your family fits into two double beds, you probably don't have much privacy anyway.

➤ If you can afford it, **booking a second room** is great with older children, particularly at a hotel that offers adjoining rooms connected by an interior door. You might even get a break on the price (usually on a weekend).

➤ At some hotels, it might be less expensive to **reserve a suite.** The kids will feel like royalty, and you might actually enjoy a little peace and quiet.

➤ Most families will find that a **refrigerator or kitchenette** pays for itself. You can stock up on breakfast supplies, and perhaps the makings of a bag lunch or two.

Strategies for Travelers with Disabilities

Not all hotels, especially older ones, have been brought up to date with access regulations. Most small hotels, budget hotels, and B&Bs are only partly or not at all in compliance with federal law. But many establishments—especially affiliates of the large national chains—have the full range of ADA-compliant accommodations, including roll-in showers, lower sinks, extra space for maneuvering wheelchairs, and so forth. Be explicit about your needs when you make your reservations. And check the recommendations in chapter 6.

What if I Didn't Plan Ahead?

Stop kicking yourself—unless it's foliage or graduation season, in which case you might want to sustain that shuffling motion until you're a couple of hundred miles away. When you're through, try one or more of the following:

Time-Savers

Make a reservation, make a reservation, make a reservation. Yes, sometimes it's an emergency, but you had time to buy this book, didn't you? Save money and save time by calling ahead.

➤ **Call the Hotel Hot Line** run by the Greater Boston Convention & Visitors Bureau (☎ **800/777-6001**). It can help make reservations even during the busiest times. It's staffed weekdays until 8pm, weekends until 4pm.

➤ **Call a reservation bureau** such as **Accommodations Express** (☎ 800/906-4685), **Hotel Reservations Network** (☎ 800/96-HOTEL), or **Citywide Reservation Services** (☎ 800/HOTEL-93).

➤ **Phone hotels from the airport** or train station. Ask *everyone* you reach who doesn't have a room available to suggest another property.

➤ If you're driving from the west, **stop at the Massachusetts Turnpike's Natick rest area** and try the reservation service at the visitor information center.

➤ **Call a B&B agency** (see "Make Yourself at Home," above) and ask if any of its properties have cancellations.

➤ **Rent a car** and head for the suburbs. I'm only half kidding.

Chapter 6

Boston Hotels from A to Z

In This Chapter

➤ Quick indexes of hotels by location and price

➤ Reviews of my favorite hotels

➤ A worksheet to help you make your choice

By now you probably have a good idea of what you want from your hotel, neighborhoods that sound promising, and how much you're willing to pay. This chapter starts with handy lists that break down the listings by location and price. Then come the reviews of my favorite hotels, listed alphabetically.

Kids This icon indicates hotels that are especially family friendly. Scattered through the chapter, you'll find boxes that point you toward accommodations particularly suited to other special interests. The chapter wraps up with a worksheet to help you sort out your choices.

Each review includes a dollar sign icon indicating the price range (the more dollar signs, the more you pay), lists the neighborhood, and gives the rack rate. Remember that you don't have to pay the rack rate—this is to give you a sense of which hotels fit in which categories. The breakdown, using the least expensive double room in the summer as a yardstick:

$$\begin{aligned}
\$ &= \text{less than } \$100 \\
\$\$ &= \$100 \text{ to } \$175 \\
\$\$\$ &= \$175 \text{ to } \$250 \\
\$\$\$\$ &= \$250 \text{ and up}
\end{aligned}$$

Quick Picks: Boston Hotels at a Glance
Hotel Index by Location

Back Bay East

Boston Park Plaza Hotel, $$$

Four Seasons Hotel, $$$$

Radisson Hotel Boston, $$$

The Ritz-Carlton, $$$$

Back Bay West

Chandler Inn Hotel, $$

The Colonnade Hotel, $$$$

Eliot Hotel, $$$$

The Fairmont Copley Plaza Hotel, $$$$

Hostelling International—Boston, $

The Lenox Hotel, $$$$

The MidTown Hotel, $$

Newbury Guest House, $$

Sheraton Boston Hotel & Towers, $$$

The Westin Copley Place Boston, $$$

Beacon Hill

Eliot & Pickett Houses, $$

Holiday Inn Select Boston Government Center, $$$

Cambridge

The Charles Hotel, $$$$

Harvard Square Hotel, $$

Sheraton Commander Hotel, $$$

Downtown Crossing

Omni Parker House, $$$

Swissôtel Boston, $$$

Downtown/Faneuil Hall Marketplace

Harborside Inn, $$

Regal Bostonian Hotel, $$$$

Downtown/Financial District

Le Meridien Boston, $$$$

Downtown/Waterfront

Boston Harbor Hotel, $$$$

Outskirts & Brookline

Anthony's Town House, $

Doubletree Guest Suites, $$$

Holiday Inn Boston Brookline, $$

Howard Johnson Hotel—Kenmore, $$

Howard Johnson Lodge Fenway, $$

Longwood Inn, $

Hotel Index by Price

$

Anthony's Town House, Outskirts & Brookline

Hostelling International—Boston, Back Bay West

Longwood Inn, Outskirts & Brookline

$$

Chandler Inn Hotel, Back Bay West

Eliot & Pickett Houses, Beacon Hill

Harborside Inn, Downtown/Faneuil Hall Marketplace

Harvard Square Hotel, Cambridge

Holiday Inn Boston Brookline, Outskirts & Brookline

Howard Johnson Hotel—Kenmore, Outskirts & Brookline

Howard Johnson Lodge Fenway, Outskirts & Brookline

The MidTown Hotel, Back Bay West

Newbury Guest House, Back Bay West

$$$

Boston Park Plaza Hotel, Back Bay East

Doubletree Guest Suites, Outskirts & Brookline

Holiday Inn Select Boston Government Center, Beacon Hill

Omni Parker House, Downtown Crossing

Radisson Hotel Boston, Back Bay East

Sheraton Boston Hotel & Towers, Back Bay West

Sheraton Commander Hotel, Cambridge

Swissôtel Boston, Downtown Crossing

The Westin Copley Place Boston, Back Bay West

$$$$

Boston Harbor Hotel, Downtown/Waterfront

The Charles Hotel, Cambridge

The Colonnade Hotel, Back Bay West

Eliot Hotel, Back Bay West

The Fairmont Copley Plaza Hotel, Back Bay West

Four Seasons Hotel, Back Bay East

Le Meridien Boston, Downtown/Financial District

The Lenox Hotel, Back Bay West

Regal Bostonian Hotel, Downtown/Faneuil Hall Marketplace

The Ritz-Carlton, Back Bay East

Boston Hotels A to Z

What follows is an opinionated selection of the best accommodations in Boston, Cambridge, and Brookline. Each offers a commendable combination of location, price, service, and comfort. For a more extensive rundown of places to stay, consult *Frommer's Boston.*

As you review the reviews, keep a marker handy and check off the ones that appeal to you. If you're traveling with others, give each person (including the kids, who will probably be thrilled to be consulted) a marker of a different color and a crack at the listings. When you get to the end of the chapter and start filling in the **worksheet,** you can easily pick out your own and everyone else's favorites.

Don't waste time trying to figure out which places are dumps; all are clean, reputable, and in safe neighborhoods. And please don't take that to mean that these are the only safe, clean places in town. These are my favorites. I hope you like them, too.

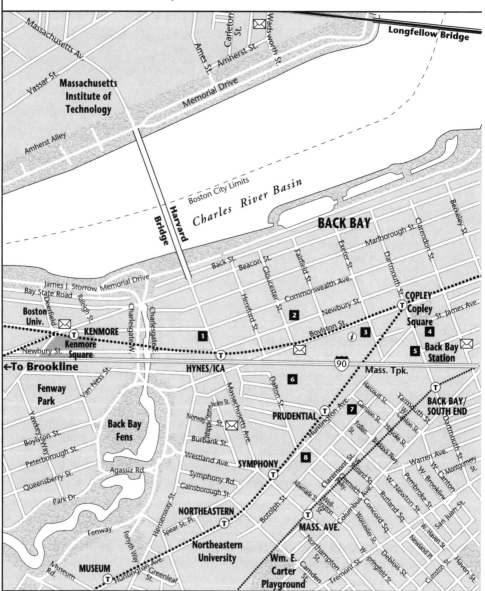

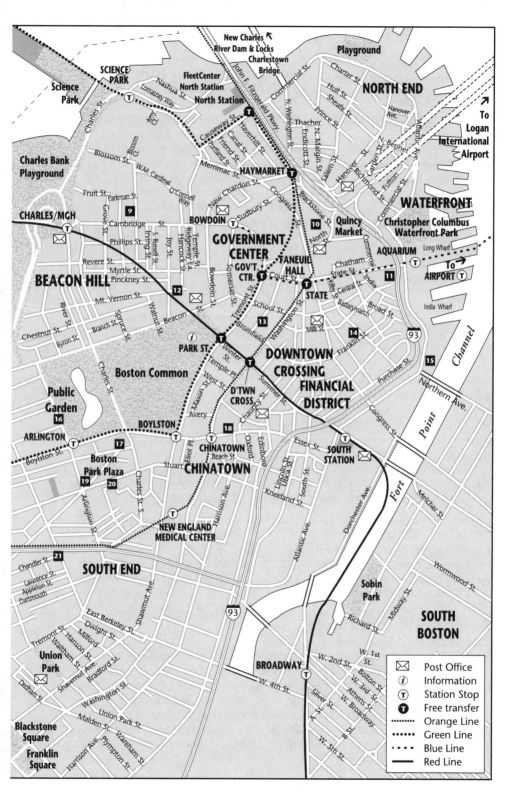

Anthony's Town House
$. Outskirts & Brookline.

A cozy atmosphere and great location offset the lack of private bathrooms at this guest house about a mile from Kenmore Square. Three rooms share one bathroom (with enclosed shower) on each of the four floors. Ask for one of the larger front rooms, which have bay windows. All rooms have air-conditioning and TV (but not phones), and downtown is about 15 minutes away on the Green Line trolley. The historic brownstone has been a family operation since 1944.

1085 Beacon St., Brookline, MA 02446. ☎ *617/566-3972. MBTA: Green Line C to Hawes St. Parking: Free. Rack rates: $48–$78 double. Extra person $10. Weekly rates. No credit cards.*

Boston Harbor Hotel
$$$$. Downtown/Waterfront.

Everything about this landmark hotel is top-notch, from the architecture to the sensational views of the harbor. Rooms are large and luxuriously appointed, with mahogany furniture and windows that open. The business amenities and fitness facilities (including a 60-foot lap pool) are state-of-the-art. The restaurant is one of the best in the city, and the Airport Water Shuttle runs to the hotel dock. This hotel is easy on the eyes, easy on the ego—easy on everything except the wallet. Children under 18 stay free in their parents' room.

70 Rowes Wharf (entrance on Atlantic Ave.), Boston, MA 02110. ☎ *800/ 752-7077 or 617/439-7000. Fax 617/330-9450. www.bhh.com. MBTA: Blue Line to Aquarium; walk 2½ blocks south. Red Line to South Station; walk 2½ blocks north. Parking: Valet $26, self $22 weekdays; weekend discounts. Rack rates: $255–$510 double; from $365 suite. Extra person $50. Weekend packages. AE, CB, DC, DISC, MC, V.*

Boston Park Plaza Hotel
$$$. Back Bay East.

You know those generic chain hotels that could be anywhere from Anchorage to Atlanta? This classic property (it opened in 1927) is their exact opposite. It has an old-fashioned feel, yet offers modern conveniences. Ongoing renovations are part of a recent emphasis on business travel, and the hotel is already a magnet for convention and tour business. Rooms vary in size and decor, and some are quite small—ask for one of the newly refurbished units. There's a **Legal Sea Foods** on the ground floor. Children under 18 stay free in their parents' room.

Dollars & Sense: Hotels with Free Parking

Anthony's Town House (Outskirts & Brookline, $)
Howard Johnson Hotel—Kenmore (Outskirts & Brookline, $$)
Howard Johnson Lodge Fenway (Outskirts & Brookline, $$)
Longwood Inn (Outskirts & Brookline, $)
The MidTown Hotel (Back Bay West, $$)
Sheraton Commander Hotel (Cambridge, $$$)

64 Arlington St., Boston, MA 02116. ☎ *800/225-2008 or 617/426-2000. Fax 617/423-1708.* **MBTA:** *Green Line to Arlington; follow Arlington Street 1 block away from the Public Garden.* **Parking:** *Valet $23, self $19.* **Rack rates:** *$175–$265 double; $375–$2,000 suite. Extra person $20. Senior discount, weekend and family packages. AE, CB, DC, DISC, MC, V.*

Chandler Inn Hotel
$$. Back Bay West.
The Chandler Inn Hotel is actually in the South End, but it offers such good value that you probably won't mind not being in the heart of the Back Bay. Rooms are pleasant and well maintained, the staff is helpful, and rates include continental breakfast. This is the largest gay-owned property in town, and it's popular with bargain-hunters of all persuasions. Children under 12 stay free in their parents' room.

26 Chandler St. (at Berkeley St.), Boston, MA 02116. ☎ *800/842-3450 or 617/482-3450. Fax 617/542-3428. www.chandlerinn.com. E-mail: inn3450@ ix.netcom.com.* **MBTA:** *Orange Line to Back Bay; turn left, walk 1 block, cross Columbus Ave., turn left onto Chandler St., walk 2 blocks.* **Parking:** *$18 in nearby public garage.* **Rack rates:** *$99–$139 double; winter discounts. Extra person $10–$20. AE, CB, DC, DISC, MC, V.*

 ## The Charles Hotel
$$$$. Cambridge.
Just off Harvard Square, this is *the* place to stay in Cambridge, assuming you can afford it. Rather than the clubby university atmosphere you might expect, it's contemporary and light filled. The austere, Shaker-style furnishings contrast agreeably with the lavish appointments—everything from superior toiletries to the audiophile's dream, a Bose Wave radio in every room. The large windows open, and the bathrooms have

The Best Hotels for Shopaholics

Chandler Inn Hotel	$$
Harborside Inn	$$
The Lenox Hotel	$$$$
Newbury Guest House	$$
The Ritz-Carlton	$$$$

TVs. Guests have the use of the pool and exercise room at the adjacent WellBridge Health and Fitness Center, and there's an excellent spa. The restaurant, **Rialto,** is the best in the Boston area, and the **Regattabar** is one of the best jazz clubs. Children under 18 stay free in their parents' room.

1 Bennett St., Cambridge, MA 02138. ☎ *800/882-1818 outside Massachusetts, or 617/864-1200. Fax 617/864-5715.* **MBTA:** *Red Line to Harvard; follow Brattle St. 2 blocks, turn left onto Eliot St. and proceed 2 blocks.* **Parking:** *Valet $18, self $16.* **Rack rates:** *$239–$315 double; $389–$2,000 suite. Extra person $20. Weekend packages. AE, CB, DC, DISC, JCB, MC, V.*

 ### The Colonnade Hotel
$$$$. Back Bay West.

This independently owned hotel is a slice of Europe, topped with an all-American swimming pool and "rooftop resort" (open seasonally). It offers lots of amenities and superb multilingual service to its well-heeled international clientele. Rooms are large, with contemporary furnishings, marble bathrooms, and windows that open. **Brasserie Jo**, in the lobby, is a spin-off of the acclaimed Alsatian restaurant in Chicago. Children under 12 stay free in their parents' room.

120 Huntington Ave., Boston, MA 02116. ☎ *800/962-3030 or 617/424-7000. Fax 617/424-1717. www.colonnadehotel.com.* **MBTA:** *Green Line E to Prudential.* **Parking:** *$20.* **Rack rates:** *$315 double; $450–$1,400 suite. Weekend packages. AE, CB, DC, DISC, MC, V.*

 ### Doubletree Guest Suites
$$$. Outskirts & Brookline.

This hotel is one of the best values in town—every unit is a large two-room suite with a living room, bedroom, and bathroom. It's equally popular with business people and families. Most bedrooms have king-size beds, and the living rooms contain full-size sofa beds, coffeemakers, and good-sized refrigerators. There is an indoor pool, fitness facilities, and a laundry room. And the jogging and bike path along the Charles River is just across the street. The only thing not to like is the less-than-central location, but there's complimentary van service to and from attractions and business areas in Boston and Cambridge. And you don't need to go out at night—the justly celebrated **Scullers Jazz Club** has two nightly shows. Children under 18 stay free in their parents' room.

400 Soldiers Field Rd. (adjacent to Mass. Pike [Massachusetts Turnpike] Allston/Cambridge exit), Boston, MA 02134. ☎ *800/222-TREE or 617/783-0090. Fax 617/783-0897.*

Lobbies Worth Gawking At

Boston Harbor Hotel	$$$$
Boston Park Plaza Hotel	$$$
Eliot Hotel	$$$$
The Fairmont Copley Plaza Hotel	$$$$

www.doubletreehotels.com. **Parking:** *$15.* **Rack rates:** *$139–$259 double. Extra person $20. Weekend packages. AAA and AARP discounts. AE, CB, DC, DISC, JCB, MC, V.*

Eliot & Pickett Houses
$$. Beacon Hill.

This B&B, in a pair of 1830s town houses near the peak of Beacon Hill, is worth the climb. Each of the 20 attractively decorated, high-ceilinged rooms has a double or queen bed. It's such a deal because you make your own breakfast (fixings are provided), and the only TV is in the den. If

The Best Hotels, Period

Hey, it's not my money.

Boston Harbor Hotel	$$$$
The Charles Hotel	$$$$
The Fairmont Copley	$$$$
Four Seasons Hotel	$$$$

you want to eat in, guests have kitchen access for other meals. The combination of location and value makes the Eliot & Pickett Houses extremely popular, so reserve well in advance. They're run by the Unitarian Universalist Association. Children under 12 stay free in their parents' room.

6 Mount Vernon Place (off Joy St. between Beacon and Mt. Vernon sts.), Boston, MA 02108. ☎ *617/248-8707. Fax 617/742-1364. www.uua.org/ep. E-mail: e&p@uua.org.* **MBTA:** *Red or Green line to Park St.; walk 1 block to State House, turn left onto Beacon St., turn right onto Joy St. at first intersection. Mt. Vernon Pl. is ½ block up on the right.* **Parking:** *$19 weekday, $7 weekend in nearby Boston Common Garage.* **Rack rates:** *$85–$125 double. Extra person $10. MC, V.*

Eliot Hotel
$$$$. Back Bay West.

A boutique hotel offers whatever management says it should, and here that's spacious suites, with the most luxurious appointments available. Units have antique furnishings, French doors to separate the living and bedrooms, and Italian marble bathrooms. Each has a fax machine, and many suites have a pantry with a microwave. Adding to the away-from-it-all aura are the location, on a residential street a block from the madness of Newbury Street, and **Clio**, the exalted restaurant in the lobby. Children under 12 stay free in their parents' room.

370 Commonwealth Ave. (at Mass. Ave.), Boston, MA 02215. ☎ *800/44-ELIOT or 617/267-1607. Fax 617/536-9114. E-mail: HotelEliot@aol.com.* **MBTA:** *Green Line B, C, or D to Hynes/ICA; turn right onto Mass. Ave., walk 1 block.* **Parking:** *Valet $20.* **Rack rates:** *$245–$295 1-bedroom suite for 2; $400–$475 2-bedroom suite. Extra person $20. AE, DC, MC, V.*

The Fairmont Copley Plaza Hotel
$$$$. Back Bay West.

Long known as the *grande dame* of Boston hotels, the Copley Plaza has become a true "grand hotel" under the stewardship of the Fairmont Hotel Group. This is another traditional hostelry, dripping with turn-of-the-century

75

Dog Gone: Hotels That Welcome Your Pet

Boston Harbor Hotel	$$$$
The Charles Hotel	$$$$
Four Seasons Hotel	$$$$
Howard Johnson Hotel—Kenmore	$$

elegance (the last century—the building dates to 1912). The large, newly restored guest rooms have reproduction Edwardian antiques and every perk you can think of (and some you probably haven't), including fax machines. The bathrooms even have oversized towels. There are two restaurants, two bars, a business center, and a fitness center, but—the only "but"— no pool. Guests have access to the nearby coed YWCA. Children under 18 stay free in their parents' room.

138 St. James Ave. (at Dartmouth St.), Boston, MA 02116. ☎ ***800/527-4727*** *or 617/267-5300. Fax 617/247-6681. www.fairmont.com. E-mail: boston@ fairmont.com.* ***MBTA:*** *Green Line to Copley or Orange Line to Back Bay.* ***Parking:*** *Valet $26.* ***Rack rates:*** *$289–$409 double; $429–$1,500 suite. Extra person $30. Weekend packages. AE, CB, DC, JCB, MC, V.*

Four Seasons Hotel
$$$$. Back Bay East.

This is the best hotel in a city full of excellent hotels. It has it all: superb location, guest rooms, public areas, health club, business center, restaurants, and especially service. And it all comes at a price. If I were traveling with someone else's credit cards, I'd head straight here. Rooms are large and impressively appointed, and all have bay windows that open. The second-floor restaurant, **Aujourd'hui,** is one of Boston's best, and the **Bristol Lounge** serves a celebrated afternoon tea (as well as lunch and dinner). Children under 18 stay free in their parents' room.

200 Boylston St., Boston, MA 02116. ☎ ***800/332-3442*** *or 617/338-4400. Fax 617/423-0154. www.fourseasons.com.* ***MBTA:*** *Green Line to Arlington; walk 1 block on Boylston St. opposite the Public Garden.* ***Parking:*** *Valet $27.* ***Rack rates:*** *$385–$610 double; from $950 one-bedroom suite; from $1,900 two-bedroom suite. Extra person $40. Weekend packages. AE, CB, DC, DISC, JCB, MC, V.*

Harborside Inn
$$. Downtown/Faneuil Hall Marketplace.

This renovated 1858 warehouse is perfectly situated for sightseers and thrifty business travelers alike. Like its sister property, the Newbury Guest House (see below), it's one of the best deals in Boston. Room rates include continental breakfast (served in the first-floor cafe). Each guest room has a queen-size bed, hardwood floors, and Oriental rugs, along with some features you'd expect at pricier hotels, including free local phone calls and voice mail. Rooms on the top floors have lower ceilings but better views. There's a small exercise room.

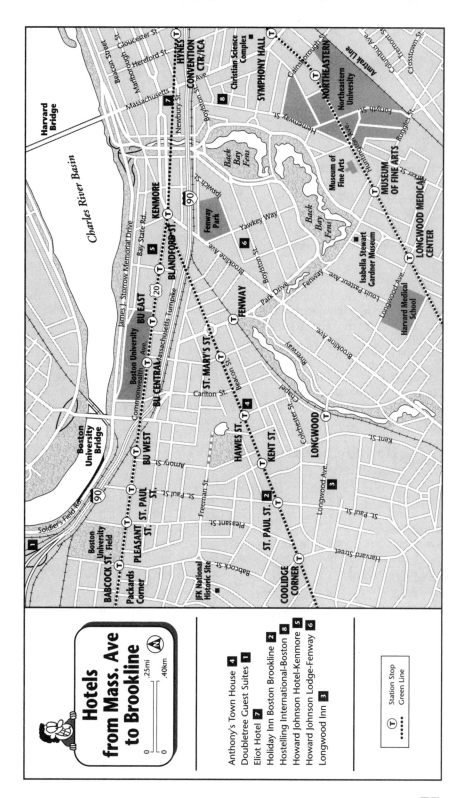

Hotels from Mass. Ave to Brookline

A

| 0 | .25mi |
| 0 | .40km |

Anthony's Town House **4**
Doubletree Guest Suites **1**
Eliot Hotel **7**
Holiday Inn Boston Brookline **2**
Hostelling International-Boston **8**
Howard Johnson Hotel-Kenmore **5**
Howard Johnson Lodge-Fenway **6**
Longwood Inn **3**

(T) Station Stop
•••••• Green Line

The Best Hotels for Watching the Marathon

Eliot Hotel $$$$
Holiday Inn Boston
  Brookline $$
The Lenox Hotel $$$$

185 State St. (between India St. and I-93), Boston, MA 02109. ☎ *617/723-7500. Fax 617/670-2010.* **MBTA:** *Blue Line to Aquarium.* **Parking:** *At least $18 weekdays in nearby public garages.* **Rack rates:** *$135–$155 double; $250 suite; winter discounts. May be higher during special events. Extra person $10. AE, CB, DC, DISC, MC, V.*

Harvard Square Hotel
$$. Cambridge.

Smack in the middle of Harvard Square, this hotel is a favorite with visiting parents and budget-conscious business travelers. Rooms aren't large but do have data ports, voice mail, hair dryers, irons, and ironing boards. The hotel was completely refurbished in 1996; it's still not the place for coddled business travelers, but the comfortable, unpretentious atmosphere can be a relief after a few hours in the Square. Children under 17 stay free in their parents' room.

110 Mount Auburn St., Cambridge, MA 02138. ☎ *800/458-5886 or 617/ 864-5200. Fax 617/864-2409. www.doubletreehotels.com.* **MBTA:** *Red Line to Harvard; follow Brattle St. 2 blocks, turn left onto Eliot St. and proceed 1 block.* **Parking:** *$16.* **Rack rates:** *$125–$180 double. Extra person $10. Corporate rates, AAA and AARP discounts. AE, DC, DISC, JCB, MC, V.*

Holiday Inn Boston Brookline
$$. Outskirts & Brookline.

This is not the Holiday Inn of your childhood. In a pleasant residential neighborhood, it offers recently redecorated rooms that are large and well appointed, with coffeemakers, hair dryers, irons, and ironing boards. There is a small indoor pool, whirlpool, sundeck, and exercise room. The bustling Coolidge Corner neighborhood is a 10-minute walk away, and downtown Boston is about 15 minutes away on the Green Line. Children under 18 stay free in their parents' room.

1200 Beacon St., Brookline, MA 02446. ☎ *800/HOLIDAY or 617/277-1200. Fax 617/734-6991. www.holiday-inn.com.* **MBTA:** *Green Line C to St. Paul St.* **Parking:** *$9.* **Rack rates:** *$145–$170 double; $200–$350 suite. Extra person $10. AE, DC, DISC, JCB, MC, V.*

Holiday Inn Select Boston Government Center
$$$. Beacon Hill.

When Holiday Inn created the "Select" brand to court business travelers, it started in Boston. Rooms here were renovated in 1994, and have fax machines and data ports. There's a business center, and two floors of rooms with upgraded business amenities. The hotel has an outdoor heated pool, small exercise room, sundeck, and coin laundry. For a picture-window view of the city or the State House, ask to be as high up as possible. Children under 18 stay free in their parents' room.

5 Blossom St. (at Cambridge St.), Boston, MA 02114. ☎ ***800/HOLIDAY** or 617/742-7630. Fax 617/742-4192. www.holiday-inn.com. **MBTA:** Red Line to Charles/MGH; walk 3 blocks on Cambridge St. **Parking:** $18. **Rack rates:** From $200 double. Extra person $20. Rollaway $20. Weekend and corporate packages; 10% AARP discount. AE, DC, DISC, JCB, MC, V.*

Hostelling International—Boston
$. Back Bay West.

If you really *just* want a place to crash after a day of sightseeing, this might be for you. The 205-bed hostel caters to students, youth groups, and other travelers in search of comfortable, no-frills lodgings. Accommodations are dorm-style, with three to six beds per room. The hostel provides a "sheet sleeping sack," or you can bring your own (sleeping bags are not permitted). To get a bed during the summer you must be a member of Hostelling International—American Youth Hostels, P.O. Box 37613, Washington, DC 20013 (☎ **202/ 783-6161;** www.hiayh.org).

12 Hemenway St., Boston, MA 02115. ☎ ***800/HOST-222** or 617/536-9455. Fax 617/424-6558. www.tiac.net/users/hienec/. E-mail: bostonhostel@juno.com. **MBTA:** Green Line B, C, or D to Hynes/ICA; turn left and walk 1 block on Mass. Ave., go right onto Boylston St. for 1 block, then left onto Hemenway St. **Parking:** You're driving to a hostel? At least $10 at public garages. **Rates:** Members $18 per bed; nonmembers $21 per bed. JCB, MC, V.*

Kids Howard Johnson Hotel— Kenmore
$$. Outskirts & Brookline.

If the location of this hotel doesn't get you, the pool and free parking might. It's right on the Green Line, surrounded by Boston University, and near Fenway Park. Rooms are standard-issue Howard Johnson's—comfortable, but nothing fancy—and some are small. The indoor swimming pool and skylit sundeck on the roof are open year-round from 11am to 9pm. Children under 18 stay free in their parents' room.

575 Commonwealth Ave., Boston, MA 02215. ☎ ***800/654-2000** or 617/267-3100. Fax 617/424-1045. www.hojo.com. **MBTA:** Green Line B to Blandford St. **Parking:** Free. **Rack rates:** $125–$225 double. Extra person $10. Senior and AAA discounts. AE, CB, DC, DISC, JCB, MC, V.*

The Best Hotels for Families

The Charles Hotel	$$$$
Doubletree Guest Suites	$$$
Four Seasons Hotel	$$$$
Holiday Inn Boston Brookline	$$
Howard Johnson Lodge Fenway	$$
Longwood Inn	$
Sheraton Boston Hotel & Towers	$$$

Kids **Howard Johnson Lodge Fenway**
$$. Outskirts & Brookline.

Listen closely—you might hear the Fenway Park crowd cheering from here. This is a basic motel on a busy street in a commercial-residential neighborhood. It's convenient to the Back Bay colleges, the Museum of Fine Arts, and the Isabella Stewart Gardner Museum. There's an outdoor pool, open 9am to 7pm in the summer, and some rooms have a microwave oven and refrigerator. Children under 18 stay free in their parents' room.

1271 Boylston St., Boston, MA 02215. ☎ *800/654-2000 or 617/267-8300. Fax 617/267-2763. www.hojo.com.* **MBTA:** *Green Line B, C, or D to Kenmore. Go left at turnstiles, right at stairs; at first intersection (½ block up), turn left onto Brookline Ave. Cross bridge, pass Fenway Park, and turn left onto Yawkey Way; take second right onto Boylston St. Total: about 10 minutes.* **Parking:** *Free.* **Rack rates:** *$115–$185 double. Extra person $10. Family packages, senior and AAA discounts. AE, CB, DC, DISC, JCB, MC, V.*

The Best Hotels for Business Travelers

Boston Harbor Hotel	$$$$
Four Seasons Hotel	$$$$
Le Meridien Boston	$$$$
Sheraton Boston Hotel & Towers	$$$
The Westin Copley Place Boston	$$$

Le Meridien Boston
$$$$. Downtown/Financial District.

This is the city's premier business hotel. If you don't need to leave the Financial District, you may not even need to leave the premises—the business amenities are that good. And if you're visiting on a weekend, you may be pleasantly surprised by the price. This is a very proper hotel with a French accent (the telephone operators say "Bonjour"), and it has a well-equipped health club with a 40-foot pool. The elegant formal restaurant, **Julien**, is perfect for a business meal, and there's a more casual cafe. Children under 12 stay free in their parents' room.

250 Franklin St. (at Post Office Sq.), Boston, MA 02110. ☎ *800/543-4300 or 617/451-1900. Fax 617/423-2844. www.lemeridien.com.* **MBTA:** *Red Line to South Station; walk 1 block north on Atlantic Ave., turn left, and follow Congress St. 3 long blocks. Or Orange Line to Downtown Crossing; walk 1 block on Washington St. side of Filene's, turn right, and follow Franklin St. 6 blocks.* **Parking:** *Valet $29, $13 Fri–Sat; self $28, $8 Fri–Sat.* **Rack rates:** *$285–$335 double; $475–$800 suite. Extra person $30. Weekend packages. AE, CB, DC, DISC, MC, V.*

The Lenox Hotel
$$$$. Back Bay West.

This hotel is aiming for the uppermost tier of Boston lodgings, and the recent completion of a $20 million renovation left it well positioned to make the push. Building on its great location, the Lenox courts business travelers with lots of amenities, including in-room fax machines (but not a pool or health club). The spacious, high-ceilinged rooms have sitting areas and lovely marble bathrooms. It'll cost you, but how's this for plush: 15 corner rooms have wood-burning fireplaces. The excellent restaurant **Anago,** in the lobby, provides the hotel's food services. Children under 18 stay free in their parents' room.

710 Boylston St. (at Exeter St.), Boston, MA 02116. ☎ ***800/225-7676*** *or 617/536-5300. Fax 617/236-0351. www.lenoxhotel.com.* **MBTA:** *Green Line to Copley; walk 1 block on Boylston St. side of Boston Public Library.* **Parking:** *$28.* **Rack rates:** *from $245 double; executive corner room with fireplace $275; fireplace suite $475. Extra person $20. Cots $20. Cribs free. Corporate and weekend packages. AE, CB, DC, DISC, JCB, MC, V.*

Longwood Inn
$. Outskirts & Brookline.

In a residential area 3 blocks from Boston, this three-story Victorian guest house offers convenient, affordable accommodations. Seventeen (of 22) units have private bathrooms, and all rooms have air-conditioning and a phone. Guests have the use of a fully equipped kitchen and common dining room, coin laundry, and TV lounge. There's an apartment that sleeps four and has a private kitchen and balcony. Tennis courts, a running track, and a playground at the school next door are open to the public.

123 Longwood Ave., Brookline, MA 02446. ☎ ***617/566-8615.*** *Fax 617/738-1070.* **MBTA:** *Green Line D to Longwood; turn left, walk ½ block to Longwood Ave., turn right and walk 2½ blocks. Or Green Line C to Coolidge Corner; walk 1 block south on Harvard St. (past Trader Joe's), turn left and go 2 blocks on Longwood Ave.* **Parking:** *Free.* **Rack rates:** *$69–$89 double; winter discounts. Weekly rates. No credit cards.*

The MidTown Hotel
$$. Back Bay West.

Free parking is the big draw (and rightly so) at this two-story hotel on a busy street 2 minutes from the Prudential Center. The newly renovated rooms are bright and attractively outfitted, but you may be outnumbered by tour groups and conventioneers. The heated outdoor pool is open from Memorial Day through Labor Day, and families can request adjoining rooms. True, this is not the lap of luxury, but it's more than acceptable, and the price is right. Children under 18 stay free in their parents' room.

220 Huntington Ave. (at W. Concord St.), Boston, MA 02115. ☎ ***800/343-1177*** *or 617/262-1000. Fax 617/262-8739.* **MBTA:** *Green Line E to Symphony; from the corner*

The Best Hotels for Romance

Eliot Hotel	$$$$
The Fairmont Copley Plaza Hotel	$$$$
Newbury Guest House	$$
Regal Bostonian Hotel	$$$$

diagonally across from Symphony Hall, walk 1 block. Or Orange Line to Mass Ave;
turn left, walk 2 blocks, turn right, and follow Huntington Ave. for 1 block. **Parking:**
Free. **Rack rates:** *$109–$179 double. Extra person $15. 10% AARP discount; gov-*
ernment employee discount subject to availability. AE, DC, DISC, MC, V.

Newbury Guest House
$$. Back Bay West.
After just a little shopping, you'll recognize the value of this bargain on
Newbury Street. This B&B in a pair of renovated town houses offers comfort-
able furnishings, a pleasant staff, and nifty architectural details. Rooms aren't
huge but are nicely appointed, and rates include a buffet breakfast served in
the ground-level dining room, which adjoins a brick patio. The Hagopian fam-
ily (which also runs the Harborside Inn, above) opened the B&B in 1991, and
it operates near capacity year-round. Reserve as early as possible.

261 Newbury St. (between Fairfield and Gloucester sts.), Boston, MA 02116.
☎ *617/437-7666. Fax 617/262-4243.* **MBTA:** *Green Line to Copley; follow*
Dartmouth St. 1 block away from Copley Square, turn left on Newbury St., and
go 2½ blocks. Or Green Line B, C, or D to Hynes/ICA; follow Newbury St. away
from Mass Ave for 2½ blocks. **Parking:** *$10 (reservation required).* **Rack rates:**
$105–$140 double. Winter discounts. May be higher during special events. Extra
person $10. Minimum 2 nights on weekends. AE, CB, DC, DISC, MC, V.

Omni Parker House
$$$. Downtown Crossing.
This is one of the city's most pleasant surprises. It's the oldest continuously
operating hotel in the country (since 1855), and just when it was starting to
show its age, Omni Hotels swooped in and spent $60 million on renovations.
You can't suddenly expand guest rooms in a 150-year-old structure, but you
can equip them with tons of modern amenities, select furniture that's not
out of scale, and arrange it so thoughtfully that the rooms feel cozy, not
cramped. The hotel has a new staffed busi-
ness center and exercise facility. Children
under 18 stay free in their parents' room.

History 101

Yes, this is the Parker House
of Parker House roll fame.
They were invented here (if
food can be said to be
"invented"), as was Boston
cream pie.

60 School St. (at Tremont St.), Boston, MA
02108. ☎ *800/THE-OMNI or 617/*
227-8600. Fax 617/742-5729. www.
omnihotels.com. **MBTA:** *Green Line to*
Government Center; follow Tremont St.
across Court St. and walk 1 block. Or Red
Line to Park St.; follow Tremont St. away
from Boston Common for 2 blocks. **Parking:**
Valet $24, self $17. **Rack rates:** *$185–*
$325 double; from $295 suite. Weekend
packages. AE, CB, DC, DISC, MC, V.

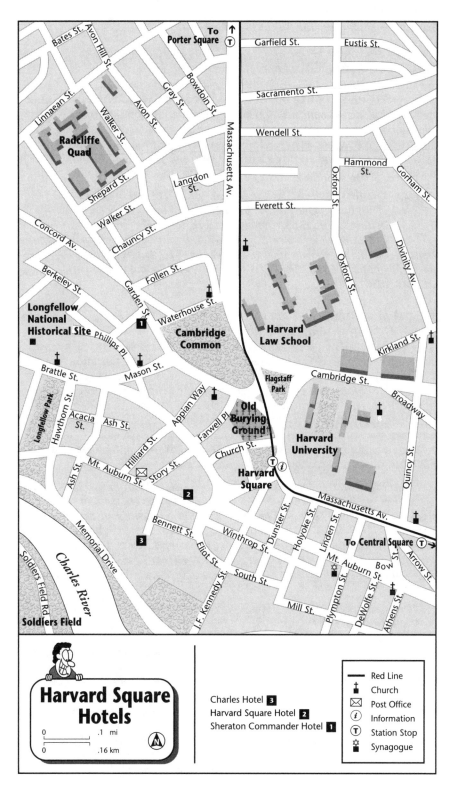

Radisson Hotel Boston
$$$. Back Bay East.
This hotel offers proof that business travelers don't have to break the bank to make a good impression. A top-to-bottom renovation completed in 1997 left the Radisson in great shape, and it continues to upgrade, most recently with a staffed business center. The tastefully decorated guest rooms are among the largest in the city, and each has a private balcony. There is an indoor pool, sundeck, and exercise room. Children under 18 stay free in their parents' room.

200 Stuart St. (at Charles St. South), Boston, MA 02116. ☎ ***800/333-3333*** *or 617/482-1800. Fax 617/451-2750.* **MBTA:** *Green Line to Boylston; follow Tremont St. away from Boston Common 1 block, turn right onto Stuart St. and go 2 blocks. Or Orange Line to New England Medical Center; turn left, walk ½ block, turn left, and go 3 blocks on Stuart St.* **Parking:** *$15.* **Rack rates:** *$160–$275 double. Extra person $20. Cot $20. Cribs free. Weekend and theater packages. AE, DC, DISC, JCB, MC, V.*

Regal Bostonian Hotel
$$$$. Downtown/Faneuil Hall Marketplace.
This quirky property offers a gratifying mix of old and new. It's relatively small and doesn't have an on-premises health club, but its location and business features make it competitive with larger hotels. The newly redecorated guest rooms vary in size; all boast top-of-the-line furnishings and amenities, and bathrooms almost nice enough to live in (three words: heated towel racks). Both buildings (they date from 1824 and 1890) are soundproofed— a necessity with the Marketplace, I-93, and Haymarket so close. Guests have health club and pool privileges at the excellent Sky Club, 4 blocks away. Children under 19 stay free in their parents' room.

At Faneuil Hall Marketplace (North and Clinton sts., ½ block from I-93), Boston, MA 02109. ☎ ***800/343-0922*** *or 617/523-3600. Fax 617/523-2454. www. regal-hotels.com.* **MBTA:** *Green or Blue Line to Government Center; cross plaza with City Hall on left, walk downstairs, and follow North St. 1½ blocks. Or Orange Line to Haymarket; use Congress St. exit, go left, walk 2 blocks, turn left, and follow North St. 1½ blocks.* **Parking:** *$20.* **Rack rates:** *$245–$375 double; $500–$775 suite. Extra person $20. Rollaway $20. Weekend and other packages. AE, DC, DISC, JCB, MC, V.*

The Ritz-Carlton
$$$$. Back Bay East.
Overlooking the Public Garden, the Ritz-Carlton has attracted the "proper Bostonian" and the celebrated guest since 1927. Although the pricier Four Seasons has better amenities (notably the on-premises pool and business center), the status-conscious consider the Ritz, well, ritzier. The hotel is famous for its service. Guest rooms are lavishly appointed; some have windows that open. There's a well-equipped fitness center, and guests have access to the pool at the nearby Candela of Boston spa. The Dining Room and the Bar at the Ritz are legendary, and the lounge serves the city's best afternoon tea. Children under 12 stay free in their parents' room.

15 Arlington St., Boston, MA 02117. ☎ *800/241-3333 or 617/536-5700. Fax 617/536-1335. www.ritzcarlton.com.* **MBTA:** *Green Line to Arlington; follow Arlington St. opposite Public Garden 1 block.* **Parking:** *Valet $24.* **Rack rates:** *$265–$415 double; from $345 (and way up) suite. Extra person $20. Weekend packages. AE, CB, DC, DISC, JCB, MC, V.*

Sheraton Boston Hotel & Towers
$$$. Back Bay West.

Here's an exception to my rule about not recommending huge convention hotels (the Westin, on page 86, is another). You and 1,124 of your closest friends can stay here, and you'll each have your own room. You'll also have a huge indoor/outdoor pool with a retractable dome, access to every business and convention amenity under the sun, a large, well-equipped health club, and a 5-second commute to the Prudential Center complex. Don't expect personalized service. Do expect fairly large, freshly refurbished rooms (part of a $65 million renovation project). Children under 17 stay free in their parents' room.

39 Dalton St., Boston, MA 02199. ☎ *800/325-3535 or 617/236-2000. Fax 617/236-1702. www.sheraton.com.* **MBTA:** *Green Line B, C, or D to Hynes/ICA; walk toward rear of trolley and use Boylston St. exit, turn left, take first right onto Dalton St., and walk 1 block. Or Green Line E to Prudential; facing tower, bear left onto Belvidere St. and walk 1 block.* **Parking:** *Valet $24, self $18.* **Rack rates:** *$229–$319 double; suites from $400. Weekend packages. 25% discount for students, faculty, and retired persons with ID, depending on availability. AE, CB, DC, DISC, JCB, MC, V.*

Sheraton Commander Hotel
$$$. Cambridge.

This is the textbook definition of a traditional hotel so close to Harvard that it's practically on campus. The Sheraton Commander attracts the type of guest who finds the Charles Hotel just too trendy (not to mention expensive). The colonial-style decor begins in the elegant lobby and extends to the guest rooms, which aren't huge but are attractively furnished; all were renovated in 1996. There's a small fitness center, a sundeck, and a laundry room. And never underestimate the value of free parking near Harvard Square. Children under 18 stay free in their parents' room.

16 Garden St., Cambridge, MA 02138. ☎ *800/325-3535 or 617/547-4800. Fax 617/868-8322. www.sheraton.com.* **MBTA:** *Red Line to Harvard; take Mass. Ave. north 1 or 2 blocks to Garden St., turn left, and walk 4 blocks.* **Parking:** *Free.* **Rack rates:** *$159–$279 double; $330–$550 suite. Extra person $20. AE, CB, DC, DISC, JCB, MC, V.*

Swissôtel Boston
$$$. Downtown Crossing.

If you're traveling on a weekend, don't say, "Three dollar signs? Next!" The Swissôtel hops with business travelers during the week, then offers appealing weekend packages. It's a European-style establishment, with elegant furnishings,

The Best Hotels if You Have a Disability

The Charles Hotel	$$$$
Doubletree Guest Suites	$$$
Eliot & Pickett Houses	$$
The Westin Copley Place Boston	$$$

proper service, and everything a traveling tycoon might need for a corporate takeover. Then she (or he) can repair to the indoor pool, sun terrace, or fitness center. Guest rooms are large enough to have sitting areas, and all have fax machines. Children under 12 stay free in their parents' room.

1 Ave. de Lafayette (off Washington St.), Boston, MA 02111. ☎ *800/621-9200 or 617/451-2600. Fax 617/451-0054. www.swissotel.com.* **MBTA:** *Red or Orange line to Downtown Crossing; walk 1 long block along Washington St. side of Macy's and turn left. Green Line to Boylston; follow Tremont St. 1 block opposite Boston Common, turn right onto Avery St., left onto Washington, right onto Ave. de Lafayette.* **Parking:** *Valet $26; self $22 weekdays, $8 weekends.* **Rack rates:** *$235–$260 double; from $440 suite. Extra person $25. Weekend packages. AE, CB, DC, DISC, JCB, MC, V.*

The Westin Copley Place Boston
$$$. Back Bay West.
Ordinarily I wouldn't sing the praises of a chain megahotel, but this is an exception (as is the Sheraton Boston, above). The Westin fills its 800 rooms with travelers of every stripe by offering something for everyone. It boasts the full range of business amenities and an excellent health club with a pool, and adjoins the Copley Place–Prudential Center shopping complex. Guest rooms are large and well appointed, and all have windows that open. The hotel is home to two first-class restaurants, the **Palm** and **Turner Fisheries.** And the views from the 36-story tower are amazing. Children under 18 stay free in their parents' room.

10 Huntington Ave. (at Dartmouth St.), Boston, MA 02116. ☎ *800/WESTIN-1 or 617/262-9600. Fax 617/424-7483. www.westin.com.* **MBTA:** *Green Line to Copley; follow Dartmouth St. 1 block opposite Copley Square. Or Orange Line to Back Bay; enter through Copley Place mall.* **Parking:** *Valet $24.* **Rack rates:** *$189–$305 double; from $350 suite. Extra person $20–$30. Weekend packages. AE, CB, DC, DISC, JCB, MC, V.*

Help! I'm So Confused!
Take a deep breath.

For some people, this is a cinch. If your parents met at the dear departed Merry-Go-Round Bar at the old Copley Plaza, or you live to rack up points at a certain chain, you know where you're headed. Everyone else has homework to do.

Flip through the listings again, and enter the names of the hotels you checked off on the worksheet that follows. Do the same (in the correct colors, if you're really compulsive) with the choices of everyone else who took a turn. Now move on to "compare and contrast." Fill in the little boxes, then scan the columns to see how everyone's selections stack up. Hash it out with your traveling companions, if you want them in on the decision-making process—this is an excellent way for kids who are old enough to learn about budgeting and compromise. Rank your choices roughly, and when your preferences become clear, note them in order in the column on the far right. Now you're ready to start calling around, or to present your travel agent with your well-researched preferences.

Hotel Preferences Worksheet

Hotel	Location	Price per night

Advantages	Disadvantages	Your Ranking (1–10)

Part 3

Learning Your Way Around Boston

Planes approaching Boston usually swing around and come in over the Atlantic, affording air travelers a dazzling view that looks like something out of a snow globe. The magic bubble bursts as soon as the wheels touch down. A tide of people sweeps you through the terminal, pausing at the baggage carousel, and spits you out onto the sidewalk.

In this section you'll learn how to get from that sidewalk (or the train station) to wherever you're going. After you drop off your stuff, you need to get your bearings. I'll outline your transportation options, describe the neighborhoods, and even be a good sport and suggest other places to get information.

Your first time in a new city can be a tad scary. Try to hang on to that exhilarating first impression, and I'll try to help make the transition as painless as possible.

Chapter 7

Getting Your Bearings

In This Chapter

➤ Point A to point B (from the airport to your bed)

➤ A beautiful day in the neighborhoods

➤ Where to learn more

Boston is an infuriating place if you like your streets straight and parallel, your intersections four-cornered and square, and your compass helpful. Adopt a looser attitude, and soon the crazy-quilt geography will feel perfectly natural—or you'll like exploring so much that you just won't care. One of the pluses of visiting a relatively small city is that you can never get *that* lost.

Logan's Run: Airport Information

Logan International Airport ("Logan" to its friends) is across the harbor in East Boston, just 3 miles from downtown. It consists of five terminals, A through E. In A through D, which serve domestic carriers, gates are on the upper level, baggage claim and ground transportation on the first. Terminals A, C, and E have information booths, and all five have ATMs.

The Massachusetts Port Authority coordinates airport transportation (☎ **800/ 23-LOGAN;** www.massport.com). The toll-free line provides information about getting to the city and to many nearby suburbs. It's available 24 hours a day and staffed weekdays 8am to 7pm.

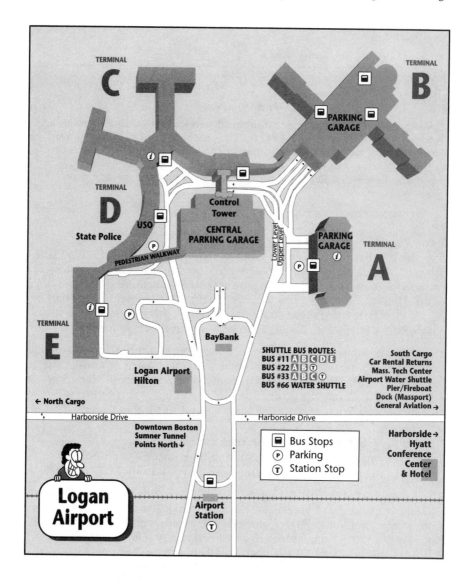

Get Me Outta Here! Leaving Logan

When you reach ground level, you have several options. Follow signs in the terminal for the transportation you've selected, and they'll direct you to the exit closest to the correct spot on the curb. Except at odd hours, such as very early on weekend mornings, driving (in a cab, bus, or car) is the slowest way to get downtown.

93

Time-Savers

Unless you have serious mobility difficulties (or you ignored the packing advice in chapter 4 and brought along the contents of your hope chest), I strongly recommend that you take the subway or water shuttle to and from the airport, particularly at busy times. Downtown Boston traffic is so unpredictable that you can land in a big tie-up at just about any hour—a terrible way to begin or end your vacation.

T for You, You for T: Taking the Subway

Free **shuttle buses** connect the terminals to the MBTA (the "T") Blue Line subway's airport station, which is aboveground. Buses run on four routes in a continuous loop from 5:30am to 1am every day, year-round. Take the no. 22 or no. 33 shuttle bus to the station, *not* the no. 11 (terminal-to-terminal) or no. 66 (dock). At the station, you'll need to buy a token for 85¢ (or a visitor passport—see chapter 8). The line can be long but moves quickly.

The Blue Line stops at Aquarium, on the Waterfront, then at State Street and Government Center, downtown points where you can exit or transfer (free) to the other lines. The trip to Government Center takes about 10 minutes. If you're going to Cambridge, switch to the Green Line at Government Center, take it one stop, and transfer *again* at Park Street to the Red Line.

By the Sea, by the Sea: Water Transportation

The trip downtown in a weather-protected **boat** takes 7 minutes, dock to dock. Take the no. 66 shuttle bus from any terminal to the Logan ferry dock.

The **Airport Water Shuttle** (☎ 617/330-8680) runs to Rowes Wharf, on Atlantic Avenue behind the Boston Harbor Hotel. It leaves every 15 minutes from 6am to 8pm on weekdays, and every 30 minutes on Friday until 11pm, Saturday 10am to 11pm, and Sunday and national holidays (except January 1, July 4, Thanksgiving, and December 25) 10am to 8pm. The one-way fare is $10 for adults and children 12 and up, $5 for senior citizens, free for children under 12.

Harbor Express (☎ 617/376-8417) runs between the airport and Long Wharf, near the Aquarium T station, 24 times a day on weekdays between 5:30am and 9pm (Friday until 11pm), and less frequently on weekends. There's no service on Thanksgiving and December 25. The one-way fare is $10.

Call Me a Cab. Okay, You're a Cab.

Taxis queue up at every terminal. Join the line, if there is one, at the cab stand. The uniformed dispatcher will wave a taxi to an open space at the curb, then call for the party at the head of the line. Don't worry if there's no cab when it's your turn—the pool is large, and except at the busiest times, you shouldn't have to wait more than a few minutes.

The trip takes anywhere from 10 to 40 minutes, depending on the time of day and how congested the approaches to the tunnels are. If you must travel during rush hour, allow extra time. The fare to downtown or the Back Bay should be about $18 to $24, including the $2 toll and $1.50 airport fee, which the passenger pays. (See chapter 8 for more information on taxis.)

Call Me a Limo. Okay, You're . . .

To arrange **limousine** service, call ahead for a reservation, especially at busy times. Your hotel can recommend a company, or try **Carey Limousine Boston** (☎ **800/336-4646** or 617/623-8700) or **Commonwealth Limousine Service** (☎ **800/558-LIMO** outside Massachusetts, or 617/787-5575).

On the Bus

Buses run between every terminal and Gate 25 at South Station, on Atlantic Avenue near the waterfront. They leave every 15 to 30 minutes from 7:15am (with an extra run on weekends and holidays at 6:25am) to 10:15pm. The last bus leaves Logan at 11:15pm. The one-way fare is $6, free for children under 12. Look for a bus with a SOUTH STATION sign on it, and pay onboard.

If traffic from the airport to downtown is bad, the area around South Station (ground zero for the Big Dig) usually isn't in great shape either. If you need to continue in a cab, taking the bus might not save too much time, but it's great if you're connecting to the commuter rail. If you plan to take the Red Line, which has a South Station stop, you're saving the hassle of two transfers (for an extra $5.15).

In the Driver's Seat

The major **car-rental** companies all operate shuttle vans. If your flight is delayed and you're arriving very late, call the company's toll-free number and ask that the office be alerted to expect a customer. At any hour, be sure you have your confirmation number.

You might not want to pick up a car immediately. If it's going right into a hotel garage, consider waiting until you need it. If you need it now, the staff at the car-rental office can map a route that incorporates the latest traffic patterns (there's construction at the airport as well as downtown). Because the distance you're covering is so short, it's basically a straight shot, but be *positive* that you know where

Extra! Extra!

An ongoing overhaul called "Logan 2000" is messy, but it shouldn't affect you if you aren't renting a car. If you are, make sure you know where to go when you return the car, and don't worry if you screw up—the main airport road is a loop, so you can just go around again.

you're going. The route into town doesn't run through places where you can pull over and ask for directions. Well, the correct route doesn't.

Riding the Rails (And the Bus)

Arriving at South Station

South Station is on Atlantic Avenue at Summer Street, near the Waterfront and the Financial District. It serves Amtrak and the commuter rail, and is in the same complex as the bus station. When you leave the train or bus, follow signs into the terminal. Then follow signs to the Red Line subway or to taxis, or walk to your hotel if it's close enough. That's it!

You can take the Red Line to Cambridge or to Park Street, the central station of the T system. There you can make free connections to the Green, Blue (via the Green Line), and Orange (via a pedestrian passage) lines. If you take a cab at rush hour, you'll have a great view of the Big Dig and the accompanying traffic, and loads of time to enjoy it.

Arriving at Back Bay Station

Back Bay Station is on Dartmouth Street between Huntington Avenue and Columbus Avenue, straddling the Back Bay and the South End. It serves Amtrak, the commuter rail, and the MBTA Orange Line. The Orange Line connects Back Bay Station with Downtown Crossing (where there's a walkway to Park Street station) and other points.

Arriving at North Station

North Station serves the commuter rail to the North Shore, Lowell, and Fitchburg, and the MBTA Green and Orange lines. It's part of the FleetCenter complex that replaced Boston Garden. Because of the Big Dig and the redevelopment of the Garden site, you may encounter (surprise, surprise) construction.

Getting Oriented

Boston is one of the oldest cities in the country, with a street pattern that looks about like the network of wrinkles you'd expect to see on the face of a 370-year-old. With one exception (the Back Bay), the layout of the parts of town you'll probably visit makes almost no sense. Old Boston is littered with alleys, dead ends, one-way streets, streets that change names, and streets named after extinct geographical features. The glass will be half full if you think of wrong turns as chances to see something interesting that you might otherwise have missed.

A quick history lesson can help you make sense of this directional anarchy. The original settlement was where downtown is now, but with the 19th-century creation of the Back Bay and annexation of several suburbs, the city grew so large that its geographic center is now somewhere in Roxbury. South Boston *is* south of downtown, but it's east of most of the city. Likewise the West End—north of almost everywhere, but west of the North End.

Find a map and let's take a tour.

The Major Neighborhoods

These are the neighborhoods where most visitors go to see sights. The numerous residential areas outside central Boston include the Fenway, South Boston, Dorchester, Roxbury, West Roxbury, and Jamaica Plain. Also see the neighborhood capsules in chapter 5 for help with deciding where to stay.

Downtown

The neighborhood I've defined as downtown consists of these areas: the Waterfront, the North End, Faneuil Hall Marketplace and Haymarket, Downtown Crossing, the Financial District, and Government Center (the ones not mentioned in chapter 5 don't have hotels).

History 101

Well into the 19th century, when Bostonians started running out of space, they just dumped some landfill into the water and redrew the shoreline. This do-it-yourself approach reached its apex when a whole marshy estuary became the Back Bay neighborhood between 1835 and 1882.

The **Waterfront,** along Commercial Street and Atlantic Avenue, faces the Inner Harbor. Once filled with wharves and warehouses, it now boasts luxury condos, restaurants, and offices. The New England Aquarium and public docks are here. Just over the Northern Avenue Bridge is Museum Wharf, on the edge of a harbor-front neighborhood developers have dubbed the Seaport District.

The **North End,** one of the city's oldest neighborhoods, is where you'll find the Paul Revere House and the Old North Church. It's east of I-93 and within the loop formed by Commercial and North Washington streets. Home to waves of immigrants over the years, it was predominantly Italian before a recent influx of young professionals. Nevertheless, you'll hear Italian in the streets and find a wealth of Italian restaurants, cafes, and shops. The adjacent **North Station** area, around Causeway Street near the FleetCenter, is increasingly popular with the nightclub crowd.

Employees aside, Boston residents tend to be scarce at **Faneuil Hall Marketplace** (also called Quincy Market after the central building). The "festival market," in a cluster of buildings between I-93 and North, Congress, and State streets, is the city's most popular attraction. **Haymarket,** on Blackstone Street from North to Hanover streets, is the site of an open-air produce and fish market on Fridays and Saturdays. The buildings in the **Blackstone Block,** the tiny area between Blackstone, Hanover, Union, and North streets, are among the oldest in Boston.

The intersection that gives **Downtown Crossing** its name is at Washington Street where Winter Street becomes Summer Street. The Freedom Trail runs through this shopping and business district between Tremont Street, Chinatown, the Financial District, and Court and State streets.

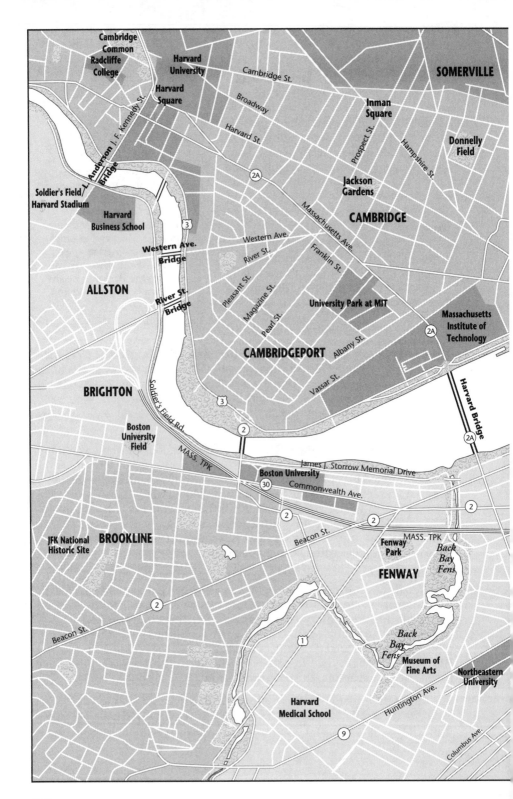

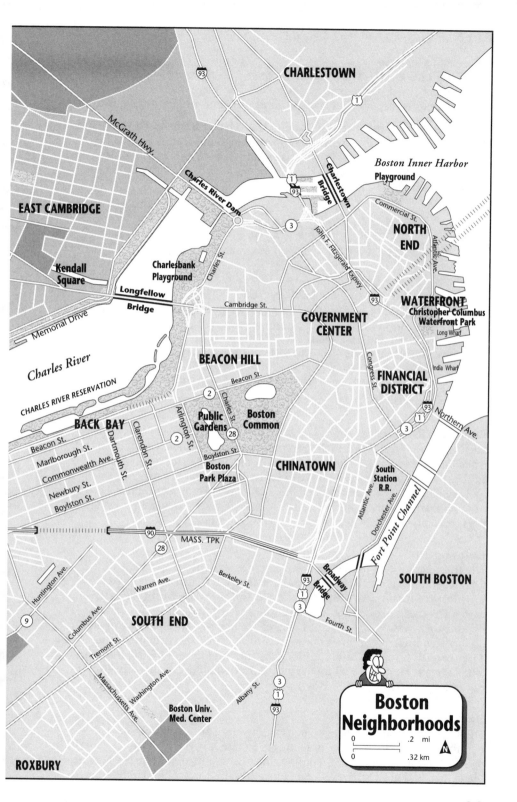

99

The **Financial District,** between I-93, State Street, Downtown Crossing, and Summer Street, is the banking, insurance, and legal center of the city. Its giant office towers loom over the Custom House and its colorful clock tower.

Government Center, between Faneuil Hall Marketplace, Beacon Hill, and Downtown Crossing, is a splash of modern design on Boston architecture's redbrick-and-granite facade. It consists mostly of state and federal office buildings and Boston City Hall, the concrete monstrosity across Congress Street from Faneuil Hall.

History 101

Washington Street—the closest thing downtown has to a main drag—follows the route of the narrow causeway that connected the Boston peninsula to the mainland in the 17th and 18th centuries. By 1824 the street had been named after George Washington; as another tribute, all street names (except Mass. Ave.) change when they cross Washington Street: For example, Bromfield becomes Franklin, Winter becomes Summer, Stuart becomes Kneeland.

Beacon Hill

Narrow, tree-lined streets and architectural showpieces, mostly in Federal style, make up this residential area in the shadow of the State House. Louisburg Square and Mount Vernon Street, two of the loveliest (and most exclusive) spots in Boston, are on Beacon Hill. Bounded by Government Center, Boston Common, and the river, it's also home to Massachusetts General Hospital, on the nominally less-tony north side of the neighborhood.

Chinatown

The third-largest Chinatown in the country is an expanding area jammed with Asian restaurants, groceries, and gift shops. It's currently between Downtown Crossing, Tremont Street, I-93, and the Mass. Turnpike extension, with a few businesses to the west and south. The "Combat Zone," or red-light district, was on the edge of this area for many years and has just about disappeared under community pressure. Still in place and thriving is the **Theater District.** Within $1\frac{1}{2}$ blocks of the intersection of Tremont and Stuart streets, you'll find all the largest professional Boston theaters. (No, it's not exactly the Great White Way.)

Back Bay

The Back Bay abounds with gorgeous architecture and chic shops. It is bounded by the Public Garden, Kenmore Square, the river, and to the south by Huntington Avenue or St. Botolph Street. Students dominate the area near Mass. Ave. and grow scarce as property values rise toward the Public Garden.

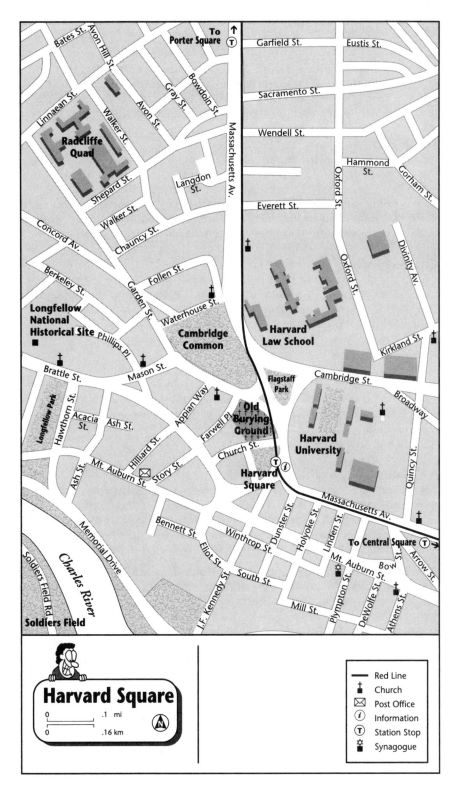

Harvard Square

0 .1 mi
0 .16 km

Red Line
Church
Post Office
Information
Station Stop
Synagogue

Commonwealth Avenue is largely residential, Newbury Street largely commercial; both are excellent places to walk around. In the Back Bay you'll find Trinity Church, the Boston Public Library, the Hancock Tower, Copley Place, the Prudential Center, and the Hynes Convention Center.

South End
Cross Stuart Street or Huntington Avenue heading south and you'll soon be in this landmark district. Packed with Victorian row houses and little parks, the South End was extensively gentrified in the 1970s and '80s. Known for its ethnic, economic, and cultural diversity, it has a large gay community and some of the best restaurants in the city. *Note:* Don't confuse the South End with South Boston, a predominantly Irish-American residential neighborhood.

Charlestown
One of the oldest areas of Boston, this is where you'll see the last two stops on the Freedom Trail, USS *Constitution* ("Old Ironsides") and the Bunker Hill Monument. Off the beaten track, Charlestown is an almost entirely white residential neighborhood with a well-deserved reputation for insularity.

Kenmore Square
The white-and-red Citgo sign above the intersection of Commonwealth Avenue, Beacon Street, and Brookline Avenue tells you you're approaching Kenmore Square. Its shops, bars, restaurants, and clubs are a magnet for students from adjacent Boston University. The college-town atmosphere goes out the window when the Red Sox are in town and baseball fans flock to historic Fenway Park, 3 blocks away.

A Cambridge Introduction
Boston and Cambridge are so closely associated that many people believe they're the same city—a notion both municipalities' residents and politicians would be happy to dispel. Cantabrigians (a native or resident of Cambridge) are often considered more liberal and better educated than Bostonians, which is another idea that's sure to get you involved in a heated discussion.

The areas of the city you're apt to visit are along the MBTA Red Line. **Harvard Square** is a magnet for students, sightseers, and well-heeled shoppers. It's an easy walk along Massachusetts Avenue southeast to **Central Square,** a rapidly gentrifying area dotted with ethnic restaurants and clubs, and north to **Porter Square,** a mostly residential neighborhood with some quirky shops like those that once characterized Harvard Square. Around **Kendall Square** you'll find MIT and many technology-oriented businesses.

Face Time: Getting Information in Person
Start by asking the concierge or front desk staff at your hotel for suggestions. Many hotels have racks full of brochures and other information.

The **Boston National Historic Park Visitor Center,** at 15 State St. (☎ **617/242-5642**), across the street from the Old State House and the State

Speech Depaaahtment

The world-famous Boston accent lands like an anvil on the ears of people expecting the vaguely British imitations so common in the movies and on TV. Rent *Good Will Hunting* if you want a realistic preview, and remember a few things: "Copley" is *Cop*-ley, not *Cope*-ley; "Quincy" is Quin-zee, not Quin-see, and it's Charles*town*, not Charles*ton*. Incidentally, it is not considered sporting to ask someone with a Boston accent to say "I parked my car in Harvard Yard." Just keep your ears open—anyone who can make the most of that sentence is capable of more vowel-related pandemonium. (And there's no parking in Harvard Yard anyway.)

Street T station, is a good resource. National Park Service rangers staff the center, dispense information, and lead free tours of the Freedom Trail. It's open daily from 9am to 5pm except January 1, Thanksgiving Day, and December 25.

The Freedom Trail begins at the **Boston Common Information Center,** at 146 Tremont St. on the Common. The center is open Monday to Saturday 8:30am to 5pm and Sunday 9am to 5pm. The **Prudential Information Center,** on the main level of the Prudential Center, is open Monday through Saturday 9am to 8pm, and Sunday 11am to 6pm. The **Greater Boston Convention & Visitors Bureau (☎ 888/SEE-BOSTON** or 617/536-4100) operates both centers.

The bureau also provides information on attractions, dining, performing arts and nightlife, shopping, and travel services through its **"Boston by Phone"** service, accessible from the main phone numbers.

There's a small information booth at **Faneuil Hall Marketplace** between Quincy Market and the South Market Building. It's outdoors and staffed in the spring, summer, and fall from 10am to 6pm Monday through Saturday, noon to 6pm Sunday.

In Cambridge, there's an information kiosk (☎ **617/497-1630**) in the heart of Harvard Square, near the T entrance at the intersection of Massachusetts Avenue, John F. Kennedy Street, and Brattle Street. It's open Monday to Saturday 9am to 5pm and Sunday 1 to 5pm.

Publications

The "Calendar" section of the Thursday *Globe,* the "Scene" section of the Friday *Herald,* and the *Boston Phoenix* list more activities than you'll possibly have time for. *Where* magazine, a free shopping and events guide with good street maps, is distributed at most hotels. *The Improper Bostonian* and *Stuff@Night* have entertainment listings and general lifestyle coverage; they're free at newspaper boxes around town.

Getting
Around
Boston

Boston calls itself "America's Walking City," and it proudly lives up to the name. It's also the home of the oldest subway system in the hemisphere. You've probably already gathered that driving is not a good choice in central Boston, but you may need to bring a car into town anyway. This chapter includes information on all three.

Taking It to the Streets

The central city is compact—walking east to west quickly from one end to the other takes about an hour—and dotted with historically and architecturally interesting buildings and neighborhoods. The narrow, twisting streets that make driving such a headache are a treat for pedestrians, who are never far from something worth seeing. If you want someone else to point out that something, check the section on walking tours in chapter 12.

The only steep parts of town are **Beacon Hill** and one piece of the **North End**—Copp's Hill, where the Freedom Trail leads up from the Old North Church to the burying ground, then down toward Charlestown. The **Back Bay** is the only neighborhood laid out in a grid. The cross streets begin at the Public Garden with Arlington and proceed alphabetically until Mass. Ave. jumps in after Hereford.

There are three things to watch out for:

➤ The brick, cobblestone, and otherwise uneven **streets and sidewalks** all over town are brutal on footwear. Remember those walking shoes I harped on in chapter 4? This is why you packed them.

➤ Many downtown **traffic lights** give you just 7 seconds to get across the street, no matter how wide the intersection. Stay on the curb when the light is red, lest you stray into the path of danger.

➤ **Boston drivers.** They deserve their notoriety. The truly reckless are a tiny minority, but it pays to be careful. Look out for wrong-way bike messengers and skaters, too. See box below.

The Truth About Boston Drivers

It's all true. Never assume that a Boston driver will behave as you expect, especially when it comes to the rarely used turn signal. Watch out for cars that leave the curb and change lanes without signaling, that double- and triple-park in the most inconvenient places imaginable, and that travel the wrong way down one-way streets. Also watch out for bicyclists and skaters, who are just drivers without the cars. Look both ways!

The Line on the MBTA

The **Massachusetts Bay Transportation Authority,** or MBTA (☎ 617/222-3200; www.mbta.com), is known as the "T," and its logo is the letter in a circle. The MBTA runs subways, trolleys, and buses in Boston and many suburbs, as well as the commuter rail, and contracts out some water transportation. You'll hear subway stops called "T stops" and "T stations"—or just "T," as in "I'll meet you near the Aquarium T." The automated information line operates 24 hours a day, and helpful operators are available on weekdays 6:30am to 8pm, weekends 7:30am to 6pm. The Web site offers answers to just about any question and incorporates maps.

Kids Children under 5 ride the T subway and buses free with an adult, and children 5 to 11 pay half price. The commuter rail family fare—the equivalent of two adult fares—is also good for a single adult and up to four kids under 18.

The Subway & Trolley System

The **Red, Orange,** and **Blue line** subways and **Green Line** trolleys take you around Boston faster than any other mode of transportation except walking. The system is quite reliable, with the occasional exception of the ancient Green Line, and generally safe. As on any subway system, watch out for pickpockets, especially during the holiday season.

Dollars & Sense

The **MBTA visitor passport** (☎ **617/222-5218**) is good for unlimited travel on all subway lines, local buses, commuter rail zones 1A and 1B, and two ferries, plus discounts on attractions. A 1–day pass is $5 (so tokens are cheaper for fewer than six trips); it's $9 for 3 consecutive days, $18 for 7 consecutive days. You can buy one when you arrive at the Airport T stop, South Station, Back Bay Station, or North Station. They're also for sale at the Government Center and Harvard T stations; the Boston Common, Prudential Center, and Quincy Market information centers; and some hotels. On the subway, show your pass to the token clerk, who will unlock the turnstile closest to the window.

The local fare is **85¢,** and transfers are free. You need a token or a visitor passport (see "Dollars & Sense" box). You can buy tokens (get an extra for your return trip) at booths near the main entrance of every station, and from machines at many stops. Green Line subway cars become trolleys when they reach the surface, using tracks in the middle of the street, and you pay at the front of the first car. On the Green Line inbound west of Kenmore or Prudential, you can use a token, but exact change is also accepted. On some surface extensions on the Green and Red lines, the fare can be as much as $2.25.

Extra! Extra!

Green Line pointers: Each of the four lines (B, C, D, and E) starts and ends at a different stop. Riding westbound, be sure you have the right letter. If you don't, and you have to backtrack and switch. B, C, and D cars all stop at Kenmore. The crossover from the E line is all the way back at Arlington—there's no free transfer between inbound and outbound at Copley.

Subway maps are color-coded and include the commuter rail to the suburbs, depicted in purple. If you misplace the one included with this book, take your chances at a token booth. Route and fare information and timetables are available from the Web site and at Park Street station (under Boston Common), the center of the system.

The main problem with the T if you plan to go out at night is its sense of timing. Service begins at around 5:15am and shuts down between 12:30 and 1am, system-wide. The only exception is New Year's Eve, or First Night, when closing time is 2am and service is free after 8pm.

The Green Line is being renovated to make it wheelchair accessible. Most stations on other lines already are; they are indicated on system maps. To learn more, call the main information number or the **Office for Transportation Access** (☎ **800/533-6282** or 617/222-5123; TDD 617/222-5415).

The Bus System

The MBTA (☎ **617/222-3200**) also runs buses and "trackless trolleys," identifiable by their electric antennae but otherwise indistinguishable from buses. They provide service around town and to and around the suburbs. The local routes you're likeliest to need are **no. 1,** along Mass. Ave. from Dudley station in Roxbury through the Back Bay and Cambridge to Harvard Square; **no. 92** and **93,** which run between Haymarket and Charlestown; and **no. 77,** along Mass. Ave. north of Harvard Square to Porter Square, North Cambridge, and Arlington.

The local bus fare is **60¢.** Exact change is required; you can use a token, but you won't get change back. Express bus fares start at $1.50. Many buses are equipped with lifts for wheelchairs; call ☎ **800/ LIFT-BUS** for information.

History 101

Boston's subway system is the oldest in the western hemisphere. Newspaper headlines from 1897, incorporated into the decoration of the Green Line platform at Park Street, describe the inaugural run (and make it sound more exciting than the moon landing—must have been a slow news day).

Time-Savers

Look at a map with T stations superimposed on downtown before assuming that you need to head underground to get where you're going. South Station to Aquarium, for example, is a three-train trip but a 10-minute walk. You'd spend almost that long just getting to and from the platforms.

A Ferry Good Idea

The state of water transportation is in flux. Operators constantly evaluate changing demand and experiment with offerings, inaugurating routes with great fanfare, then quietly taking them out of service. At press time, two useful ferries (both included in the MBTA visitor passport) run from Lovejoy Wharf, off Causeway Street behind North Station and the FleetCenter. One runs to Long Wharf (near the Aquarium T stop) and the Charlestown Navy Yard—it's a good way to get back from "Old Ironsides" and the Bunker Hill

Monument. The other serves the World Trade Center, on Northern Avenue in South Boston. The fare is $1. Call ☎ **617/227-4321** for more information.

Time-Savers

To reach Cambridge from the Back Bay, walk to Mass. Ave. and catch the no. 1 bus, which runs from Dudley station in Roxbury to Harvard Square. Except at rush hour, it's at least a bit faster than the subway, and you don't have to transfer. The view from the bridge across the Charles River is spectacular, and you save a quarter, too.

All Hail: Getting a Taxi

Taxis are expensive and not always easy to find, but worth the trouble when you're getting thrown out of a club at 2am. If you really are getting thrown out of a club, there should be plenty of drivers cruising—they go where the business is. The rest of the time, seek out a cab stand or call a dispatcher. If it's late and you're desperate, look in front of a 24-hour business such as Dunkin' Donuts.

You can usually find cab stands near hotels. There are also busy ones at Faneuil Hall Marketplace (on North Street), South Station, Back Bay Station, and on Mass. Ave. in Harvard Square in front of BayBank (near the Coop) and Cambridge Trust (near Au Bon Pain).

To call ahead for a cab, try the **Independent Taxi Operators Association,** or ITOA (☎ **617/426-8700**); **Boston Cab** (☎ **617/536-5010**); **Town Taxi** (☎ **617/536-5000**), or **Checker Taxi** (☎ **617/536-7000**). In Cambridge, call **Ambassador Brattle** (☎ **617/492-1100**) or **Yellow Cab** (☎ **617/ 547-3000**). Boston Cab will dispatch a wheelchair-accessible vehicle; advance notice is recommended.

The fare structure: the first quarter mile (when the flag drops) costs $1.50, and each additional eighth of a mile is 25¢. "Wait time" is extra, and the passenger pays all tolls as well as the $1.50 airport fee (on trips leaving Logan only). Charging a flat rate is not allowed within Boston; the police department publishes a list of distances to the suburbs that establishes the flat rate for those trips.

Road Trip! Road Trip!

So you insist on bringing your car into town.

If you're staying in the suburbs or you have to drive for another reason, the smartest strategy is to park the car and walk or take the T. Bring along a good

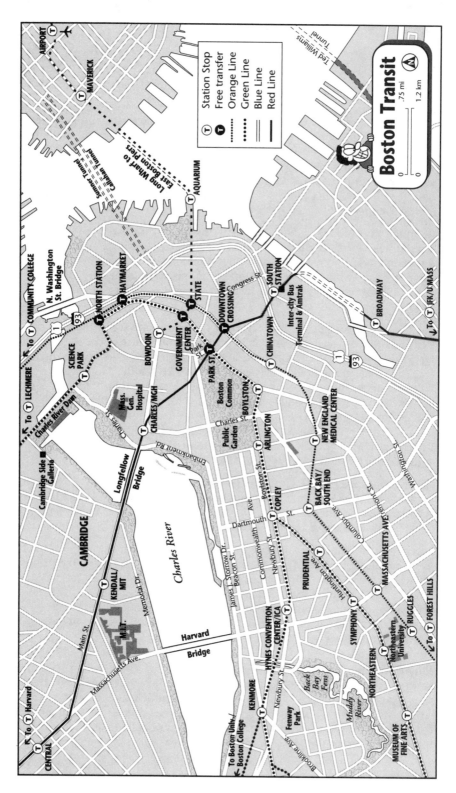

map and, if possible, a navigator, and don't expect your out-of-state plates to get you any slack. (See box "The Truth About Boston Drivers," above.) Here's what you need to know.

Parking on the street is for suckers. Most spaces are metered (and patrolled until 6pm on the dot every day except Sunday), and open to nonresidents for 2 hours or less between 8am and 6pm. The penalty is a $20 ticket. Should you blunder into a tow-away zone, retrieving the car will take at least $55 and a lot of running around. The cost of meters varies but is usually $1 an hour downtown (bring plenty of quarters). Time limits range from 15 minutes to 2 hours.

It's much easier to leave the car in a parking lot or garage and walk. With the economy booming, the daily rate may be as much as $25. Weekend rates typically are much lower, and on weekdays there's often a discounted flat rate if you enter and exit before certain times or if you park in the evening. Some restaurants offer reduced rates at nearby garages; ask when you call for reservations.

The two largest garages are under **Boston Common** and under the **Prudential Center.** The reasonably priced city-run garage under the Common (☎ **617/954-2096**) at Charles Street accepts vehicles less than 6 feet, 3 inches tall. The garage at the Prudential Center (☎ **617/267-1002**) has entrances on Boylston Street, Huntington Avenue, and Exeter Street, and on Dalton Street at the Sheraton Boston. Parking is discounted if you buy something at the Shops at Prudential Center and have your ticket stamped. A similar deal is offered at the garage at **Copley Place** (☎ **617/375-4488**), off Huntington Avenue near Exeter Street. Many businesses in **Faneuil Hall Marketplace** validate parking at the **75 State St. Garage** (☎ **617/742-7275**).

Other good-sized garages: at **Government Center** off Congress Street (☎ **617/227-0385**), at the **New England Aquarium** (☎ **617/723-1731**), at **Zero Post Office Square** (☎ **617/423-1430**), and near the Hynes Convention Center on **Dalton Street** (☎ **617/247-8006**).

Everything I've said about Boston driving goes double for Harvard Square. It has a handful of incredibly expensive garages and lots and many tempting university spaces from which a car can be towed in the blink of an eye. You might score a metered space (maximum stay, 30 minutes to 2 hours) if you drive around enough, but don't count on it. If you can handle the walk, cross the bridge at Memorial Drive and John F. Kennedy Street and park on North Harvard Street or Western Avenue.

Law & Order: Rules of the Road

You may turn right at a red light after stopping when traffic permits, unless a sign is posted saying otherwise (as it often is). Seat belts are mandatory for adults and children, and infants and children under 5 must be strapped into car seats. You can't be stopped just for having an unbelted adult in the car, but a youngster on the loose is reason enough to pull you over.

Under state law, pedestrians in the crosswalk have the right of way, and vehicles already in a rotary (traffic circle or roundabout) have the right of way. Congratulations—you now know more state traffic laws than the average Boston driver.

Dollars & Sense

If you're staying in the suburbs to save money, $25 to park defeats the purpose. Juggle your schedule—parking fees are cheaper (and attractions more crowded) on weekends than on weekdays. Or turn into a commuter—the staff at your hotel can help you with the logistics. If you must park at a suburban train station, you'll probably be on the road early, because the lots fill up quickly. If you don't have to drive, consider waiting until after rush hour. Make sure you know the schedule for your return trip, too.

Part 4

Boston's Best Restaurants

You might come to Boston expecting to subsist on New England clam chowder, baked beans, seafood, and Boston cream pie (actually, not a terrible fate). But the stereotype of the Waspy New Englander happy with a lifetime of boarding-school chow was never accurate, and for about the last 25 years it's been downright laughable. Yes, Boston had something called the "codfish aristocracy," but it's also where Julia Child's TV career originated. "The French Chef" got the ball rolling, and over the years an army of worthy successors has turned the Boston dining scene into one of the best and most dynamic in the country.

In this section you'll get the lowdown on Boston and Cambridge restaurants, from old-line seafood favorites to cutting-edge bistros. We'll point you toward places where you can dine with frugal students, spendthrift corporate raiders, and everyone in between. And because the sightseeing pedestrian is unlikely to want a fancy lunch, we'll point you toward some great eat-and-run spots.

Visitors always ask, "Where do people who live here go to eat?" Turn the page and find out.

Chapter 9

The Lowdown on the Boston Dining Scene

In This Chapter

➤ Dining traditions and trends

➤ How much money to bring

➤ When to eat, what to tip, what to wear, what else to know

The diversity of cultures and backgrounds in the Boston area translates to a lively dining scene with lots of competition. Boston has more than its share of celebrity chefs and their protégés and groupies, but also a good number of restaurants that have thrived for many years. The places worth seeking out are popular not because they're trendy but because they're so good at what they do. My list of personal favorites incorporates both, and it tops 100 restaurants; after much agonizing, 36 of them are reviewed in chapter 10. The information in this chapter, the reviews, and the lists of snacking hot spots and national and local chains in chapter 11 will help you find your favorites.

What's Cooking

Fresh seafood is cooking, everywhere from the stuffiest private clubs to the cheapest ethnic storefronts. Of course you can have meat or poultry, of course you can go vegetarian, and yes, you can just get a burger. But when friends of friends call to ask me for a dining suggestion, they almost always want fresh seafood.

Local ingredients—such as Ipswich and Essex clams, Wellfleet oysters, and world-famous Atlantic lobsters—abound, and the rest of the undersea world is fair game. Always remember to ask about daily specials. Many chefs greet the dawn at the fish market, and you can reap the rewards *and* sleep in. Another place that's a magnet for sleepy culinary types is the produce market. Fresh local produce abounds on an increasing number of menus during even slightly warm weather. (Visitors in the dead of winter will marvel at the versatility of squash.)

There's no particular "Boston style," but many disparate menus show signs of the same influences, thanks in part to the rampant cross-pollination of local kitchen staffs. For the past few years, Asian influences have been second in popularity only to vegetarian options, with Southwestern touches a close third. Vertical food seems to be on the way out, and good-sized helpings have elbowed out dainty portions. If there's one thing New Englanders value, it's value.

Without Reservations

If you can't get a table but you just can't leave town without checking out a certain restaurant, ask if you can eat at the bar without a reservation. Some places offer a less expensive bar menu, some let you order off the regular menu, and some do both. You're on the scene if there's a last-minute cancellation, but it won't be intimate, and it might be smoky. Some good choices: **Anago** (Back Bay West, $$$$), the **Blue Room** (Cambridge, $$$$), **Chez Henri** (Cambridge, $$$), **Grill 23 & Bar** (Back Bay East, $$$$), **Hamersley's Bistro** (South End, $$$$), and **Rialto** (Cambridge, $$$$).

Studying the Classics

Boston's oldest restaurants date from 1826 and 1827, and at a couple of other spots you could be forgiven for thinking that the gentlemen at the next table inherited their seats from their great-grandfathers. For a classic Boston experience, seek out **Durgin-Park** (1827; see chapter 10), **Locke-Ober** (1875), 3 and 4 Winter Place, off Winter Street at Downtown Crossing (☎ 617/542-1340); **Ye Olde Union Oyster House** (1826), 41 Union St., near Faneuil Hall Marketplace (☎ 617/227-2750); or the **Ritz-Carlton Dining Room** (1927; a baby!), 15 Arlington St., across from the Public Garden (☎ 617/536-5700).

Two classic establishments on the South Boston waterfront near the Fish Pier are in a class by themselves, extremely popular with tourists all the time and a (predominantly male) power-broker crowd at lunch. They're reliable places for simple seafood, and their dining rooms have spectacular water views: **Jimmy's Harborside Restaurant,** 242 Northern Ave. (☎ 617/423-1000), and **Anthony's Pier 4,** 140 Northern Ave. (☎ 617/423-6363).

Celebrity Chefs

Readers of national food and travel magazines and viewers of the TV Food Network will probably recognize most of these names. As you might expect, all of them own and run excellent restaurants. They aren't cheap, but this might be the only arena left in our society where reputation actually is a reliable indicator of talent. You'll need a reservation everywhere except Olives (which accepts them only for parties larger than five) and the East Coast Grill (parties larger than four, Sunday through Thursday only).

The big names and where you'll find them: **Lydia Shire** and **Susan Regis** at **Biba,** 272 Boylston St. (☎ **617/426-7878**), and **Pignoli,** 79 Park Plaza (☎ **617/338-7500**), both Back Bay East; **Chris Schlesinger** at the **East Coast Grill,** 1271 Cambridge St., Inman Square, Cambridge (☎ **617/491-6568**); **Gordon Hamersley** at **Hamersley's Bistro,** 553 Tremont St., South End (☎ **617/423-2700**); **Todd English** at **Olives,** 10 City Sq., Charlestown (☎ **617/242-1999**), and **Stan Frankenthaler** at **Salamander,** 1 Athenaeum St., at First Street, Kendall Square, Cambridge (☎ **617/225-2121**).

Location! Location! Location!

In just the past month, I've eaten at two thriving restaurants located where there supposedly isn't enough foot traffic to support a profitable business. Central Boston's small size means that quality is widespread—"all the way across town" is not all that far, so curious diners don't have to invest a lot of time to check out a promising new place. And almost every part of town is a residential area or is next to one, so there are plenty of solid neighborhood restaurants.

Boston has no "Restaurant Row," no single "hot" area (forced to choose, though, most people would say the **South End**), and just two ethnic enclaves homogeneous enough to be worth mentioning. The only parts of town where you won't pass plenty of eateries when you're out exploring are most of the Back Bay north of Newbury Street and a few pockets of the Financial District.

In **Cambridge, Harvard Square** offers a good mix of places where students go with other students and places where civilians see visiting parents eating with their kids.

The Top Locations (in Altitude)

First, a disclaimer: I'm not criticizing the food at either of these elegant places—it's quite good. But the fact is, you're paying extra for the view at the **Bay Tower** and **Top of the Hub.** If you can't get a reservation for a table *by the window* (the odds are better at the Bay Tower), just have a drink in the lounge, and eat somewhere else.

The Bay Tower (☎ **617/723-1666**) is on the 33rd floor of 60 State St., overlooking Faneuil Hall Marketplace, the Waterfront, and the airport. It serves dinner Monday through Saturday, and jackets are required for men in the dining room. Top of the Hub (☎ **617/536-1775**) is on the 52nd floor of the Prudential Tower, 800 Boylston St., Back Bay West. It serves lunch Monday through Saturday, Sunday brunch, and dinner daily.

The Trendiest Tables

In some circles, it's quite the thing to complain that you have to go to New York to get a decent meal. Not only is that not true, but it's not even true that you have to go to New York to see the beautiful people. With apologies to Louis Armstrong, if you gotta ask if you're trendy, you're not.

The hottest places this week (they could be different next week) are **Aquitaine,** 569 Tremont St. (☎ **617/424-8577**), in the South End; **Mistral,** 221 Columbus Ave., also in the South End (☎ **617/867-9300**); and **No. 9 Park,** 9 Park St. (☎ **617/742-9991**), on Beacon Hill near the State House.

Ethnic Enclaves

Head to the **North End,** Boston's Little Italy (but it's *never* called that), for good Italian food in every price range. In **Chinatown,** thanks to a recent influx of immigrants and trend-spotting restaurateurs, you'll find excellent Chinese, Japanese, Vietnamese, and even Malaysian food, all at reasonable prices.

In **Cambridge,** ethnic restaurants thrive all over the city, with a particularly good and affordable mix along Mass. Ave. in **Central Square.**

The Price Is Right

The dollar signs that accompany the reviews in chapter 10 give you an idea of what dinner for one with an appetizer, main course, dessert, one drink, tax, and tip will cost. The listings also include a price range for main courses. The dollar signs represent estimates—ordering caviar, lobster, and a glass of wine that's older that you are will boost the total, and some fiscally responsible measures can push it down. (See the next section.)

Here's a breakdown of the categories.

➤ **$ (dirt cheap)** restaurants fill you up and turn you loose. The food and decor are simple but perfectly adequate. Expect to pay no more than $20 a person, and usually more like $15.

➤ **$$ (inexpensive)** places are great choices. Many are ethnic; all dish up fine food in comfortable surroundings. A full meal tops out at $30 a person.

➤ **$$$ (medium)** restaurants leave you feeling you've been *out* to dinner. The experience of excellent food, an attractive setting, and congenial service is well worth $30 to $45 a head.

➤ **$$$$** (**expensive**) restaurants are among the best in town (one of them, Rialto, is my pick for *the* best). Brilliant cuisine, a lovely setting, and refined service add up to at least $45 per person, with two exceptions. The once-in-a-lifetime experience of **L'Espalier** (which serves a fixed-price dinner only) or **Aujourd'hui** will run you at least $75.

Tourist Traps

Of course restaurant owners love to win awards, and many display the accompanying certificates. Look a little closer at the dates—if the last Golden Kilt Award at Harry's House of Haggis is from 1988, chances are the place has seen better days, and the award-winning chef (if not Harry himself) has moved on.

What if My Appetite Is Bigger Than My Wallet?

So your budget doesn't include $50 or $75 for dinner every night—not to worry. (Neither does mine.) Split an appetizer, split a dessert, order beer instead of wine, and you'll hear your credit card sigh with relief. Or skip the alcohol altogether—the markup is outrageous. Tell the kids that only adults drink anything but water in restaurants. Eat at your first-choice restaurant at lunch instead of dinner, save a ton of money, and savor the experience for the rest of the day.

Finally, remember that *dining* (as opposed to eating) out every night can be as tiring as too much running around. Why not venture into the less-expensive categories and see how the other half lives? You might enjoy it.

Speak Up!

This is the dining version of the pep talk in chapter 5. It begins with a story a friend told after an expensive dinner: "The service was bad. The waiter forgot to put ice in the bucket with the wine." The next sentence was not, "He didn't bring any when we asked"—that was the whole story! And it is unfortunate, but it's not bad service, because the omission wasn't intentional. If something goes wrong, politely call it to the server's attention. Wait a reasonable interval, then ask the host, hostess, or maître d' for help. If nothing happens, *then* the service is bad, and *then* the tip should reflect it.

Math Quiz: Tipping

The Massachusetts meal tax is 5%, so if you can do even a little multiplying, you're golden: Tip three to four times the tax. Remember that waiters and waitresses don't make much in wages—the bulk of their earnings comes in tips. Don't leave less than 15% unless the service was awful, and round up, not down. If you're with a large group (six or eight or more), the restaurant may calculate the service charge for you—check before paying. (And see "Speak Up!" above.)

Important note: The waitresses at Durgin-Park are *supposed* to act put-upon (or worse). If that bothers you, don't go there.

You Look Fine, Let's Go: What to Wear

Remember in chapter 4 when you packed that coat and tie or nice outfit? Dinner at a medium or expensive restaurant is the time to break it out. At less expensive places, just about anything goes. And at a few restaurants (noted in individual reviews) men are required to wear jackets at dinner.

True, you ought to be able to show up in a robe and slippers and be treated like a celebrity. The fact is, if you're tucking into a $35 veal chop in a denim jacket, the sweaty clothes you wore all day, and a baseball cap, the cap might as well say TOURIST on it. You're already carrying around a book that says *Complete Idiot*—please, be a visitor, not a tourist.

Got a Match? A Word on Smoking

Not so fast, Bogie. Even as we speak, the smoking lobby is being legislated into submission (remember, Massachusetts is one of the states suing the tobacco companies). A pending law will ban smoking in many Boston restaurants with more than 25 seats; smaller places don't permit it at all. Cambridge is also headed in that direction. Call ahead for details if you absolutely must light up. You'll probably wind up in or near the bar.

It's All in the Timing: Reservations & Hours

When a listing says reservations are recommended or required, that means for dinner. At lunch at fancier spots, a party of two usually won't have to wait long, if at all, but a reservation is a good idea for large groups.

Time-Savers

Your one assignment was to make a reservation at the latest white-hot boîte, and you forgot. Your concierge may be able to bail you out by calling in a favor from the maître d' or owner. If he or she does come through, a $5 to $10 tip is in order.

On Friday and Saturday night, you *must* have a reservation at any restaurant that takes them, sometimes a month or more in advance. If you already know where you want to eat or one of the reviews really speaks to you, call right away. If you see a write-up in a national magazine, it's probably too late already. In any case, it never hurts to call and ask if there have been any cancellations, especially if you're with just one other person.

Boston is a seriously early city, even on weekends. Don't count on getting a table even by showing up before the rush (before 7 in a normal city). In Boston, "early" is 5:30 or 6. And don't count on being able to slip in late without calling first. Most places won't seat you after 10pm on weeknights, 11pm on weekends.

Chapter 10

Boston Restaurants from A to Z

In This Chapter

➤ Indexes by location, price, and cuisine

➤ Reviews of my favorites

➤ The best places for families, romance, business, and more

Just reading about getting to Boston and getting around, you probably worked up an appetite. Well, now you'll really be hungry. After much hand-wringing, I've whittled my list of favorite restaurants down to a manageable three dozen. This chapter begins with indexes by location, price, and cuisine. Then come the reviews, listed alphabetically and including boxes that point out places especially suited to romance, business, families, and even chowder hounds. Chapter 11 includes some suggestions for quick meals (food fast, not fast food).

This icon indicates places that are especially family friendly. In chapter 11, parents will find listings for various national and local chains that also welcome children. An observation: In all but the most expensive restaurants, many children rise to the occasion with little more than some minor fidgeting. Sound them out, and if everyone is willing to make a good-conduct pledge, you may be pleasantly surprised.

The reviews include a dollar sign icon as well as a price range for main courses. The icons indicate the approximate price of dinner for one with appetizer, main course, dessert, one drink, tax, and tip. Remember that these are just ranges—you can easily go wild in a cheap place or take it easy in a pricey one and knock the total into the next category. The ranges:

$$\begin{array}{rcl} \$ & = & \text{under } \$20 \\ \$\$ & = & \$20 \text{ to } \$30 \\ \$\$\$ & = & \$30 \text{ to } \$45 \\ \$\$\$\$ & = & \text{over } \$45 \end{array}$$

Quick Picks: Restaurants at a Glance
Restaurant Index by Location

Back Bay East
Aujourd'hui, $$$$
Grill 23 & Bar, $$$$
Legal Sea Foods, $$$

Back Bay West
Anago, $$$$
Café Jaffa, $
Casa Romero, $$$
Legal Sea Foods, $$$
L'Espalier, $$$$

Beacon Hill
Istanbul Café, $$

Cambridge/Central Square
Green Street Grill, $$$

Cambridge/Harvard Square
Bartley's Burger Cottage, $
Border Café, $$
Chez Henri, $$$
Rialto, $$$$

Cambridge/Inman Square
Jae's, $$$
S&S Restaurant, $

Cambridge/Kendall Square
Blue Room, $$$$

The Helmand, $$
Legal Sea Foods, $$$

Cambridge/Somerville
Dalí, $$
Redbones, $$

Chinatown
Buddha's Delight, $
Grand Chau Chow, $$

Downtown Crossing
Maison Robert, $$$$

Faneuil Hall Marketplace
Durgin-Park, $$
Zuma's Tex-Mex Café, $$

Kenmore Square
Elephant Walk, $$$

North End
Daily Catch, $$
Giacomo's, $$$
Lo Conte's, $$
Mamma Maria, $$$$
Piccola Venezia, $$

South End
Addis Red Sea, $
Icarus, $$$$
Jae's, $$$

South Station

Les Zygomates, $$$

Theater District

Galleria Italiana, $$$$

Jae's, $$$

Waterfront

Billy Tse Restaurant, $$

Waterfront/South Boston

Daily Catch, $$

Jimbo's Fish Shanty, $

Restaurant Index by Price

$

Addis Red Sea, South End

Bartley's Burger Cottage,
Cambridge/Harvard Square

Buddha's Delight, Chinatown

Café Jaffa, Back Bay West

Jimbo's Fish Shanty,
Waterfront/South Boston

S&S Restaurant, Cambridge/
Inman Square

$$

Billy Tse Restaurant,
Waterfront

Border Café,
Cambridge/Harvard Square

Daily Catch, North End,
Waterfront/South Boston

Dalí, Cambridge/Somerville

Durgin-Park, Faneuil Hall
Marketplace

Grand Chau Chow,
Chinatown

The Helmand,
Cambridge/Kendall Square

Istanbul Café, Beacon Hill

Lo Conte's, North End

Piccola Venezia, North End

Redbones,
Cambridge/Somerville

Zuma's Tex-Mex Café, Faneuil
Hall Marketplace

$$$

Casa Romero, Back Bay West

Chez Henri,
Cambridge/Harvard Square

The Elephant Walk, Kenmore
Square

Giacomo's, North End

Green Street Grill,
Cambridge/Central Square

Jae's, Cambridge/Inman
Square, South End, Theater
District

Legal Sea Foods, Back Bay
West, Back Bay East,
Cambridge/Kendall Square

Les Zygomates, South Station

$$$$

Anago, Back Bay West

Aujourd'hui, Back Bay East

The Blue Room,
Cambridge/Kendall Square

Galleria Italiana, Theater
District

Grill 23 & Bar, Back Bay East

Icarus, South End

L'Espalier, Back Bay West

Maison Robert, Downtown
Crossing

Mamma Maria, North End

Rialto, Cambridge/Harvard
Square

123

Restaurant Index by Cuisine

Afghan

The Helmand,
Cambridge/Kendall Square, $$

American

Bartley's Burger Cottage,
Cambridge/Harvard Square, $

Durgin-Park, Faneuil Hall
Marketplace, $$

Grill 23 & Bar, Back Bay East,
$$$$

Barbecue

Redbones,
Cambridge/Somerville, $$

Cambodian

The Elephant Walk, Kenmore
Square, $$$

Caribbean

Green Street Grill,
Cambridge/Central
Square, $$$

Contemporary American

Anago, Back Bay West, $$$$

Aujourd'hui, Back Bay
East, $$$$

Chinese

Billy Tse Restaurant,
Waterfront, $$

Buddha's Delight, Chinatown, $

Grand Chau Chow,
Chinatown, $$

Cuban

Chez Henri,
Cambridge/Harvard
Square, $$$

Deli

S&S Restaurant,
Cambridge/Inman Square, $

Eclectic

The Blue Room,
Cambridge/Kendall Square,
$$$$

Icarus, South End, $$$$

Ethiopian

Addis Red Sea, South End, $

French

Chez Henri,
Cambridge/Harvard
Square, $$$

The Elephant Walk, Kenmore
Square, $$$

L'Espalier, Back Bay
West, $$$$

Les Zygomates, South
Station, $$$

Maison Robert, Downtown
Crossing, $$$$

Italian

Daily Catch, North End,
Waterfront/South Boston, $$

Galleria Italiana, Theater
District, $$$$

Giacomo's, North End, $$$

Lo Conte's, North End, $$

Mamma Maria, North
End, $$$$

Piccola Venezia, North End, $$

Korean

Jae's, Cambridge/Inman
Square, South End, Theater
District, $$$

Mediterranean

Rialto, Cambridge/Harvard Square, $$$$

Mexican

Casa Romero, Back Bay West, $$$

Middle Eastern

Café Jaffa, Back Bay West, $

New England

Durgin-Park, Faneuil Hall Marketplace, $$

L'Espalier, Back Bay West, $$$$

Pan-Asian

Billy Tse Restaurant, Waterfront, $$

Jae's, Cambridge/Inman Square, South End, Theater District, $$$

Seafood

Daily Catch, North End, Waterfront/South Boston, $$$

Giacomo's, North End, $$$

Jimbo's Fish Shanty, Waterfront/South Boston, $

Legal Sea Foods, Back Bay West, Back Bay East, Cambridge/Kendall Square, $$$

Southwestern

Border Café, Cambridge/Harvard Square, $$

Zuma's Tex-Mex Café, Faneuil Hall Marketplace, $$

Spanish Tapas

Dalí, Cambridge/Somerville, $$

Sushi

Jae's, Cambridge/Inman Square, South End, Theater District, $$$

Turkish

Istanbul Café, Beacon Hill, $$

Vegetarian

Buddha's Delight, Chinatown, $

Vietnamese

Buddha's Delight, Chinatown, $

My Favorite Boston Area Restaurants

Addis Red Sea
$. South End. ETHIOPIAN.
Unusual cuisine in an exotic, subterranean setting for not too much money—what's not to like? You sit on stools at *mesobs*, traditional Ethiopian tables. Wash your hands! Ethiopian food is served family style on a platter, without utensils. The waitress covers the platter with a layer of *injera*, a spongy, tangy bread, and spoons the food on top of it. Tear off a piece of *injera* and use it to scoop up a mouthful of the stewlike main courses. You choose—with or without meat, spicy or mild. Even the tamest vegetable dishes are flavorful and filling.

125

Boston Dining

0 _____ .5 mi
0 _____ .8 km

Addis Red Sea **50**
Anago **6**
Anthony's Pier 4 **29**
Aquitaine **48**
Aujourd'hui **36**
The Bay Tower **22**
Bertucci's **19**
Biba **34**
Billy Tse Restaurant **17**
Buddha's Delight **39**
Cafe Fleuri **26**

Café Jaffa **4**
Casa Romero **2**
China Pearl **42**
Daily Catch **28**
Durgin-Park **20**
The Elephant Walk **1**
Empire Garden Restaurant **40**
Fuddrucker's **37**
Galleria Italiana **38**
Giacomo's **15**
Golden Palace Restaurant **41**
Grand Chau Chow **43**
Grill 23 & Bar **46**
Ground Round **8**
Hamersly's Bistro **49**
Icarus **47**
Istanbul Cafe **23**
Jae's **11**
Jimbo's Fish Shanty **31**
Jimmy's Harborside
  Restaurant **30**
Legal Sea Foods **7**

Legal Sea Foods **9**
Legal Sea Foods **45**
L'Espalier **3**
Les Zygomates **44**
Locke-Ober **32**
Lo Conte's **13**
Maison Robert **25**
Mamma Maria **16**
Mistral **10**
No. 9 Park **24**
Olives **12**
Piccola Venezia **14**
Pignoli **35**
The Ritz-Carlton
  Dining Room **33**
Rowes Wharf Restaurant **27**
TGI Friday's **5**
Top of the Hub **8**
Ye Olde Union
  Oyster House **18**
Zuma's Tex-Mex Café **21**

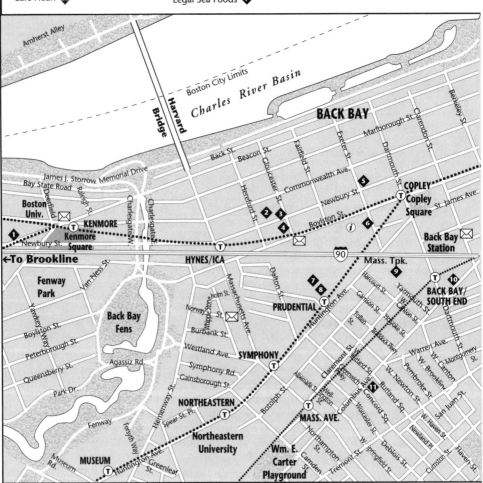

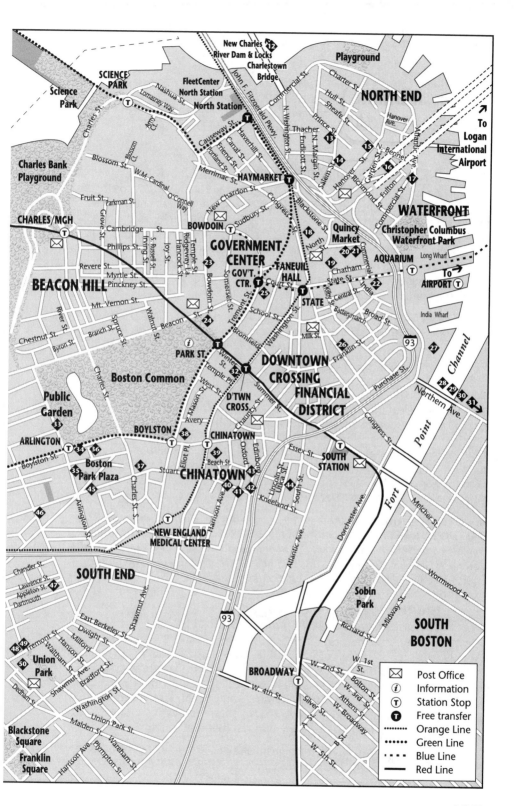

544 Tremont St., at Clarendon St., opposite Boston Center for the Arts. ☎ *617/
426-8727. Reservations not necessary.* **MBTA:** *Orange Line to Back Bay; use
Clarendon St. exit (at back of outbound train), turn right, walk 5 blocks to Tremont
St.* **Main courses:** *$8.95–$12.95. AE, MC, V.* **Open:** *Dinner daily.*

Anago
$$$$. Back Bay West. CONTEMPORARY AMERICAN.
Originally a tiny bistro in Cambridge, Anago made the transition to the big
time flawlessly. Bold, inventive dishes make good use of the region's fresh
produce, seafood, and meats, often served roasted. The kitchen's creative
style never strays into "hey-look-at-me" territory—you can schedule a business lunch, romantic dinner, or family brunch here with equal confidence.
The menu isn't long, but it doesn't need to be when everything is this good.
Desserts are sublime, service is friendly but polite, and the tall wide room is
surprisingly quiet.

In the Lenox Hotel, 710 Boylston St., at Exeter St. ☎ *617/266-6222. Reservations
recommended at dinner.* **MBTA:** *Green Line to Copley; walk 1 block on Boylston St.
side of Boston Public Library.* **Main courses:** *Dinner $17–$32. AE, DC, MC, V.*
Open: *Lunch weekdays, Sun brunch, dinner daily.*

Aujourd'hui
$$$$. Back Bay East. CONTEMPORARY AMERICAN.
On the second floor of the city's premier luxury hotel, the most beautiful
restaurant in town has floor-to-ceiling windows overlooking the Public
Garden. Even if it were under a pup tent, though, the incredible service and
food would make Aujourd'hui a hit with its special-occasion and expense-
account clientele. Yes, the cost is astronomical, but how often is it true that
you get what you pay for? Here, it is.

In the Four Seasons Hotel, 200 Boylston St., opposite the Public Garden. ☎ *617/
451-1392. Reservations recommended (imperative on holidays).* **MBTA:** *Green
Line to Arlington; walk 1 block on Boylston St. opposite the Public Garden.* **Main
courses:** *Dinner $35–$45. AE, CB, DC, MC, V.* **Open:** *Breakfast and dinner
daily, lunch weekdays, Sun brunch. Valet parking available.*

⭐Kids⭐ Bartley's Burger Cottage
$. Cambridge/Harvard Square. AMERICAN.
Great burgers and the best onion rings in the world make Bartley's a perennial
favorite with a cross section of Cambridge, from Harvard students to regular
folks. It's a high-ceilinged, crowded room plastered with signs and posters.
Burgers bear the names of local and national celebrities; the names change,
but the ingredients stay the same. Anything you can think of to put on
ground beef is available here, from American cheese to béarnaise sauce. There
are also some good dishes (like veggie burgers) that don't involve meat.

1246 Massachusetts Ave., between Plympton and Bow sts. ☎ *617/354-6559.
Reservations not necessary.* **MBTA:** *Red Line to Harvard; with the Harvard Coop at*

your back, walk up Mass. Ave. 3½ blocks. **Main courses:** *$7 or less. No credit cards.* **Open:** *Mon–Sat 11am–10pm.*

Billy Tse Restaurant
$$. Waterfront. CHINESE/PAN-ASIAN.

An Asian restaurant on the edge of the Italian North End might seem incongruous, but this casual, economical spot makes a good break from pizza and pasta. You can choose from excellent renditions of the usual dishes and more adventurous selections. The kitchen has a flair for fresh seafood—be sure to check the daily specials. Lunch specials, served until 4pm, are a great deal for a mountain of food. Ask to sit near the French doors that open to the street.

240 Commercial St., at Fleet St. ☎ **617/227-9990.** *Reservations recommended at dinner on weekends.* **MBTA:** *Blue Line to Aquarium; turn right and follow Atlantic Ave. 4 blocks, cutting through Waterfront Park. Or Green or Orange Line to Haymarket; follow the Freedom Trail to Hanover and Fleet sts., turn right, and go 3 long blocks (to traffic light).* **Main courses:** *$5–$19.95; lunch specials $5.50–$7.50. AE, DC, DISC, MC, V.* **Open:** *Mon–Thurs 11:30am–11:30pm, Fri–Sat 11:30am–midnight, Sun 11:30am–11pm.*

The Brunch Bunch

Many restaurants serve an excellent Sunday brunch, but for decadence befitting a medieval head of state, seek out a top hotel for a buffet of monstrous proportions. Expect to spend $42 to $50 a head for adults, about half that for children. At the first three, ask for a table by the window. You definitely need a reservation. You definitely don't need a big dinner.

➤ **Aujourd'hui,** in the Four Seasons Hotel, 200 Boylston St. (☎ 617/451-1392).

➤ The **Rowes Wharf Restaurant,** in the Boston Harbor Hotel, 70 Rowes Wharf (☎ 617/439-3995).

➤ The **Ritz-Carlton Dining Room,** 15 Arlington St. (☎ 617/536-5700).

➤ **Café Fleuri** at Le Meridien Boston, 250 Franklin St. (☎ 617/451-1900).

The Blue Room
$$$$. Cambridge/Kendall Square. ECLECTIC.

The Blue Room is a foodie paradise in the midst of high-tech heaven. The cuisine is a rousing combination of aggressive flavors, and the crowded dining room is not as noisy as it looks through the glass front wall. Many dishes are roasted, grilled, or braised, with at least two vegetarian choices. The roast chicken, served with garlic mashed potatoes, is world-class. In warm weather, there's seating on the brick patio.

1 Kendall Sq., off Hampshire St. ☎ **617/494-9034.** *Reservations recommended.* **MBTA:** *Red Line to Kendall; cross through the Marriott lobby, turn left, follow Broadway 2 long blocks (across the train tracks), bear right onto Hampshire St. and walk ½ block.* **Main courses:** *$16–$26. AE, CB, DC, DISC, MC, V.* **Open:** *Dinner daily, Sun brunch. Validated parking available.*

Border Café
$$. Cambridge/Harvard Square. SOUTHWESTERN.
This insanely crowded Harvard Square hangout combines a festival atmosphere with generous portions of tasty, if not completely authentic, food. The menu features Cajun, Tex-Mex, and some Caribbean specialties, and the beleaguered wait staff keeps the chips and salsa coming. Of course fajitas are popular here—sizzling noisily in a large iron frying pan, they just add to the din. Set aside a couple of hours, be in a party mood, and ask to be seated downstairs if you want to be able to hear your companions.

32 Church St., at Palmer St. ☎ **617/864-6100.** *Reservations not accepted.* **MBTA:** *Red Line to Harvard; use Church St. exit (at front of outbound train), go right at turnstiles, walk 1 block.* **Main courses:** *$7–$14. AE, MC, V.* **Open:** *Mon–Thurs 11am–1am, Fri–Sat 11am–2am, Sun noon–11pm.*

Buddha's Delight
$. Chinatown. VEGETARIAN/VIETNAMESE/CHINESE.
This bare-bones restaurant doesn't serve meat, poultry, fish, or dairy (some beverages have condensed milk), but it does serve tofu and gluten—magically fried or barbecued to taste like chicken, pork, beef, and even lobster. Cuong Van Tran learned the secrets of vegetarian cooking from Buddhist monks in a temple outside Los Angeles. The results are delicious, healthy, and inexpensive. The house specialties are always good, as are soups, chow fun, and stir-fried noodles.

Best Places to Indulge a Sweet Tooth

Anago (Back Bay West, $$$$)
Dalí (Cambridge/Somerville, $$)
Grill 23 & Bar ($$$$, Back Bay East)
Icarus (South End, $$$$)
Jae's (Theater District, $$$)
Jimbo's Fish Shanty (Waterfront/South Boston, $)
Redbones (Cambridge/Somerville, $$)
Zuma's Tex-Mex Café (Faneuil Hall Marketplace, $$)

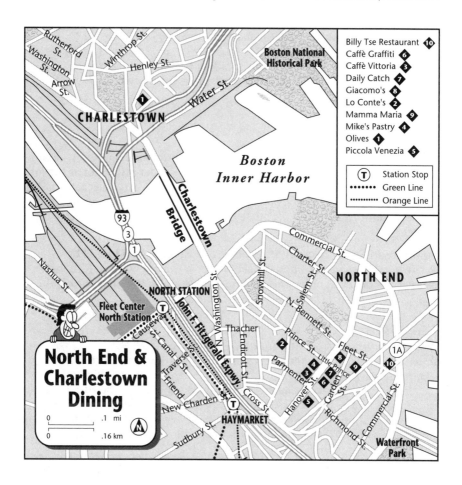

Billy Tse Restaurant ❿
Caffè Graffiti ❻
Caffè Vittoria ❸
Daily Catch ❼
Giacomo's ❽
Lo Conte's ❷
Mamma Maria ❾
Mike's Pastry ❹
Olives ❶
Piccola Venezia ❺

Ⓣ Station Stop
•••••• Green Line
•••••••• Orange Line

Boston Inner Harbor

CHARLESTOWN

NORTH END

NORTH STATION

Fleet Center North Station

North End & Charlestown Dining

0   .1 mi
0   .16 km

HAYMARKET

Waterfront Park

5 Beach St., at Washington St. ☎ *617/451-2395. Reservations not necessary.* **MBTA:** *Orange Line to Chinatown; follow Washington St. (past the China Trade Center) 1 block.* **Main courses:** *$6–$12. No credit cards.* **Open:** *Sun–Thurs 11am–10pm, Fri–Sat 11am–11pm.*

Café Jaffa
$. Back Bay West. MIDDLE EASTERN.
Yes, it looks like a yuppie pizza place, and it draws a young crowd. They come for the low prices, high quality, and large portions of traditional Middle Eastern offerings such as falafel, baba ghanoush, and hummus, as well as burgers and steak tips. Lamb, beef, and chicken kebabs come with Greek salad, rice pilaf, and pita bread. For dessert, try the baklava if it's fresh (give it a pass if not).

131

48 Gloucester St., between Boylston and Newbury sts. ☎ *617/536-0230.*
Reservations not necessary. **MBTA:** *Green Line B, C, or D to Hynes/ICA; use*
Newbury St. exit, turn right, walk 2 blocks, turn right. **Main courses:**
$4.25–$9.75. AE, DC, DISC, MC, V. **Open:** *Mon–Thurs 11am–10:30pm, Fri–Sat*
11am–11pm, Sun 1–10pm.

Casa Romero

$$$. Back Bay West. MEXICAN.
The tiled floor, heavy wood furnishings, dim lighting, and authentic decora-
tions give Casa Romero a real Mexican feel—you're definitely not at the local
Tex-Mex counter. The food is excellent, both authentic (try the cactus salad)
and accessible, with generous portions of spicy-hot and milder dishes; the
friendly staff will help you negotiate the menu. In the summer, reserve a
table in the walled garden.

30 Gloucester St., off Newbury St., entrance in alley. ☎ *617/536-4341.*
Reservations recommended. **MBTA:** *Green Line B, C, or D to Hynes/ICA; use*
Newbury St. exit, turn right, walk 2 blocks, turn left. **Main courses:** *$12–$21.*
DISC, MC, V. **Open:** *Dinner daily.*

Chez Henri

$$$. Cambridge/Harvard Square. FRENCH/CUBAN.
A dark, elegant space, Chez Henri shows how good fusion cuisine can be.
The regularly changing menu concentrates on French bistro-style food with
Cuban accents. Entrees include generous portions of meat and fish, with
unusually creative side dishes. The fixed-price menu includes one of two
appetizers and one of two entrees as well as dessert—the crème brûlée is magnificent. The food at the bar is Cuban, as are the strong specialty drinks.

1 Shepard St., off Mass. Ave. ☎ *617/354-8980. Reservations accepted only for*
parties of 6 or more. **MBTA:** *Red Line to Harvard; take Mass. Ave. north 3 blocks*
past Cambridge Common. **Main courses:** *$14.95–$18.95; three-course fixed-*
price menu $28; bar food $4.95–$7.95. AE, DC, MC, V. **Open:** *Dinner and bar*
food daily, Sun brunch.

Best Bets for Families

Also see the listings of national and local chains in chapter 11.

Bartley's Burger Cottage (Cambridge/Harvard Square, $)
Durgin-Park (Faneuil Hall Marketplace, $$)
Grand Chau Chow (Chinatown, $$)
Jimbo's Fish Shanty (Waterfront/South Boston, $)
Redbones (Cambridge/Somerville, $$)
S&S Restaurant (Cambridge/Inman Square, $)

Daily Catch
$$. Waterfront/South Boston. SEAFOOD/ITALIAN.
This Fish Pier institution is a basic storefront, where the staff sometimes seems overwhelmed and it can take forever to get a table, but the food is marvelous. Garlic haters, this is not for you. Calamari (squid) is the house specialty, prepared at least eight ways—even the standard garlic-and-oil pasta sauce has ground-up squid in it. All food is prepared to order, and some dishes come to the table in the frying pans in which they were cooked.

The original Daily Catch, a tiny space in the **North End** at 323 Hanover St. (☎ **617/523-8567**), keeps the same hours but doesn't accept credit cards or reservations.

261 Northern Ave., opposite the Fish Pier. ☎ *617/338-3093. Reservations accepted only for parties of 8 or more.* **MBTA:** *Red Line to South Station; walk north on Atlantic Ave. 2 blocks, turn right onto New Northern Ave. Bridge, and proceed about 1 mile. Total 25 minutes, or a $5 cab ride.* **Main courses:** *$10–$18. AE.* **Open:** *Sun–Thurs noon–10:30pm, Fri–Sat noon–11pm.*

Dalí
$$. Cambridge/Somerville. SPANISH TAPAS.
This is a fun, noisy spot for tapas—little plates of hot or cold meat, seafood, vegetable, and cheese creations that burst with flavor. You'll probably wait at the bar (sometimes an hour or more) for a table. The payoff is the delectable tapas offerings, 32 on the menu and nine monthly specials, all perfect for sharing. If you want to experiment and order in stages, that's fine. And desserts are so good that you won't want to share. (For a conventional full meal, this is a $$$ experience.)

415 Washington St., Somerville. ☎ *617/661-3254. www.tiac.net/users/dali. Reservations not accepted.* **MBTA:** *Red Line to Harvard; pass through Harvard Yard, follow Kirkland St. from back of Memorial Hall to intersection of Washington and Beacon sts. It's a $5 cab ride.* **Tapas:** *$2.50–$7.50.* **Main courses:** *$17–$21. AE, DC, MC, V.* **Open:** *Dinner daily.*

Kids Durgin-Park
$$. Faneuil Hall Marketplace. NEW ENGLAND.
For huge portions of delicious food, a rowdy atmosphere where CEOs share tables with students, and famously cranky waitresses who can't seem to bear the sight of any of it, people have flocked to Durgin-Park since 1827. It's everything it's cracked up to be—a tourist magnet that attracts hordes of locals, where everyone's disappointed when the waitresses are pleasant (they often are). This is the time to try *very* traditional New England fare, like baked beans, strawberry shortcake, and Indian pudding. The line stretches down a flight of stairs and moves quickly. You'll probably wind up seated at a long table with other people (smaller tables are available).

340 Faneuil Hall Marketplace, in the North Market building. ☎ *617/227-2038. Reservations not accepted.* **MBTA:** *Green or Blue Line to Government Center, or*

Orange Line to Haymarket, and follow the crowds. **Main courses:** *$4.95–$17.95, specials $15.90–$24.95. AE, CB, DC, DISC, MC, V.* **Open:** *Lunch and dinner daily; dinner menu starts at 2:30pm.*

The Elephant Walk

$$$. Kenmore Square. FRENCH/CAMBODIAN.

People will tell you about the Elephant Walk as though it's a great insider tip. Then why is it so crowded? This madly popular spot has a two-part menu, but the boundary is porous. Many of the Cambodian dishes have part-French names, and the Asian influence shows on the French side. In any language, it's all delicious, and the pleasant staff will help if you need guidance. Many dishes are available with tofu substituted for animal protein. The plant-filled front room is quieter than the main dining room.

900 Beacon St., at St. Mary's St., 4 blocks past Kenmore Sq. ☎ **617/247-1500.** *Reservations recommended at dinner Sun–Thurs, not accepted Fri–Sat.* **MBTA:** *Green Line C to St. Mary's St.* **Main courses:** *Dinner $9.50–$18.50. AE, DISC, MC, V.* **Open:** *Lunch Mon–Sat; dinner daily.*

Galleria Italiana

$$$$. Theater District. ITALIAN.

This slice of the Abruzzi region is one of the city's best and most popular Italian restaurants. The co-owners hail from the small town of Orsogna, and use their native region's strong flavors and hearty ingredients to exceptionally good effect. The handmade pastas are spectacular. For an authentic final course, try the cheese plate. The staff has the pretheater routine down, but the experience is more enjoyable if you dine fashionably late (for Boston, not for Italy—after the 8pm curtain) and take your time.

177 Tremont St., at Avery St. ☎ **617/423-2092.** *Reservations recommended at dinner.* **MBTA:** *Green Line to Boylston; cross Tremont St. and walk ½ block opposite Boston Common.* **Main courses:** *$20–$30. AE, DC, DISC, MC, V.* **Open:** *Breakfast and lunch weekdays; dinner Tues–Sun.*

Giacomo's

$$$. North End. ITALIAN/SEAFOOD.

This is the place with the line out front, especially on weekends. No reservations, cash only, a tiny dining room with an open kitchen—what's the secret? The food is terrific, there's plenty of it, and don't underestimate the we're-all-in-this-together atmosphere. Take the chef's advice or assemble your dish from the list of ingredients on the board. Salmon in pesto cream sauce is a keeper, as is shrimp with anything. Service is friendly but incredibly swift—those people waiting in 90° heat or an ice storm want your seat.

355 Hanover St., at Fleet St. ☎ **617/523-9026.** *Reservations not accepted.* **MBTA:** *Green or Orange Line to Haymarket; cross under Expressway, turn right, follow Cross St. to Hanover St., turn left, walk 3 full blocks.* **Main courses:** *$15–$24. No credit cards.* **Open:** *Dinner daily.*

Grand Chau Chow
$$. Chinatown. CHINESE.

This is one of the best and busiest restaurants in Chinatown, with an encyclopedic menu. In the large fish tanks, you can watch your main dish swimming around (if you have the heart). Stick to seafood and you can't go wrong—clams with black bean sauce is a specialty. Lunch specials are a great deal, but skip the chow fun, which quickly turns gelatinous.

A North End Tip

Many North End restaurants don't serve dessert and coffee—they're just too small. Head to one of the cafes listed in chapter 11 for a cappuccino and a sweet.

45 Beach St., at Harrison Ave. ☎ *617/ 292-5166. Reservations accepted only for parties of 10 or more.* **MBTA:** *Orange Line to Chinatown; walk 1 block on Washington St. (past the China Trade Center), turn left, and go 2½ blocks on Beach St.* **Main courses:** *$5–$22. AE, DC, DISC, MC, V.* **Open:** *Sun–Thurs 10am–3am, Fri–Sat 10am–4am.*

Green Street Grill
$$$. Cambridge/Central Square. CARIBBEAN.

You wanted a place where locals go, and here it is. Pass through Charlie's Tap, a neighborhood bar, to the austere dining room and get ready for Caribbean food that's among the tastiest and hottest in town. If you can take the heat, you'll be in heaven (some dishes have as many as five kinds of peppers); if not, ask the helpful staff to steer you toward something less incendiary. Grilled seafood is done quite well here, and the wide variety of beers can help put out the fire.

280 Green St., between Magazine and Pearl sts. ☎ *617/876-1655. Reservations not accepted.* **MBTA:** *Red Line to Central Square; from the south (even-numbered) side of Mass. Ave., walk 1 block to Green St.* **Main courses:** *$12.95–$17.95. AE, MC, V.* **Open:** *Dinner daily.*

Grill 23 & Bar
$$$$. Back Bay East. AMERICAN.

Its versatility makes this the best steakhouse in town. The usual slabs of meat are expertly prepared, of course. They coexist peacefully with bolder entrees that would fit in at any cutting-edge hot spot, and the fish dishes rival those at any seafood restaurant. The bountiful à la carte side dishes are uniformly wonderful, as are the desserts. *But* (two big caveats) smoking is not only allowed but also encouraged—a humidor makes the rounds—and the room can get quite noisy.

161 Berkeley St., at Stuart St. ☎ *617/542-2255. www.grill23.com. Reservations recommended.* **MBTA:** *Green Line to Arlington; follow Boylston St. 1 block away from the Public Garden, turn left, walk 2 full blocks.* **Main courses:** *$22–$30. AE, CB, DC, DISC, MC, V.* **Open:** *Dinner daily. Valet parking available.*

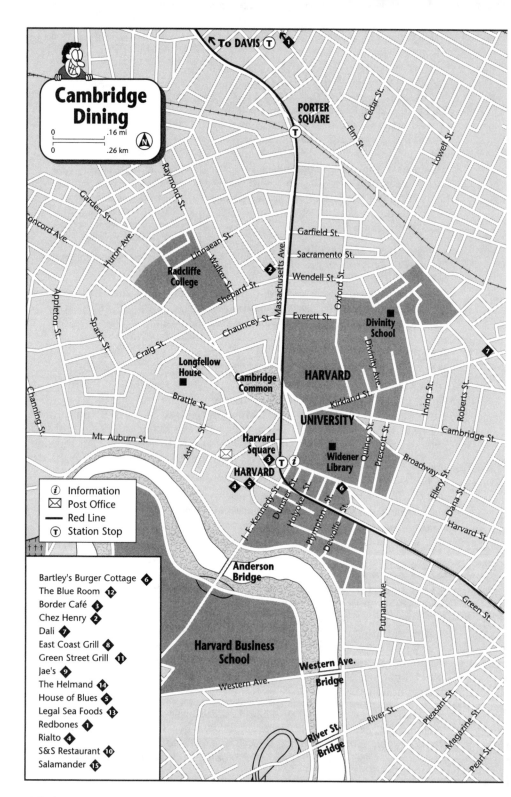

Cambridge Dining

0   .16 mi

0   .26 km

To DAVIS ⓣ ①

PORTER SQUARE ⓣ

Garden St.

Concord Ave.

Raymond St.

Huron Ave.

Linnaean St.

Walker St.

Shepard St.

Cedar St.

Elm St.

Lowell St.

Garfield St.

Sacramento St.

Wendell St.

Radcliffe College ②

Appleton St.

Sparks St.

Craig St.

Chauncey St.

Everett St.

Oxford St.

Divinity School ■

Divinity Ave.

Channing St.

Longfellow House ■

Brattle St.

Cambridge Common

HARVARD

Kirkland St.

UNIVERSITY

Irving St.

Roberts St.

Cambridge St.

⑦

Mt. Auburn St.

Ash St.

Harvard Square ③ ⓣ ⓘ

HARVARD

④ ⑤

Widener Library ■

Quincy St.

Prescott St.

Broadway

Ellery St.

Dana St.

J. F. Kennedy St.

Dunster St.

Holyoke St.

Plympton St.

Bow St.

Dewolfe St.

⑥

Harvard St.

Anderson Bridge

Putnam Ave.

Green St.

Information ⓘ

Post Office ✉

Red Line ▬

Station Stop ⓣ

Harvard Business School

Western Ave.

Western Ave. Bridge

Pleasant St.

Magazine St.

River St.

River St. Bridge

Pearl St.

Bartley's Burger Cottage ⑥
The Blue Room ⑫
Border Café ③
Chez Henry ②
Dali ⑦
East Coast Grill ⑧
Green Street Grill ⑪
Jae's ⑨
The Helmand ⑭
House of Blues ⑤
Legal Sea Foods ⑬
Redbones ①
Rialto ④
S&S Restaurant ⑩
Salamander ⑮

136

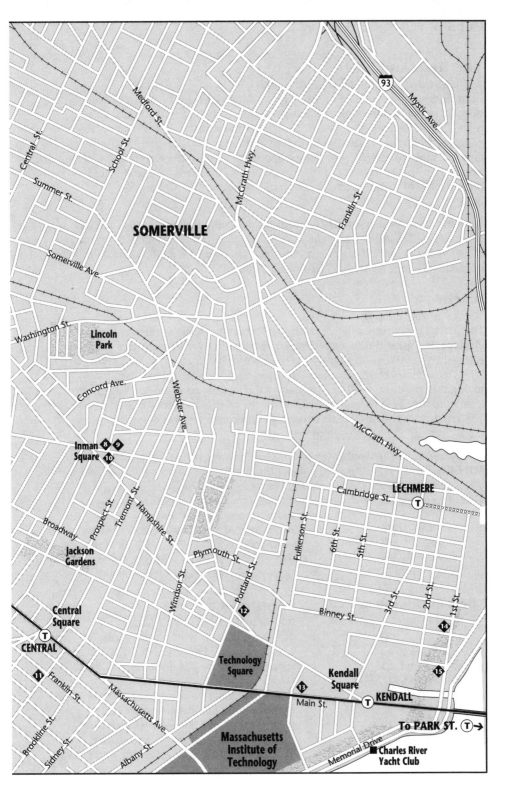

137

The Helmand
$$. Cambridge/Kendall Square. AFGHAN.
Even in cosmopolitan Cambridge, Afghan food is a novelty, and an exceptionally welcome one. This spacious, elegant setting belies the reasonable prices. The courteous staff patiently answers questions about the food, which is distinctly Middle Eastern with Indian and Pakistani influences. Many vegetarian dishes are offered; when meat appears it's often one element of a dish rather than the centerpiece. The delectable bread is made in a wood-fired brick oven while you watch. For dessert, don't miss the Afghan version of baklava.

143 First St., at Bent St. ☎ **617/492-4646.** *Reservations recommended.* **MBTA:** *Green Line to Lechmere; walk behind train, pass through tunnel on right, proceed 6½ short blocks on First St., passing CambridgeSide Galleria mall.* **Main courses:** *$8.95–$15.95. AE, MC, V.* **Open:** *Dinner daily.*

Icarus
$$$$. South End. ECLECTIC.
This shamelessly romantic subterranean restaurant deftly combines every element of a great dining experience. It has lasted over 20 years in a wildly competitive market and slightly out-of-the-way location, and that's saying a lot. The regularly changing menu leans on choice local seafood, poultry, meats, and produce, used in imaginative dishes that seem more like alchemy than cooking. Be sure you save room for one of the unbelievable desserts. The fixed-price "Square Meal" consists of three courses plus dessert with no more than 30% of calories from fat.

3 Appleton St., off Tremont St. ☎ **617/426-1790.** *Reservations recommended.* **MBTA:** *Green Line to Arlington; follow Arlington St. away from the Public Garden, across the Mass. Pike. (about 6 blocks), bear right onto Tremont St. and go 1 long block. Or Orange Line to Back Bay; use Clarendon St. exit (at back of outbound train), turn right, walk 4 blocks, turn left onto Appleton St. and go 2 blocks.* **Main courses:** *$19.50–$29.50; "Square Meal" $42. AE, CB, DC, DISC, MC, V.* **Open:** *Dinner daily. Valet parking available.*

Best Bets for Romance

Aujourd'hui
(Back Bay East, $$$$)
Casa Romero
(Back Bay West, $$$)
Icarus (South End, $$$$)
L'Espalier
(Back Bay West, $$$$)
Mamma Maria
(North End, $$$$)

Istanbul Café
$$. Beacon Hill. TURKISH.
This little place is worth seeking out. The scent of Middle Eastern spices hits you as soon as you open the door, and the food ranges from familiar and unusually good to just unusual (and also good). Traditional Middle Eastern fare shares the menu with many lamb dishes and Turkish pizza, which is odd but delicious. The baklava is perfect with a Turkish coffee.

The always-helpful service can sometimes be slow, but for once that's not a complaint—you'll want to linger.

37 Bowdoin St., at Derne St. ☎ **617/227-3434.** *Reservations not necessary.* **MBTA:** *Red or Green Line to Park; climb hill 1 block, go around to right side of State House (Bowdoin St.), walk 1½ blocks.* **Main courses: $9–$15.** *AE, MC, V.* **Open:** *Mon–Thurs 11am–10pm, Sat 11am–11pm, Sun noon–10pm.*

Jae's
$$$. Theater District. KOREAN/SUSHI/PAN-ASIAN.

This 3-story food festival serves sushi on the first floor, Korean and pan-Asian dishes on the second, and Korean barbecue on the third. It's fun and busy (service can be slow), with a bountiful menu that ranges from artfully prepared sushi to bountiful noodle dishes to traditional Korean fare—you just can't go wrong. Desserts are curiously European in style, and quite delicious.

There are other branches of Jae's in the **South End,** 520 Columbus Ave. (☎ **617/421-9405**), and **Cambridge's Inman Square,** 1281 Cambridge St. (☎ **617/497-8380**), that are smaller but equally busy.

212 Stuart St., off Arlington St. ☎ **617/451-7788.** *Reservations recommended at dinner.* **MBTA:** *Green Line to Arlington; follow Arlington St. 1–2 blocks away from the Public Garden and turn left onto Stuart St.* **Main courses: $8.25–$20.95; sushi from $5.25.** *AE, DC, MC, V.* **Open:** *Lunch Mon–Sat; dinner daily; Sun noon–10pm.*

Kids Jimbo's Fish Shanty
$. Waterfront/South Boston. SEAFOOD.

Under the same management as the landmark Jimmy's Harborside across the street, Jimbo's serves decent portions of good, fresh seafood to office workers, tourists, and bargain-hunters. Ask your server for a suggestion—someone who calls you "pal" or "honey" isn't holding back. You can also order fish or beef skewers, and pasta dishes (at dinner only) with varied sauces, including a lobster cream version. The decadent desserts generally involve ice cream and chocolate, so save room. And watch out for the model trains suspended from the low ceiling.

245 Northern Ave., opposite the Fish Pier. ☎ **617/542-5600.** *Reservations not necessary.* **MBTA:** *Red Line to South Station; walk north on Atlantic Ave. 2 blocks, turn right onto New Northern Ave. Bridge, and proceed about 1 mile. Total 25 minutes, or a $5 cab ride.* **Main courses: $6–$14.** *AE, DC, MC, V.* **Open:** *Mon–Thurs 11:30am–9:30pm, Fri–Sat 11:30am–10pm, Sun noon–8pm.*

Best Bets Before the Theater

Galleria Italiana
(Theater District, $$$$)
Grand Chau Chow
(Chinatown, $$)
Jae's (Theater District, $$$)
Les Zygomates
(South Station, $$$)

Legal Sea Foods
$$$. Back Bay West and other locations. SEAFOOD.

This is *the* place in Boston to go for seafood. Not the fanciest, cheapest, or trendiest seafood—it's the freshest. This family-owned business has an international reputation for serving only top-quality fish and shellfish prepared in every imaginable way. The menu includes regular selections (scrod, haddock, bluefish, salmon, shrimp, calamari, and lobster, among others) plus whatever looked good at the market that morning, and it's all splendid. The clam chowder is famous, and some consider the fish chowder even better. I suggest the Prudential Center branch because it takes reservations (at lunch only), a deviation from a long tradition. See box "Legal Proceedings" for other locations.

800 Boylston St., in the Prudential Center. ☎ *617/266-6800. Reservations recommended at lunch, not accepted at dinner.* **MBTA:** *Green Line E to Prudential. Or Green Line B, C, or D to Hynes/ICA; use Boylston St. exit and walk toward tower on Boylston St. 1½ blocks.* **Main courses:** *Dinner $13.95–$23.95. AE, CB, DC, DISC, MC, V.* **Open:** *Mon–Thurs 11am–10:30pm, Fri–Sat 11am–11:30pm, Sun noon–10pm. SEAFOOD.*

L'Espalier
$$$$. Back Bay West. NEW ENGLAND/FRENCH.

Yes, it's a ton of money, and no, you won't care. This restaurant promises and delivers a unique experience. It occupies the second floor of an 1886 town house, creating the illusion that you're in a formal (but most inviting) home. The food, an exploration of the freshest and most interesting ingredients available, is magnificent. Ask to see the desserts even if you have one of the superb soufflés (which are ordered with dinner). Or try the celebrated cheese tray, which always includes at least two local cheeses.

30 Gloucester St., off Newbury St. ☎ *617/262-3023. www.lespalier.com. Reservations required.* **MBTA:** *Green Line B, C, or D to Hynes/ICA; use Newbury St. exit, turn right, walk 2 blocks, turn left.* **Main courses**: *Fixed-price menu $65*

Legal Proceedings

Three of the 11 other Legal Sea Foods branches:

➤ Boston Park Plaza Hotel, 35 Columbus Ave., off Arlington Street (☎ 617/426-4444).

➤ Copley Place, second shopping level (☎ 617/266-7775).

➤ Kendall Square, Cambridge, 5 Cambridge Center, at Main and Ames streets (☎ 617/864-3400).

(four courses). Tasting menu (seven courses; whole tables only) $82. AE, DISC, MC, V. **Open:** *Dinner Mon–Sat. Valet parking available.*

Best Bets for Business

Anago (Back Bay West, $$$$)
Grill 23 & Bar (Back Bay East, $$$$)
Legal Sea Foods (Cambridge/Kendall Square, $$$)
Les Zygomates (South Station, $$$)
Maison Robert (Downtown Crossing, $$$$)

Les Zygomates
$$$. South Station. FRENCH.

Pick your way across the Big Dig wasteland to this delightful, Parisian-style (without the attitude) bistro and wine bar. The great selection of wines is available by the bottle, the glass, and the 2-ounce "taste." The efficient staff will guide you to a good accompaniment for the wonderful food. Salads are excellent, and main courses are hearty and filling but not heavy. Try not to fight over the desserts. And Sunday through Thursday night, you can linger over a glass of wine and listen to live jazz.

129 South St., between Tufts and Beach sts. ☎ *617/542-5108. www.winebar.com. Reservations recommended.* **MBTA:** *Red Line to South Station; cross Atlantic Ave., turn left, walk 1 block to East St., turn right, walk 1 block to South St. Or ask a construction worker.* **Main courses:** *$12–$20. Fixed-price lunch $11, fixed-price dinner (Sun–Thurs only) $19. AE, CB, DC, DISC, MC, V.* **Open:** *11am–1am weekdays, 6pm–1am Sat–Sun. Valet parking available at dinner.*

Lo Conte's
$$. North End. ITALIAN.

This is a neighborhood place, with chummy service and large portions of excellent food. The glorified-storefront dining rooms get noisy on busy nights. Salads and appetizers aren't cheap, but portions are large and quality generally high (pass on the cold antipasto, though). Main dishes are about what you'd expect, and the "House Specials" include the best chicken, broccoli, and ziti in town. The daily specials taste as good as they sound—try something with seafood.

116 Salem St., between Cooper and Prince sts. ☎ *617/720-0339 or 617/720-3550. Reservations recommended at dinner.* **MBTA:** *Green or Orange Line to Haymarket; cross under Expressway and follow Salem St. 4½ short blocks.* **Main courses:** *$10.50–$16.95. AE, DC, DISC, MC, V.* **Open:** *Sun–Thurs 11:30am–10pm, Fri–Sat 11:30am–11pm.*

141

Foodie Faves

Anago (Back Bay West, $$$$)
Galleria Italiana
(Theater District, $$$$)
Icarus (South End, $$$$)
L'Espalier (Back Bay
West, $$$$)
Maison Robert (Downtown
Crossing, $$$$)
Rialto (Cambridge/
Harvard Square, $$$$)

Maison Robert
*$$$$. Downtown Crossing.
FRENCH.*
This world-class French restaurant has been a legend since it opened in Old City Hall in 1971. The Robert family helped put Boston on the culinary map, and rather than resting on its laurels, the magnificent restaurant continues to evolve. Chef Jacky Robert (the owners' nephew) turns out food that's classic but dramatic, with some unexpected but welcome Asian influences. The formal dining room is spectacular, and the cozy **Ben's Café** on the ground floor is more casual and less expensive than the upstairs room, with terrace seating in the summer.

45 School St., at Province St., between Tremont and Washington sts. ☎ *617/227-3370. www.maisonrobert.com. Reservations recommended.* **MBTA:** *Green Line to Government Center; follow Tremont St. across Court St., walk 1 block and turn left onto School St.* **Main courses:** *Dinner $17–$32; cafe $14–$28. AE, CB, DC, MC, V.* **Open:** *Lunch weekdays; dinner Mon–Sat. Valet parking available at dinner.*

Mamma Maria
$$$$. North End. ITALIAN.
In a town house overlooking North Square and the Paul Revere House, this traditional-looking restaurant offers innovative cuisine and level of sophistication you might not expect in the North End. The menu changes seasonally and includes fantastic daily pasta specials (as appetizers and main courses). Fresh seafood is always a good bet. The excellent entrees are unlike anything else in this neighborhood, except in their generous size. And don't worry if someone suddenly starts crying—it's just another marriage proposal.

3 North Sq., at Prince St. ☎ *617/523-0077. Reservations recommended.* **MBTA:** *Green or Orange Line to Haymarket; cross under Expressway, turn right, follow Cross St. to Hanover St., turn left. Walk 2 full blocks, go right onto Prince St. and walk 1 block.* **Main courses:** *$18–$28. AE, DC, DISC, MC, V.* **Open:** *Dinner daily. Valet parking available.*

Piccola Venezia
$$. North End. ITALIAN.
Don't walk past Piccola Venezia just because it's one of the first places you see in the North End. The menu has a good mix—homey food, which tends to be heavy on red sauce, and more sophisticated dishes—and portions are large. This is a good place to try traditional Italian-American favorites such as polenta (home-style, not the yuppie croutons available at so many other places), *baccala* (reconsti-tuted salt cod), or the house specialty, tripe.

263 Hanover St. ☎ ***617/523-3888.*** *Reservations recommended at dinner.* **MBTA:** *Green or Orange Line to Haymarket; cross under Expressway, turn right, follow Cross St. to Hanover St., turn left and walk ½ block.* **Main courses:** *$10–$20; lunch specialties $5.25–$7.95. AE, DISC, MC, V.* **Open:** *Daily 11am–10pm (lunch menu weekdays only).*

Kids Redbones
$$. Cambridge/Somerville. BARBECUE.

The wacky walls of this raucous dining room sport old photos, T-shirts, and hand-lettered signs to study while you wait for your food. The full range of barbecue and its running mates (like catfish and grilled chicken) comes with appropriate side dishes, alone or in any combination you want. The chummy staff can help you decide. Portions are enormous, so pace yourself. You'll want to try the wonderful appetizers, sides, and desserts. There's a huge beer selection. Sit upstairs if you can—Underbones, downstairs, is more of a bar.

55 Chester St., off Elm St., Somerville. ☎ ***617/ 628-2200.*** *Reservations accepted only for parties of 11 or more, Sun–Thurs.* **MBTA:** *Red Line to Davis; right at turnstiles, right at exit; walk 3 blocks on Elm St. and turn right onto Chester St.* **Main courses:** *$7–$14. No credit cards.* **Open:** *Lunch and dinner daily. Valet parking.*

> **Best Bets for Chowder**
>
> Legal Sea Foods
> (Back Bay East, $$$$)
> Legal Sea Foods
> (Back Bay West, $$$$)
> Legal Sea Foods (Cambridge/
> Kendall Square, $$$$)
> *Catch my drift?*

Rialto
$$$$. Cambridge/Harvard Square. MEDITERRANEAN.

People constantly ask where I would go if money were no object, and I say Rialto. If it isn't the best restaurant in the Boston area, it's close. It attracts a chic crowd, but it's not a "scene" in the sense that out-of-towners will feel left behind. Chef Jody Adams's extraordinary food is the real draw. The menu changes regularly, always incorporating seasonal ingredients in ways that conjure sunnier climes—think more garlic and vegetables, less butter and cream. Fish is always good here, but generally, if you like all the ingredients in a particular dish, you're in very good hands.

1 Bennett St., in the Charles Hotel. ☎ ***617/661-5050.*** *Reservations recommended.* **MBTA:** *Red Line to Harvard; follow Brattle St. 2 blocks, turn left onto Eliot St. and proceed 2 blocks.* **Main courses:** *$20–$29. AE, DC, MC, V.* **Open:** *Dinner daily.*

Kids S&S Restaurant
$. Cambridge/Inman Square. DELI.

Inman Square is a bit of a hike from the T, but you'd never know it. This wildly popular brunch spot draws what seems to be half of Cambridge at busy times on weekends. The menu includes fantastic omelettes, fruit salad, and all sorts of pancakes and waffles. Be early for brunch, or plan to stand around people-watching and getting hungry. Or be a maverick and come during the week—everything's good then, too. The full menu offers traditional deli items, plus hearty American fare. You can order breakfast anytime.

1334 Cambridge St., at Hampshire St. ☎ **617/354-0777.** *Reservations not accepted.* **MBTA:** *Red Line to Harvard; use Church St. exit (at front of outbound train), turn left at turnstiles. Then take no. 69 bus (Harvard–Lechmere) to Inman Square, or walk ⁷⁄₁₀ mile up Cambridge St. It's a $5 cab ride.* **Main courses:** *$2.95–$10.95. No credit cards.* **Open:** *Mon–Sat 7am–midnight, Sun 8am–midnight; Sat brunch 7am–4pm, Sun brunch 8am–4pm.*

Best Bets for Vegetarians

The Blue Room (Cambridge/Kendall Square, $$$$)
Buddha's Delight (Chinatown, $)
The Elephant Walk (Kenmore Square, $$$)
Istanbul Café (Beacon Hill, $$)
Rialto (Cambridge/Harvard Square, $$$$)

Zuma's Tex-Mex Café
$. Faneuil Hall Marketplace. SOUTHWESTERN.
Because of its great location, Zuma's could probably get away with serving so-so food and still draw enormous crowds. But it's excellent, with guacamole and salsa cruda made from scratch, and tortilla chips cut and fried throughout the day right in the dining room. The casual spot is popular with local office workers, who congregate at the noisy bar (the table area is marginally quieter). Portions are large, especially considering the low prices. The Key lime pie and the margaritas are deservedly acclaimed.

7 N. Market St., Faneuil Hall Marketplace, North Market building, lower level. ☎ **617/367-9114. MBTA:** *Reservations not accepted. Green or Blue Line to Government Center, or Orange Line to Haymarket, and follow the crowds.* **Main courses:** *$4.97–$13.99. AE, CB, DC, DISC, MC, V.* **Open:** *Mon–Thurs 11:30am–11pm, Fri–Sat 11:30am–midnight, Sun noon–10pm.*

Chapter 11

Quick Bites & Other Tasty Morsels

In This Chapter

➤ Linking to the chains

➤ What's all this about a tea party?

➤ Where to go for dim sum

➤ Where to rev up and cool off

In chapters 9 and 10 you learned where to have a meal in Boston that leaves you with that "only in Boston" feeling. For a more generic feel (hey, sometimes you need that, too), Boston also has outlets of national and regional chains. In this chapter you'll find quick lists of those, plus suggestions if you want afternoon tea, dim sum, coffee and pastries, or ice cream.

Back on the Chain Gang

The national chains are pretty well represented in Boston, and they are all kid-friendly. There's a **Hard Rock Cafe** at 131 Clarendon St. in the Back Bay (☎ **617/424-ROCK;** MBTA: Orange Line to Back Bay). It's fun, but you probably already know that.

The original **House of Blues** is at 96 Winthrop St. in Harvard Square, Cambridge (☎ **617/491-BLUE;** MBTA: Red Line to Harvard). See the listing in chapter 20.

The **TGI Friday's** at 26 Exeter St., at Newbury Street, in the Back Bay (☎ **617/266-9040;** MBTA: Green Line to Copley) courts children with a special activity pack that might buy parents a moment's peace.

The **Ground Round** chain of family restaurants has a lively branch at the Prudential Center, 800 Boylston St. (☎ **617/247-0500**; MBTA: Green Line E to Prudential).

Fuddrucker's serves burgers and other grilled items in the Theater District at 137 Stuart St. (☎ **617/723-3833**; MBTA: Green Line to Boylston), not far from the Common and the Public Garden. Make as much noise as you want—this is also a rowdy business-lunch spot.

Hello, Stranger: Local Chain Restaurants

Kids The **Bertucci's** chain of pizzerias appeals to children and adults equally. The wood-fired brick ovens are visible from many tables, the rolls (made from pizza dough) are great, and the pizza and pastas range from basic to quite sophisticated. There are convenient branches at **Faneuil Hall Marketplace** (☎ **617/227-7889**; MBTA: Blue or Green Line to Government Center or Orange Line to Haymarket); in the **Back Bay** at 43 Stanhope St., around the corner from the Hard Rock Cafe (☎ **617/247-6161**; MBTA: Orange Line to Back Bay); and in **Harvard Square** at 21 Brattle St., Cambridge (☎ **617/864-4748**; MBTA: Red Line to Harvard).

Souper Salad appeals to time-pressed office workers who flock to the bounteous salad bars, sit down or take out, and zip back to their desks. That's just the right attitude for a determined sightseer, too. Three downtown branches are especially convenient to the Freedom Trail: **Government Center**, 3 Center Plaza (☎ **617/367-6067**; MBTA: Green or Blue Line to Government Center); **Downtown Crossing**, 82 Summer St. (☎ **617/426-6834**; MBTA: Red or Orange Line to Downtown Crossing); and the **Financial District**, 103 State St. (☎ **617/227-9151**; MBTA: Blue or Orange Line to State).

Extra! Extra!

On the run? Can't get the kids to agree on anything? Don't forget the **food courts** at Faneuil Hall Marketplace, the Shops at the Prudential Center, and the CambridgeSide Galleria mall (5 minutes from the Museum of Science).

Boston Tea Party, Part Two

This is Boston, the only city that has a whole tea party named after it, and the tradition of afternoon tea at a plush hotel is alive and well. Pots of tea and individual food items are available à la carte, but for the full effect, order light or full tea with all the trimmings.

The **Bristol Lounge** at the Four Seasons Hotel, 200 Boylston St. (☎ **617/ 351-2053**), serves an excellent tea every day from 3 to 4:30pm. The **Ritz- Carlton,** 15 Arlington St. (☎ **617/536-5700**), serves the city's most cele- brated tea in the elegant Ritz Lounge every day from 3 to 5:30pm. **Intrigue** at the Boston Harbor Hotel, 70 Rowes Wharf, at Atlantic Avenue (☎ **617/ 439-7000**), is across the street from the site of the original Boston Tea Party. It serves tea at on weekdays from 2:30 to 4:30pm. And **Swans Court,** in the lobby of the Boston Park Plaza Hotel, 64 Arlington St. (☎ **617/426-2000**), serves tea daily from 3 to 5pm.

Yum, Yum, Dim Sum

Many restaurants in Chinatown offer dim sum, a traditional midday meal featuring a wide variety of appetizer-style dishes: steamed buns, dumplings, spare ribs, sticky rice, spring rolls, sweets, and more. The wait staff wheels around carts laden with tempting morsels, and you order by pointing (unless you know Chinese). They stamp your check with the symbol of the dish, adding about $1 to $3 to your tab. Unless you're ravenous or you order à la carte items from the regular menu, the grand total won't be more than about $10 per person. This is a great group activity, especially on weekends, when the variety is wider than on weekdays and you'll see two and three genera- tions of families sharing dishes. The top three dim sum destinations:

➤ **Empire Garden Restaurant,** 690–698 Washington St., second floor (☎ **617/482-8898**).

➤ **Golden Palace Restaurant,** 14 Tyler St. (☎ **617/423-4565**).

➤ **China Pearl,** 9 Tyler St., second floor (☎ **617/426-4338**).

For Caffeine Fiends

As in most other American cities, you can't get far in Boston or Cambridge without seeing a **Starbucks,** but for coffee, tea, pastries, and hanging out, there are plenty of less generic options. (And if you just want good coffee, **Dunkin' Donuts** is still the champ.) All of them keep long hours and don't discourage loiterers.

My North End cafe favorites include **Caffè Graffiti,** 307 Hanover St., **Caffè dello Sport,** 308 Hanover St., and **Caffè Vittoria,** 296 Hanover St. There's also table service at **Mike's Pastry,** 300 Hanover St. Find what you want in the case, *then* sit down and order. (The cannoli are said to be President Clinton's favorite.)

Elsewhere in Boston, there's **Curious Liquids Café,** 22B Beacon St., on Beacon Hill, and **Trident Booksellers & Café,** 338 Newbury St., in the Back Bay. In Cambridge, you'll find the **1369 Coffeehouse,** 1369 Cambridge St., Inman Square, and 757 Mass. Ave., Central Square; and **Algiers Coffeehouse,** 40 Brattle St., Harvard Square (☎ **617/492-1557**), which also serves tasty Middle Eastern food. Or ride the Red Line to Somerville. People of all ages hang out the **Someday Café,** 51 Davis Sq.

147

I Scream, You Scream . . .

Bostonians *love* their ice cream, year-round—lines form even when there's 2 feet of snow on the ground. You'll find some of the best confections in Boston at **Emack & Bolio's,** 290 Newbury St.; **Herrell's,** 224 Newbury St.; and **JP Licks,** 352 Newbury St., all in the Back Bay, and **Steve's Ice Cream,** Quincy Market, Faneuil Hall Marketplace.

In Cambridge, try **Herrell's,** 15 Dunster St., Harvard Square; **Toscanini's,** 899 Main St., Central Square, and 1310 Mass. Ave., Harvard Square; and **Christina's,** 1255 Cambridge St., Inman Square.

Part 5

Ready, Set, Go!
Exploring Boston

Now you're ready to sleep, get around town, and eat—all things you do at home every day. What was the point of this trip, anyway? Oh, yeah—to explore America's past. And to see some of the art world's timeless treasures. And to blow your allowance at Filene's Basement. And to investigate the scientific arena and the undersea universe and Harvard Yard. And on the second day . . .

Let's face it: Unless you're ready to move here, you'll have to pick and choose among the countless activities the Boston area offers. This section will help you pick, choose, and schedule. When it comes to sightseeing, no single place is a "must" for everyone, and we'll help you work out your personal can't-miss list. This is the fun part of planning—you have to have a bed, some food, and a way to reach them. You don't "need" a swan-boat ride.

Here you'll find a guide to the city's top attractions, with special attention to the Freedom Trail. I'll also point you toward some less-famous and equally fascinating attractions. Maybe Filene's Basement should be one (maybe it should be on the Freedom Trail), but it's in the shopping chapter with other top retail destinations. Finally, I'll suggest some of my favorite itineraries, which combine a manageable number of attractions and diversions, and help you design your own.

Chapter 12

Should I Just Take a Guided Tour?

In This Chapter

➤ The pros and cons of guided tours

➤ Tours on land, on water, and on both

➤ Special-interest tours

Guided tours have their time and place. If you have only a day, if you have a special interest, or if you have mobility problems, a guided tour might be for you. If you have a week, if you aren't passionate about a particular subject, or if you dislike being part of a group, you might be better off on your own.

In Boston, there are four major varieties of guided tour: walking, trolley (actually a bus chassis with a trolley-style body), cruise, and Boston Duck Tours.

➤ **Walking tours** show you the sights up close. Boston is a city of small pleasures—a peek down a crooked alley, the artisanship of an iron railing—and on a walking tour, you'll get a good sense of that. But they don't go everywhere, usually last less than 2 hours, and involve (you guessed it) a lot of walking. Most regularly scheduled walking tours aren't given in the winter.

➤ A narrated **trolley tour** can give you an overview before you focus on specific attractions, or you can use the all-day pass to hit as many places as possible in 8 hours or so. The 1-day sightseeing tour included in many package deals is almost certainly one of these. If you're unable to walk long distances, to travel with children, or are short on time, a trolley tour can be worth the money. Do bear in mind that it's still a bit of a hike from trolley stops to some attractions, notably those in the North End. And moving in a pack, with a little sticker on your shirt (it allows you to reboard), you'll *really* feel like a tourist. But they do operate year-round.

➤ **Sightseeing cruises** offer a unique perspective and breathtaking views. Trips around the harbor run right by the airport (a must if aviation freaks are along), teach you a little about Boston's maritime history, and make a nice break from walking or driving. But they're not comprehensive, don't last all that long, and aren't available in the winter.

➤ **Boston Duck Tours,** the only amphibious operation in town, offers a lot of fun for a lot of money (see below).

Dollars & Sense

Keep a running tally of admission fees in your head, and you may start to feel a little dizzy. Not to worry—here are two great tips.

➤ If you're staying more than 2 or 3 days, you'll want an **Arts/Boston coupon book** (☎ **617/423-4454,** ext. 23; www.boston.com/artsboston). It offers discounts on admission to many museums and attractions in Boston and the suburbs. Couples and families can take good advantage of the reduced rates for all the destinations included in the CityPass (see below) and many others, such as the Computer and Children's museums, Boston Duck Tours, Beantown and Old Town trolleys, and the Concord and Peabody Essex museums. It's not worth the money (currently $9) for single travelers, because many of the coupons offer two-for-one deals. They're on sale at **BosTix** booths at Faneuil Hall Marketplace (on the south side of Faneuil Hall; closed Monday), in Copley Square (at the corner of Boylston and Dartmouth streets), and in Harvard Square (in the Holyoke Center arcade at 1350 Mass. Ave.), over the phone, and through the Web site.

➤ If you plan to concentrate on the included attractions, a **CityPass** offers great savings. It's a booklet of tickets (so you can go straight to the entrance) to the John F. Kennedy Library & Museum, New England Aquarium, Museum of Fine Arts, Museum of Science, Isabella Stewart Gardner Museum, and John Hancock Observatory. At press time the price (adults, $26.50; seniors, $20.50; children 13 to 18, $13.50) offers a 50% savings if you visit all six. The passes, good for 9 days from the date of purchase, are on sale at participating attractions, the visitor information centers on Boston Common and at the Prudential Center, through the Greater Boston Convention & Visitors Bureau (☎ **800/SEE-BOSTON**), and from www. citypass.net.

Step Right This Way: Guided Walking Tours

Check the Thursday *Globe* "Calendar" section for special-interest and one-shot walking tours keyed to events or anniversaries that fall during your visit.

National Park Service rangers lead free 90-minute Freedom Trail walking tours as many as four times a day during busy periods, once daily in the winter. They cover the "heart" of the trail, from the Old South Meeting House to the Old North Church. You don't need a reservation, but call for schedules. Tours leave from the Visitor Center, 15 State St. (☎ **617/242-5642;** MBTA: Orange or Blue Line to State), off Washington Street across from the Old State House.

The best private walking tour provider is the nonprofit educational corporation **Boston By Foot** (☎ **617/367-2345,** or 617/367-3766 for recorded information; www.bostonbyfoot.com). From May through October, Boston by Foot gives historical and architectural tours that focus on particular neighborhoods or themes. The rigorously trained guides are volunteers who encourage questions. All tours are $8 per person, and tickets may be purchased from the guide. The 90-minute tours take place rain or shine; reservations are not required. The regularly scheduled tours (all excursions from Faneuil Hall meet at the statue of Samuel Adams on Congress Street):

➤ The **"Heart of the Freedom Trail"** tour starts at Faneuil Hall Tuesday through Saturday at 10am.

➤ Tours of **Beacon Hill** begin at the foot of the State House steps on Beacon Street weekdays at 5:30pm, Saturday at 10am, and Sunday at 2pm.

➤ **"Boston Underground"** (a look at subterranean technology, including crypts, the subway, and the depression of the Central Artery) starts at Faneuil Hall Sunday at 2pm.

➤ The **Victorian Back Bay** tour meets on the steps of Trinity Church at 10am Friday and Saturday.

➤ Tours of the **Waterfront** leave from Faneuil Hall on Friday at 5:30pm and Sunday at 10am.

➤ The **North End** tour meets at Faneuil Hall on Saturday at 2pm.

The **Society for the Preservation of New England Antiquities** (☎ **617/227-3956;** www.spnea.org) offers a fascinating tour that describes and illustrates life in the mansions and garrets of Beacon Hill in 1800. "Magnificent and Modest," a 2-hour program, costs $10 and starts at the Harrison Gray Otis House, 141 Cambridge St. (see chapter 14), at 11am on Saturday and Sunday from May through October. The price includes a tour of the Otis House, and reservations are recommended.

The **Historic Neighborhoods Foundation** (☎ **617/426-1885**) offers 90-minute walking tours in several neighborhoods, including Beacon Hill, the North End, Chinatown, the Waterfront, and the Financial District. The programs highlight points of interest while covering history, architecture, and topographical development. Schedules and offerings change with the season. Tours usually cost about $6 per person; call for schedules and meeting places of tours during your visit.

The **Boston Park Rangers** (☎ 617/635-7383) offer free guided walking tours of the "Emerald Necklace," the loop of green spaces designed by pioneering American landscape architect Frederick Law Olmsted. The tours include Boston Common, the Public Garden, the Commonwealth Avenue Mall, the Muddy River in the Fenway, Olmsted Park, Jamaica Pond, the Arnold Arboretum, and Franklin Park. The full 6-hour walk is offered only a few times a year, but 1-hour tours about a particular location or theme take place year-round. Call for topics and schedules.

On the Road Again: Trolley Tours

This is an extremely busy and competitive business, with various firms offering various stops in an effort to stand out. All cover the major Boston attractions and offer informative narratives and anecdotes in their 90- to 120-minute tours; most provide a map and offer free all-day reboarding if you want to visit an attraction and continue later.

Tourist Traps

A tour is only as good as its guide, and quality can vary, especially on trolley tours. Every few years a local TV station or newspaper runs an "exposé" about tourists being shocked that a guide passed off something wacky as fact. So take anything that sounds implausible with a grain of salt, but remember that many outlandish things about Boston are actually true. (For example, Trinity Church *is* built on pilings, and Edgar Allan Poe's *The Fall of the House of Usher* is based on a true story of adulterous lovers buried alive by the cuckolded husband.)

Trolley tickets cost $18 to $24 for adults, $12 or less for children. Boarding spots can be found at hotels, historic attractions, and tourist information centers. There are busy waiting areas near the New England Aquarium and near the corner of Boylston Street and Charles Street South, where the Common meets the Public Garden. Each company paints its cars a different color.

➤ Orange-and-green **Old Town Trolleys** (☎ 617/269-7150) are the most numerous, and Old Town is the only company that offers a separate tour of Cambridge.

➤ Minuteman Tours' **Boston Trolley Tours** (☎ **617/269-3626**) are blue. This is the only company that includes Cambridge in its loop—great if you plan to visit both cities the same day, not worth the extra money if you don't.

➤ **Beantown Trolleys** (☎ **800/343-1328** or 617/236-2148) are red. It's part of Gray Line, the Starbucks of the tour business.

➤ **CityView Luxury Trolleys** (☎ **617/363-7899,** or 800/525-2489 outside the 617 area code) are silver. This is the only company that will allow you to make a reservation.

➤ The **Discover Boston Multilingual Trolley Tours** (☎ **617/ 742-1440**) vehicles are white. It conducts tours in Japanese, Spanish, French, German, and Italian.

Just Add Water: Harbor & River Tours

The maritime sightseeing season runs from April through October, with spring and fall offerings often restricted to weekends. If you're prone to sea-sickness, check the size of the vessel for your tour *before you buy your tickets;* larger boats provide more cushioning and comfort than smaller ones. See chapter 14 for information on whale watching.

Dollars & Sense

You don't have to take a tour to take a cruise. The **MBTA** (as in the subway) ferry between Long Wharf and the Charlestown Navy Yard costs $1 and is free if you have a visitor passport.

The largest company is **Boston Harbor Cruises,** 1 Long Wharf (☎ **617/227-4321** or 617/227-4320). Excursions leave from Long Wharf, off Atlantic Avenue between the New England Aquarium and the Marriott. The 90-minute historic sightseeing cruises, which tour the Inner and Outer Harbor, depart at 11am, 1pm, 3pm, and 7pm (the sunset cruise). Tickets are $12 for adults, $10 for seniors, $8 for children under 12. The 45-minute *Constitution* cruise takes you around the Inner Harbor and docks at the Charlestown Navy Yard so you can go ashore and visit "Old Ironsides." Tours leave every hour on the half hour from 10:30am to 4:30pm, and from the Navy Yard on the hour from 11am to 5pm. The cruise is $7 for adults, $6 for seniors, and $5 for children. The company offers service to Georges Island, where free water-taxi service to the rest of the Boston Harbor Islands is available (see chapter 14).

Massachusetts Bay Lines (☎ **617/542-8000**) offers 55-minute harbor tours on the hour from 10am to 6pm; the price is $8 for adults, $5 for children and seniors. The 90-minute sunset cruise departs at 7pm. Tickets are $15 for adults, $10 for children and seniors. Cruises leave from Rowes Wharf, off Atlantic Avenue behind the Boston Harbor Hotel.

The **Charles Riverboat Company** (☎ 617/621-3001) operates out of the CambridgeSide Galleria mall, on First Street in East Cambridge. Its 55-minute narrated cruises around the lower Charles River basin depart on the hour from noon to 5pm. Once a day, a 55-minute tour goes in the opposite direction, through the Charles River locks to Boston Harbor. It starts at 10:30am. Tickets for either tour are $8 for adults, $6 for seniors, $5 for children 2 to 12.

The elegant three-level *Odyssey* (☎ 617/654-9700; www.odyssey-cruises. com) serves meals with its cruises; prices range from $27 for the "Midnight Prom Cruise" to $40 for Sunday brunch to $75 for Saturday dinner. Trips leave from Rowes Wharf, and reservations are recommended. The ***Spirit of Boston,*** a sleek 192-foot ship operated by Bay State Cruises (☎ 617/457-1450; www. spiritcruises.com), offers lunch and dinner cruises. Prices start at $35 for lunch and $60 for dinner. Trips leave from the World Trade Center, on Northern Avenue near the Fish Pier. Reservations are recommended.

Tourist Traps

Whoa! You don't have to be an animal-rights activist to think twice about the horse-drawn carriages that clog the streets around Faneuil Hall Marketplace. In August 1997, a carriage horse went berserk in downtown traffic and was so badly injured that it had to be euthanized. Until the city and the drivers can find the horses a route that's away from the Big Dig, why be even a small cog in that wheel?

Duck, Duck, Loose: An Amphibious Tour

The most unusual way to see the sights is with **Boston Duck Tours** (☎ 800/ 226-7442 or 617/723-DUCK). You board a "duck"—a reconditioned Second World War amphibious landing craft—on the Huntington Avenue side of the Prudential Center. The 80-minute narrated tour hits the high points, including Trinity Church, the Boston Public Library, the North End, Faneuil Hall, and the Old State House. The real high point comes when the brightly painted duck lumbers down a ramp and splashes into the Charles River for a spin around the basin. The tours are pricey but great fun.

Tickets, available inside the Prudential Center, are $20 for adults, $16 for seniors and students, $10 for children 4 to 12, and 25¢ for children under 4. Tours run every 30 minutes from 9am to one hour before sunset. Reservations are not accepted (except for groups of 16 or more), and tickets usually sell out, especially on weekends. Try to buy same-day tickets early in the day, or plan ahead and ask about the limited number of tickets available two days in advance. There are no tours from December through March.

Independent Tours: Special-Interest Tours

Kids **Boston By Foot** has a special program, **Boston By Little Feet,** geared to children 6 to 12 years old. The 60-minute walk gives a child's-eye view of the architecture along the Freedom Trail and of Boston's role in the American Revolution. Children must be accompanied by an adult, and a map is provided. Tours run from May through October and meet at the statue of Samuel Adams on the Congress Street side of Faneuil Hall, Saturday at 10am, Sunday at 2pm, and Monday at 10am, rain or shine. The cost is $6 per person.

Kids The **Historic Neighborhoods Foundation** offers a 90-minute "Make Way for Ducklings" tour ($7 adults, $5 children 5 and up, under 5 free). It's popular with children and adults, follows the path of the Mallard family described in Robert McCloskey's famous book, and ends at the Public Garden. Call for schedules.

National Park Service rangers lead free 2-hour walking tours of the 1.6-mile **Black Heritage Trail** daily in the summer and by request the rest of the year. The tour covers sites on Beacon Hill that are part of the history of 19th-century Boston, including stations of the Underground Railroad, homes of famous citizens, and the first integrated public school. Tours leave from the **Boston African American National Historic Site** Visitor Center, 46 Joy St. (☎ 617/742-5415). You can also explore on your own, using a brochure that includes a map and descriptions of the buildings.

The **Boston Women's Heritage Trail** is a walking route with stops at homes, churches, and social and political institutions associated with 20 influential women. You can buy a guide at the National Park Service Visitor Center at 15 State St., at local bookstores, and at historic sites, such as the Paul Revere House and the Old South Meeting House. For more detailed information, call ☎ 617/522-2872.

Old Town Trolley (☎ 617/269-7150) offers specialty tours on various topics. At press time, these include "JFK's Boston," which visits sights related to the late president; a brew pub tour; a chocolate-tasting tour, and a seafood tour. Call for information, schedules, and reservations.

Chapter 13

The Top Sights from A to Z

> ### In This Chapter
>
> ➤ Attractions indexed by location and type
>
> ➤ The lowdown on the Freedom Trail
>
> ➤ Full listings of the other top attractions
>
> ➤ A worksheet to help you plan your day(s)

Finally! With everything else arranged, you're ready to hit the streets. This chapter starts with indexes. They list the top sights by location and by type (museums, churches, and so forth). The next section breaks out the Freedom Trail into a separate series of entries, so that you don't have to keep flipping through the book as you walk along. After that come listings of the other big sights. And don't forget that chapter 14 has more listings of specialized, equally enjoyable, attractions and activities.

Get the markers back out, and let everyone read up and weigh in on activities. Rank them (color-coding again, if necessary) on a scale of one to five—one for "can't leave town without it," down to five for "take it or leave it." The **worksheet** at the end of the chapter will help you rank everything. As you proceed through the rest of the section, we'll fit it all into your schedule.

Kids The trusty family-friendly icon crops up all over this chapter. True, it's not Disney, but Boston is definitely not the open-air history lecture your kids might be dreading.

Quick Picks: Top Attractions at a Glance
The Top Sights by Neighborhood

🏃 = Freedom Trail Stop

Back Bay

John Hancock Observatory

Prudential Center Skywalk

Public Garden

Swan Boats

Beacon Hill

🏃 Boston Common

🏃 Massachusetts State House

🏃 Park Street Church

Robert Gould Shaw Memorial

Cambridge

Harvard Square

Harvard University

John Harvard Statue

Charlestown

🏃 Bunker Hill Monument

Charlestown Navy Yard

USS *Cassin Young*

🏃 USS *Constitution*

Dorchester

John F. Kennedy Library & Museum

Downtown

Benjamin Franklin's Birthplace

🏃 Benjamin Franklin Statue

🏃 Boston Common

🏃 Boston Massacre Site

Central Burying Ground

🏃 Faneuil Hall

Faneuil Hall Marketplace

🏃 First Public School Site

🏃 King's Chapel and Burying Ground

New England Holocaust Memorial

🏃 Old City Hall

🏃 Old Corner Bookstore

🏃 Old Granary Burying Ground

🏃 Old South Meeting House

🏃 Old State House

🏃 Park Street Church

Robert Gould Shaw Memorial

Faneuil Hall Marketplace

🏃 Faneuil Hall

New England Holocaust Memorial

Fenway

Isabella Stewart Gardner Museum

Museum of Fine Arts

Museum Wharf

Boston Tea Party Ship & Museum

Children's Museum

Computer Museum

North End

🏃 Copp's Hill Burying Ground

🏃 Old North Church

🏃 Paul Revere House

Pierce/Hichborn House

St. Stephen's Church

158

Science Park

Museum of Science

Waterfront

Boston Tea Party Ship & Museum

Children's Museum

Computer Museum

New England Aquarium

Index by Type of Attraction

🚶 = Freedom Trail Stop

Churches

🚶 King's Chapel and Burying Ground, Downtown

🚶 Old North Church, North End

🚶 Park Street Church, Downtown/Beacon Hill

St. Stephen's Church, North End

Graveyards

Central Burying Ground, Downtown

🚶 Copp's Hill Burying Ground, North End

🚶 King's Chapel Burying Ground, Downtown

🚶 Old Granary Burying Ground, Downtown

Historic Buildings

🚶 Faneuil Hall, Downtown

Faneuil Hall Marketplace, Downtown

🚶 Massachusetts State House, Beacon Hill

🚶 Old City Hall, Downtown

🚶 Old Corner Bookstore, Downtown

🚶 Old South Meeting House, Downtown

🚶 Old State House, Downtown

🚶 Paul Revere House, North End

Pierce/Hichborn House, North End

Miscellaneous Attractions

Charlestown Navy Yard, Charlestown

Harvard University, Cambridge

New England Aquarium, Waterfront

Monuments & Memorials

🚶 Boston Massacre Site, Downtown

Benjamin Franklin's Birthplace, Downtown

🚶 Benjamin Franklin Statue, Downtown

🚶 Bunker Hill Monument, Charlestown

🚶 First Public School Site, Downtown

John Harvard Statue, Cambridge

Robert Gould Shaw Memorial, Beacon Hill

New England Holocaust Memorial, Downtown/Faneuil Hall Marketplace

Museums

Boston Tea Party Ship & Museum, Waterfront/Museum Wharf

Children's Museum, Waterfront/Museum Wharf

Computer Museum, Waterfront/Museum Wharf

Isabella Stewart Gardner Museum, Fenway

John F. Kennedy Library & Museum, Dorchester

Museum of Fine Arts, Fenway

Museum of Science, Science Park

Old State House, Downtown

Neighborhoods

Beacon Hill

Harvard Square, Cambridge

North End

Parks & National Parks

Boston Common, Downtown

Charlestown Navy Yard, Charlestown

Public Garden, Back Bay

Ships & Boats

Boston Tea Party Ship & Museum, Waterfront/Museum Wharf

Charlestown Navy Yard, Charlestown

Swan Boats, Back Bay

USS *Cassin Young*, Charlestown

USS *Constitution*, Charlestown

Views

Bunker Hill Monument, Charlestown

John Hancock Observatory, Back Bay

Prudential Center Skywalk, Back Bay

The Thin Red Line: Walking the Freedom Trail

For out-of-towners navigating Boston's mazelike streets, the Freedom Trail can feel like a lifeline. The trail, a 3-mile red line on the sidewalk, links 16 destinations of historical interest. They all have elegant white signposts, but it's probably easier to look for the line of red paint or painted bricks. First laid out in 1958, it runs from Boston Common through downtown and the North End to Charlestown. The sights are public and private, indoor and outdoor, landlocked (two are *in* the sidewalk) and waterborne (one is a battleship). In this section they're listed in the usual order, with directions at the end of each listing pointing you toward the next site.

Break out the sturdy shoes and water bottle—this is at least a 2-hour excursion if you don't linger anywhere. You might want to start with a free 90-minute walking tour given by a National Park Service ranger (see chapter 12). To explore on your own, make your way to the visitor information center at 146 Tremont St. (**MBTA:** Red or Green Line to Park Street) and pick up a map. You're already at the first stop.

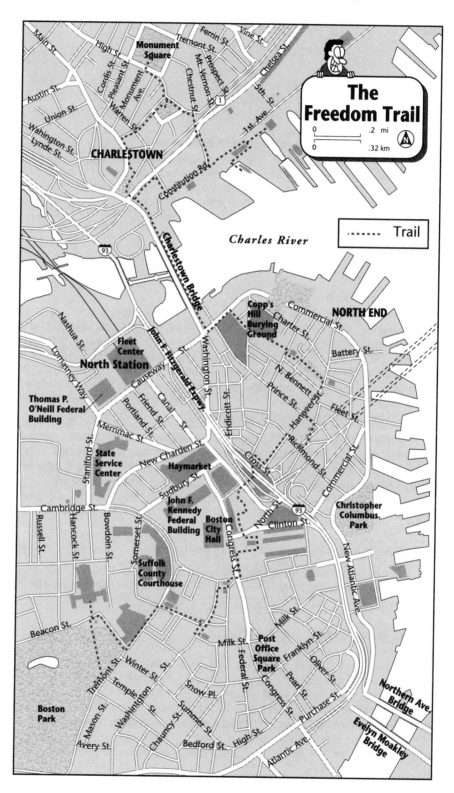

The Freedom Trail

0   .2 mi
0   .32 km

.... Trail

Charles River

CHARLESTOWN

Monument Square

Main St.
High St.
Tremont St.
Ferrin St.
Vine St.
Chelsea St.
5th St.
1st Ave.

Austin St.
Union St.
Wahington St.
Lynde St.

Cordis St.
Pleasant St.
Monument Ave.
Chestnut St.
Mt. Vernon St.
Prospect St.
Warren St.

Constitution Rd.

Charlestown Bridge

John F. Fitzgerald Espwy.

Washington St.

Copp's Hill Burying Ground

NORTH END

Commercial St.
Charter St.
Battery St.
N. Bennett St.
Prince St.
Hanover St.
Fleet St.
Richmond St.
Commercial St.

Fleet Center
North Station

Thomas P. O'Neill Federal Building

Nashua St.
Lomasney Way
Causeway St.
Canal St.
Friend St.
Portland St.
Merrimac St.
Endicott St.
Cross St.

Staniford St.
New Charden St.
Sudbury St.

State Service Center

Haymarket

John F. Kennedy Federal Building

Boston City Hall

North St.

Clinton St.

Christopher Columbus Park

Cambridge St.
Russell St.
Hancock St.
Bowdoin St.
Somerset St.

Suffolk County Courthouse

Congress St.

New Atlantic Ave.

Beacon St.

Boston Park

Tremont St.
Temple St.
Mason St.
Washington St.
Winter St.
Chauncy St.
Snow Pl.
Summer St.
Bedford St.
High St.
Milk St.
Federal St.
Congress St.
Pearl St.
Purchase St.
Oliver St.
Franklyn St.
Milk St.

Post Office Square Park

Avery St.

Atlantic Ave.

Northern Ave. Bridge

Evelyn Moakley Bridge

161

Freedom Trail Freedom

You don't have to walk the trail all at once, inspect every plaque and artifact, limit yourself to the designated stops, or even go in order. Break it into chunks over a couple of days if that works for you. Go against the flow—start in Charlestown and work backward. Wander onto a promising-looking street and ask a passerby to point you back to the trail when you're ready. Stop for a cappuccino. This is not homework, it's not "Beat the Clock," and there won't be a test at the end, so enjoy and explore.

1. Boston Common
Downtown/Beacon Hill

The country's oldest park (purchased by the town in 1634 and set aside as common land in 1640) has served over the years as a cow pasture, military camp, and all-around municipal front yard. Look around at the Central Burying Ground, off Boylston Street between Tremont and Charles streets, and the rest of the monuments and memorials. Cows have been banned since 1830, which seems to be one of the few events related to the Common that isn't commemorated with a plaque.

One of the loveliest markers is up the hill from the T station. At Beacon Street is a gorgeous bas-relief memorial designed by **Augustus Saint-Gaudens** to celebrate the deeds (indeed, the very existence) of Col. **Robert Gould Shaw** and the Union Army's **54th Massachusetts Colored Regiment,** which fought in the Civil War. You may remember the story of the first American army unit made up of free black soldiers from the movie *Glory.*

Cross Beacon Street to reach the State House.

Between Beacon, Park, Tremont, Boylston, and Charles streets. Visitor information center ☎ 800/SEE-BOSTON or 617/536-4100. **MBTA:** *Red or Green Line to Park Street.*

2. Massachusetts State House
Beacon Hill

This is the "new" State House—Gov. Samuel Adams laid its cornerstone in 1795, and it opened in 1798. The great Federal-era architect **Charles Bulfinch** designed the central building of the state capitol and its landmark dome, now covered in golf leaf. The state House of Representatives meets here under a wooden fish, the **Sacred Cod.** Merchant John Rowe (Rowes Wharf bears his name) donated the carving in 1784 as a reminder of fishing's importance to the local economy. Free tours, guided and self-guided, leave from the second floor. The 60-foot monument at the rear (off Bowdoin Street) illustrates the hill's original height, before the top was shorn off to use in 19th-century landfill projects.

Whether or not you go inside, be sure to check out the many statues outside the building. Subjects range from **Mary Dyer,** a Quaker hanged on the Common in 1660 for refusing to abandon her religious beliefs, to Pres. **John F. Kennedy.**

Walk back down Park Street 1 block.

Beacon St. at Park St. ☎ *617/727-3676. MBTA: Red or Green Line to Park St.; walk up Park St. 1 block. Open: Weekdays 9am–5pm, Sat 10am–4pm. Tours Mon–Sat 10am–3:30pm.*

3. Park Street Church
Downtown/Beacon Hill
Henry James described this 1809 structure as "the most interesting mass of bricks and mortar in America." The first missionaries to Hawaii left from here in 1819; **William Lloyd Garrison** gave his first antislavery speech here on July 4, 1829; and **"America"** ("My Country 'Tis of Thee") was first sung here on July 4, 1831. This was part of the site of a huge grain storehouse that became a public building after the Revolution. In the 1790s the sails for USS *Constitution* were manufactured in that building.

Walk 1 block along Tremont Street away from the Common.

1 Park St., at Tremont St. ☎ *617/523-3383. MBTA: Red or Green Line to Park St. Open: Late June to Aug, Tues–Sat 9:30am–4pm. Year-round, services Sun 9am, 10:45am, 5:30pm.*

4. Old Granary Burying Ground
Downtown
This cemetery, established in 1660, was once part of Boston Common. You'll see the graves of patriots **Samuel Adams, Paul Revere, John Hancock,** and **James Otis;** merchant **Peter Faneuil** (spelled "Funal"), and Benjamin Franklin's parents. Also buried here are the victims of the **Boston Massacre,** and the wife of Isaac Vergoose. She is believed to be **"Mother Goose"** of nursery rhyme fame.

Extra! Extra!
Gravestone rubbing, however tempting, is illegal in Boston's historic cemeteries. (If everyone did it, there would be nothing left to rub!)

Cross at the light, turn left, and walk 1 block on Tremont Street.

Tremont St. at Bromfield St. MBTA: Red or Green Line to Park St.; walk 1 block on Tremont St. Open: Daily 8am–4pm.

5. King's Chapel and Burying Ground
Downtown

This was the **first Anglican church in Boston.** The granite edifice is also notable because it was built (1749–54) *around* the building that previously occupied the site, a wooden chapel. The Puritan colonists had little use for the royal religion, and after the Revolution this became the **first Unitarian church in America.** Unitarian Universalist services are conducted here, using the Anglican *Book of Common Prayer.*

The **burying ground,** on Tremont Street, is the oldest in the city; it dates from 1630. Among the scary colonial headstones (winged skulls are a popular decoration) are the graves of **John Winthrop,** the first governor of the Massachusetts Bay Colony; **William Dawes,** who rode with Paul Revere; **Elizabeth Pain,** the model for Hester Prynne in Nathaniel Hawthorne's novel *The Scarlet Letter;* and **Mary Chilton,** the first female colonist to step ashore on Plymouth Rock.

Walk along the School Street side of the church.

58 Tremont St., at School St. ☎ *617/523-1749.* **MBTA:** *Green or Blue Line to Government Center; walk 1 block on Tremont St.* **Open:** *Chapel, summer Mon, Fri–Sat 9:30am–4pm, Tues, Wed 9:30am–1pm; spring and fall Mon, Fri–Sat 10am–2pm; winter Sat 10am–2pm. Services Sun 11am, Wed 12:15pm. Burying ground, summer 8am–5:30pm, winter 8am–3pm.*

History 101

The institution now known as the Boston Latin School educated Cotton Mather, John Hancock, Benjamin Franklin, Samuel Adams, Charles Bulfinch, Ralph Waldo Emerson, George Santayana, Arthur Fiedler, and Leonard Bernstein, among others. (Can you tell it was all boys until recently?)

6. First Public School/Benjamin Franklin Statue
Downtown

A colorful folk-art mosaic marks the first home of the oldest public school in the country, which opened in 1634 (2 years before Harvard College). The original building (1645) was demolished to make way for the expansion of King's Chapel, and the school was moved across the street. Now called Boston Latin School, it's located in the Fenway.

Inside the fence to your left is a statue of Boston native **Benjamin Franklin** (1706–90), with plaques on the base describing his numerous accomplishments. This was the first portrait statue erected in Boston, in 1856. The lovely granite building behind the statue is **Old City Hall** (1865), designed in Second Empire style by Arthur Gilman (who laid out the Back Bay) and Gridley J. F. Bryant.

Take School Street 1 block to Washington Street.

*School St. at Province St. **MBTA:** Orange or Blue Line to State St.; walk 2 blocks on Washington St. and turn right.*

7. Old Corner Bookstore
Downtown
This building is more interesting for its past than its present. Built in 1712, it's on a plot of land that was once home to the religious reformer **Anne Hutchinson,** who was excommunicated and expelled from Boston in 1638 for heresy. In the middle of the 19th century, the little brick building held the publishing house of Ticknor & Fields. Publisher James "Jamie" Fields counted among his friends such giants as Henry Wadsworth Longfellow, James Russell Lowell, Henry David Thoreau, Ralph Waldo Emerson, Nathaniel Hawthorne, and Harriet Beecher Stowe.

Cross Washington Street, turn right, and walk 1 block (toward the clock tower).

*3 School St., at Washington St. **MBTA:** Orange or Blue Line to State St.; walk 2 blocks up Washington St.*

8. Old South Meeting House
Downtown
The Old South was a religious and political gathering place, and is best known today as the site of one of the events leading to the Revolution. On December 16, 1773, revolutionaries protesting the royal government's tax on tea started here and wound up emptying three ships' cargo into the harbor. That uprising, the **Boston Tea Party,** is commemorated here, and you can even see a vial of the tea. An interactive multimedia exhibit tells the building's fascinating story. This building dates from 1729; the original went up in 1670.

You exit at the side of the building onto Milk Street. Before you continue, look at the second floor of the building across the street and see if you recognize the bust that's worked into the facade. (Hint: It's in the middle of the words *Birthplace of Franklin.*)

Return to Washington Street and walk 2 blocks (start by passing in front of the Old South).

310 Washington St. ☎ *617/482-6439. **MBTA:** Orange or Blue Line to State St.; walk 3 blocks up Washington St. **Admission:** $3 adults, $2.50 seniors, $1 children 6–12, free for children under 6. **Open:** Daily Apr–Oct 9am to 5:30pm; Nov–Mar weekdays 10am–4pm, weekends 10am–5pm.*

9. Old State House
Downtown
Built in 1713, the Old State House served as the seat of the colonial government of Massachusetts before the Revolution and as the state's capitol until 1797. For many years, it was considered a tall building. From its balcony the

Declaration of Independence was first read to Bostonians on July 18, 1776. The exterior decorations are particularly interesting—the gilded lion and unicorn, symbols of British rule, are reproductions. The originals were ripped down and burned the day the Declaration of Independence was read. Inside you'll find the Bostonian Society's **museum of the city's history.** There's an introductory video on the history of the building, and regularly changing exhibits.

Walk toward Devonshire Street (where the T station is) and cross onto the traffic island.

206 Washington St., at State St. ☎ *617/720-3290.* **MBTA:** *Blue or Orange Line to State St.* **Admission:** *$3 adults, $2 seniors and students, $1 children 6–18, free for children under 6.* **Open:** *Daily 9:30am–5pm.*

10. Boston Massacre Site
Downtown
Look on the traffic island in State Street for a ring of cobblestones. It marks the approximate site of the Boston Massacre, a skirmish on March 5, 1770, that helped consolidate the spirit of rebellion in the colonies. Angered at the presence of royal troops in Boston, colonists threw snowballs, garbage, rocks, and other debris at a group of redcoats. The soldiers panicked and fired into the crowd, killing five men (their graves are in the Old Granary Burying Ground).

Cross State Street, then Congress Street. Turn left and walk 1 block to the foot of the hill.

State St. at Devonshire St. **MBTA:** *Blue or Orange Line to State St.*

Speech Depaaahtment
The fine old French Huguenot name "Faneuil" more or less rhymes with "Daniel," and it's also pronounced *Fan*-yoo-ul. Peter Faneuil's gravestone, in the 18th-century tradition of phonetic funerary arts, reads "Funal."

11. Faneuil Hall
Downtown/Faneuil Hall Marketplace
You'll hear the whole marketplace called Faneuil Hall (and sometimes Quincy Market), but this is the actual hall, the "Cradle of Liberty." Built in 1742, and enlarged using a Charles Bulfinch design in 1805, Faneuil Hall was given to the city by the merchant Peter Faneuil. The hall rang with speeches by orators such as **Samuel Adams**—whose statue is on the Congress Street side—in the years leading to the Revolution, and with speeches by abolitionists, temperance advocates, and women's suffragists in the years after. The upstairs is still a public meeting (and sometimes concert) hall and the downstairs area is a market, all according to Faneuil's will. National Park Service rangers give **free 20-minute talks** every half-hour in the second-floor auditorium and operate a visitor center on the first floor.

Cross North Street onto Union Street. The glass towers in this small park are the **New England Holocaust Memorial** (1995)—a moving reminder, in the midst of attractions that celebrate freedom, of the consequences of a world without it. The apparently decorative pattern on the glass is six million random numbers, one for each Jew who died during the Holocaust.

At Hanover Street, turn right and walk 2 short blocks. Follow the trail or signs under the elevated highway, cross at the light, and turn right. Walk 1 block and turn left onto Hanover Street. At the first traffic light, turn right onto Richmond Street, walk 1 block, and turn left into North Square.

Dock Square (Congress St. off North St.). ☎ *617/242-5675.* **MBTA:** *Green or Blue Line to Government Center, or Orange Line to Haymarket.* **Admission:** *Free.* **Open:** *Second floor daily 9am–5pm; ground floor Mon–Sat 10am–9pm, Sun noon–6pm.*

> ### Extra! Extra!
> Faneuil Hall Marketplace, with its shops and food court, makes a good place to pause. It has the last public rest rooms on the route until you reach Charlestown—make sure the children take advantage. And if you want to split the Freedom Trail into two parts, this is a logical dividing point.

12. Paul Revere House
North End

One of the most pleasant stops on the Freedom Trail, the Paul Revere House presents history on a human scale. Revere set out for Lexington from here on the evening of April 18, 1775, a feat immortalized in **Henry Wadsworth Longfellow's poem "Paul Revere's Ride"** (*Listen my children and you shall hear / Of the midnight ride of Paul Revere . . .*). The oldest house in downtown Boston, it was built around 1680, bought by Revere in 1770, and put to a number of uses before being turned into a museum in the early 20th century. The self-guided tour allows you to set your own pace and gives a good sense of 18th-century life.

Across the cobblestone courtyard is the home of Revere's Hichborn cousins, the **Pierce/Hichborn House.** The 1711 Georgian-style home is a rare example of 18th-century middle-class architecture. It's suitably furnished and shown only by guided tour (usually twice a day at busy times). Call for schedules.

Turn left as you leave and walk 1 block to Prince Street. If you like, take a few steps onto Garden Court Street and look for no. 4, on the right. The private residence was the **birthplace of Rose Fitzgerald,** later Kennedy, the president's mother. Walk 1 block on Prince Street, turn right, and walk 2 blocks on Hanover Street. Cross the street and proceed across the plaza past the Paul Revere statue.

Extra! Extra!

As you walk along Hanover Street, you'll see a white steeple ahead on the right. Don't join in the chorus of "That must be the Old North Church"—it's **St. Stephen's** (1804), the only **Charles Bulfinch**–designed church still standing in Boston. The bell came from Paul Revere's foundry in 1805 (for $800).

19 North Sq., at North St. ☎ **617/523-2338. MBTA:** *Green or Orange Line to Haymarket. Cross under elevated highway and follow directions above.* **Admission:** *$2.50 adults, $2 seniors and students, $1 children 5–17.* **Open:** *Apr 15–Oct 9:30am–5:15pm; Nov–Apr 14 9:30am–4:15pm. Closed Mon Jan–Mar.*

13. Old North Church
North End

Officially known as Christ Church, this is the oldest church building in Boston; it dates from 1723. The original steeple was the one where sexton **Robert Newman** hung two lanterns on the night of April 18, 1775, to indicate to **Paul Revere** that British troops were setting out for Lexington and Concord in boats across the Charles River, not on foot (**"One if by land, two if by sea"**). The 175-foot spire is an exact copy of the original. There are markers and plaques throughout; note the bust of **George Washington,** reputedly the first memorial to the first president. The **gardens** on the north side of the church (dotted with more plaques) are open to the public. The quirky **gift shop** and museum (☎ **617/523-4848**), in a former chapel, is open daily 9am to 5pm, and all proceeds go to support the church.

Cross Salem Street onto Hull Street and walk uphill (noting the 10-foot-wide private home at no. 44, the narrowest house in Boston).

193 Salem St., at Hull St. ☎ **617/523-6676.** *www.oldnorth.com.* **MBTA:** *Green or Orange Line to Haymarket; cross under elevated highway and walk 6 blocks on Salem St.* **Admission:** *Free; donations appreciated.* **Open:** *Daily 9am–5pm; services (Episcopal) Sun 9am, 11am, 4pm.*

History 101

Small world: Robert Newman, who hung the lanterns in the steeple of the Old North Church to signal to Paul Revere, was a great-grandson of George Burroughs, one of the victims of the Salem witch trials of 1692.

14. Copp's Hill Burying Ground
North End

The second-oldest graveyard (1659) in the city, this is the burial place of **Cotton Mather** and his family, **Robert Newman,** and **Prince Hall.** Hall, a prominent member of the free black community that occupied the north slope of the hill in colonial times, fought at Bunker Hill and established the first black Masonic lodge. The highest point in the North End,

Copp's Hill was the site of the British batteries that destroyed the village of Charlestown during the Battle of Bunker Hill, June 17, 1775. You can see Charlestown (look for the masts of USS *Constitution*) across the Inner Harbor.

Follow Hull Street down the hill, turn left, and take Commercial Street to North Washington Street. Turn right, cross the bridge, turn right, and follow the trail into the Charlestown Navy Yard. Total: about 1 mile.

Between Hull, Snowhill, and Charter sts. **MBTA:** *Green or Orange Line to North Station. Follow Causeway St. to North Washington St., where it becomes Commercial St. Walk 2 blocks, turn right, and climb the hill.* **Open:** *Daily 9am–5pm.*

15. USS *Constitution*
Charlestown

"Old Ironsides," one of the U.S. Navy's six original frigates, never lost a battle. Active-duty sailors in 1812 dress uniforms lead tours, a nod to *Constitution*'s prominent role in the **War of 1812.** The frigate earned its nickname during an engagement on August 19, 1812, with the French warship *Guerrière,* whose shots bounced off its thick oak hull as if it were iron. "Old Ironsides" sailed under its own power in 1997 for the first time since 1881, drawing international attention. Tugs tow it into the harbor every **Fourth of July** and turn it to ensure that the ship weathers evenly.

Safety First

Notice that there's no crosswalk on Commercial Street at Hull Street—it's a blind spot for motorists and an *extremely* dangerous place to jaywalk. Take the extra minute and cross at North Washington or Charter Street.

The **Constitution Museum** (☎ 617/426-1812), just inland from the vessel, has several **participatory exhibits** that allow visitors to **hoist a flag, fire a cannon,** and learn more about the ship. Also at the navy yard, National Park Service rangers (☎ 617/242-5601) staff an information booth and give free 1-hour guided tours of the base. Turn left as you leave the museum (or right as you leave the ship) to reach **USS *Cassin Young,*** a refurbished World War II destroyer. Rangers give **45-minute tours** (call for times), and unescorted visitors can look around on the deck. Admission is free.

Leave the Navy Yard through gate 4 and climb the hill, following the Freedom Trail along Tremont Street. You're heading for the Bunker Hill Monument (you can't miss it).

Charlestown Navy Yard, off Constitution Rd. ☎ *617/242-5670.* **MBTA:** *Green or Orange Line to North Station; follow Causeway St. to North Washington St., turn left, and cross bridge. Total: about 15 min.* **Admission:** *Tours free; museum $4 adults, $3 seniors, $2 children 6–16, free for children under 6.* **Open:** *Constitution tours daily 9:30am–3:50pm. Museum daily June–Labor Day 9am–6pm; Mar–May and day after Labor Day–Nov 10am to 5pm; Dec–Feb 10am–3pm.*

169

History 101

The Marquis de Lafayette (1757–1834), a hero of the American and French revolutions, helped lay the Bunker Hill Monument's cornerstone in 1825. He is buried in Paris under soil taken from Bunker Hill.

16. Bunker Hill Monument
Charlestown

This 221-foot granite obelisk honors the memory of the colonists who died in the **Battle of Bunker Hill** (actually fought on Breed's Hill—hey, it was dark) on June 17, 1775. They lost the battle, but nearly half of the British troops were killed or wounded, a circumstance that contributed to the Crown's decision to abandon Boston 9 months later. The top of the momument is at the end of a flight of 294 stairs—the long climb ends in a good view, but there's no elevator, and you also get an eyeful of I-93. In the lodge at the base of the monument, staffed by park rangers, there are dioramas and exhibits.

Monument Sq., at Tremont St. ☎ *617/242-5644.* **MBTA:** *Ferry to and from Long Wharf (use shuttle bus from the Navy Yard, near "Old Ironsides"). Or no. 92 or 93 bus along Main St. (foot of the hill) to and from Haymarket. Or Orange Line to Community College; cross Rutherford Ave. and walk toward the monument.* **Admission:** *Free.* **Open:** *Daily, monument 9am–4:30pm, visitor center 9am–5pm.*

The Other Top Attractions

Beacon Hill

Climbing "the Hill," with its narrow streets and picturesque brick and brownstone architecture, is like traveling back in time. Beacon and Mount Vernon streets run from the State House downhill to commercially dense Charles Street, but if ever there was an area where there's no need to head in a straight line, it's this one. Your travels might take you past former homes of Louisa May Alcott (10 Louisburg Sq.), Henry Kissinger (1 Chestnut St.), Julia Ward Howe (13 Chestnut St.), Edwin Booth (29A Chestnut St.), or Robert Frost (88 Mount Vernon St.). One of the oldest black churches in the country, the African Meeting House, is at 8 Smith Court.

Between Beacon St., Embankment Rd., Cambridge St., and Park St. **MBTA:** *Red Line to Charles/MGH or Green Line to Park St.*

Boston Tea Party Ship & Museum
Waterfront/Museum Wharf

On December 16, 1773, a public meeting of independent-minded Bostonians led to the symbolic act of resistance commemorated here. The brig *Beaver II* is a full-size replica of one of the three merchant ships that the colonists, poorly disguised as Indians, emptied on the night of the raid. It's anchored alongside a museum with exhibits on the "tea party." The audio and video displays (including a 15-minute film), dioramas, and information panels tell the story of the uprising. You can dump your own bale of tea into Boston Harbor (a museum staffer retrieves it), and drink some complimentary tax-free tea (iced in summer, hot in winter).

Congress St. Bridge, off Dorchester Ave. ☎ *617/338-1773. E-mail: bostps@ historictours.com. MBTA: Red Line to South Station. Walk north on Atlantic Ave. 1 block (past the Federal Reserve Bank), turn right onto Congress St., and walk 1 block. Admission: $8 adults, $6.40 students, $4 children 4–12, free for children under 4. Open: Daily Mar–Nov 9am–dusk (about 6pm in summer, 5pm in winter). Closed Thanksgiving, Dec–Feb.*

Children's Museum
Waterfront/Museum Wharf

Children up to the age of 12 or so are sure to find something interesting here—and teens and adults who feared being bored out of their skulls will happily be proven wrong. Exhibits are very much hands-on. Some favorites: "Boats Afloat," which has an 800-gallon play tank and a replica of the bridge of a working boat; the "Dress-Up Shop," a souped-up version of playing in Grandma's closet; and rooms where children can race golf balls on tracks through various structures and create soap bubbles in water tanks. The "Climbing Sculpture" is a giant maze designed especially for children (adults may get stuck). You can also explore a Japanese house and a subway car from Kyoto, Boston's sister city. Children under 4 and their caregivers have a special room, "Playspace," that's packed with toys and activities.

Museum Wharf (300 Congress St., at Sleeper St.). ☎ *617/426-8855. MBTA: Red Line to South Station. Walk north on Atlantic Ave. 1 block (past the Federal Reserve Bank), turn right onto Congress St., and cross the bridge. Admission: $7 adults, $6 children age 2–15 and seniors, $2 children age 1, free for children under 1; Fri 5–9pm, $1 for all. Open: Sept–June Tues–Sun 10am–5pm, Fri until 9pm; June–Aug daily 10am–5pm, Fri until 9pm. Closed Jan 1, Thanksgiving, Dec 25, and Mon Sept–June, except Boston school vacations and holidays.*

Computer Museum
Waterfront/Museum Wharf

This is the world's premier computer museum, with exhibits that tell the story of computers from their origins in the 1940s to the latest in PCs and virtual reality. That might sound a little dull—it's absolutely not. The signature exhibit, the Walk-Through Computer 2000, is a networked multimedia machine 50 times larger than the real thing. The computer's as large as a two-story house, and the humans enjoying the 30 hands-on activities are the equivalent of crayon-size. Other exhibits include access to real and simulated computer networks, weather forecasting, financial markets, air-traffic control, robots, the history of the computer, and the practical and recreational uses of the PC. In all, you'll find more than 170 hands-on exhibits, two theaters, and countless ideas to try at home.

171

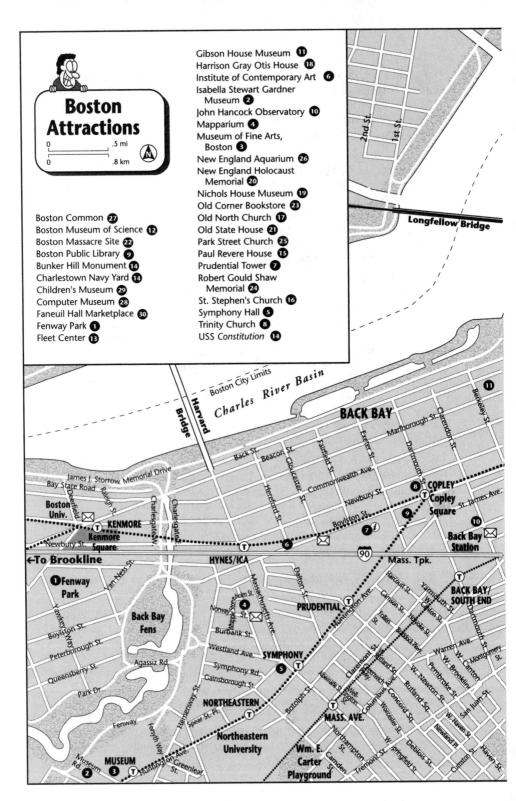

Boston Attractions

Gibson House Museum **11**
Harrison Gray Otis House **18**
Institute of Contemporary Art **6**
Isabella Stewart Gardner
  Museum **2**
John Hancock Observatory **10**
Mapparium **4**
Museum of Fine Arts,
  Boston **3**
New England Aquarium **26**
New England Holocaust
  Memorial **20**
Nichols House Museum **19**
Old Corner Bookstore **23**
Old North Church **17**
Old State House **21**
Park Street Church **25**
Paul Revere House **15**
Prudential Tower **7**
Robert Gould Shaw
  Memorial **24**
St. Stephen's Church **16**
Symphony Hall **5**
Trinity Church **8**
USS *Constitution* **14**

Boston Common **27**
Boston Museum of Science **12**
Boston Massacre Site **22**
Boston Public Library **9**
Bunker Hill Monument **14**
Charlestown Navy Yard **14**
Children's Museum **29**
Computer Museum **28**
Faneuil Hall Marketplace **30**
Fenway Park **1**
Fleet Center **13**

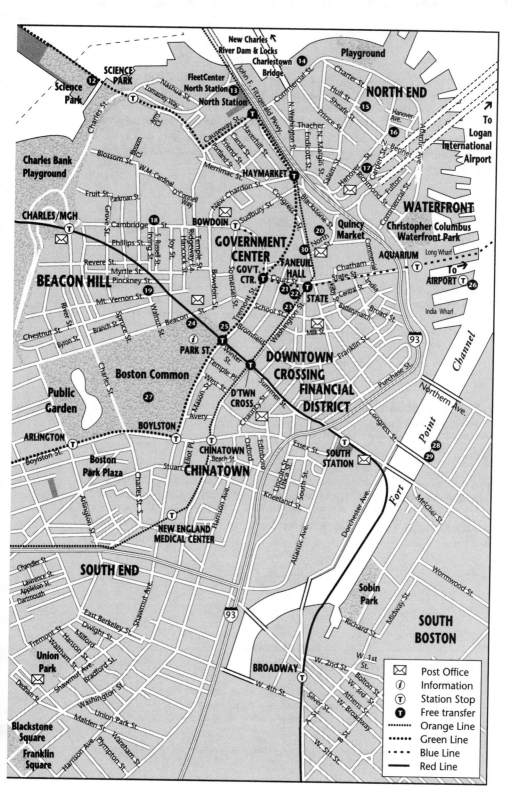

Museum Wharf (300 Congress St., at Sleeper St.). ☎ *617/426-2800 or 617/ 423-6758 for the "Talking Computer." www.tcm.org.* **MBTA:** *Red Line to South Station. Walk north on Atlantic Ave. 1 block (past the Federal Reserve Bank), turn right onto Congress St., and cross the bridge.* **Admission:** *$7 adults, $5 seniors, students, and children 3–18, free for children under 2. Sun 3–5pm, half price.* **Open:** *Summer daily 10am–6pm; fall, winter, spring Tues–Sun and Mon during Boston school holidays and vacations 10am–5pm.*

Time-Savers

Summer weekends are the busiest times for just about every Boston-area attraction. In July and August, resign yourself to having lots of company wherever you go. The rest of the year, be at your number-one choice when it opens (on a weekday, if possible) and you'll probably enjoy some measure of privacy, at least for a while.

 ## Faneuil Hall Marketplace
Downtown

The original "festival market" boasts a great mixture of shops, chain stores, knickknack-laden pushcarts, food stands, restaurants, bars, and public spaces. The five buildings teem with crowds shopping, eating, performing, watching performers, and just people-watching. In the central building, **Quincy Market** (you'll hear the whole complex called by that name as well), is a food court that runs the length of the building. In the plaza between the **South Canopy** and the South Market building is an **information kiosk.** See the Freedom Trail listings, above, for information about **Faneuil Hall.**

Extra! Extra!

A considerably less elegant shopping destination operates a stone's throw from Faneuil Hall Marketplace all day Friday and Saturday. The action at the produce and fish stalls of **Haymarket,** on Blackstone Street between North and Hanover streets (cross near the flower market and turn right), represents the last vestige of the days when Quincy Market was the pounding heart of the city's food trade. Bring a camera.

Between North, Congress, and State sts. and I-93. ☎ *617/338-2323.* **MBTA:** *Green or Blue Line to Government Center; cross the plaza, walk down the stairs, and cross Congress St. Or Orange Line to Haymarket; follow Congress St. (with I-93 on your left) 2 to 3 blocks.* **Open:** *Marketplace Mon–Sat 10am–9pm, Sun noon–6pm. Colonnade food court opens earlier; some restaurants open early for Sun brunch and close at 2am daily.*

Kids Harvard Square
Cambridge

Town and gown meet at this lively intersection, where you'll get a taste of the improbable mix of people drawn to the crossroads of Cambridge. This is a shopping destination (see chapter 15 for suggestions) that's also popular with sightseers, street performers, and procrastinating students. It's especially colorful on weekend afternoons. Stop at the information booth near the main T entrance (toward the back of outbound trains), where trained volunteers dispense information and brochures, or just set out on your own. The three main streets and the side streets that connect them all make great places for wandering.

Extra! Extra!
Standing near the Harvard Square information booth, look up at the third floor of the brick building across the intersection of John F. Kennedy and Brattle streets. Find the sign for "Dewey Cheetham & Howe" (say it out loud). National Public Radio's hilarious show "Car Talk" originates here.

Intersection of Mass. Ave., John F. Kennedy St., and Brattle St. ☎ *617/497-1630 (information booth).* **MBTA:** *Red Line to Harvard.* **Open:** *Mon–Sat 9am–5pm, Sun 1–5pm (information booth).*

Harvard University
Cambridge

Harvard is the oldest college in the United States, established in 1636 to train young men for the ministry. The university now includes 10 graduate and professional schools in more than 400 buildings scattered around Cambridge and Boston. The areas surrounded by brick walls along Mass. Ave. and Quincy and Cambridge streets make up **Harvard Yard,** the oldest part of the campus. The Yard is where you'll find the **John Harvard Statue,** one of the most photographed objects in the Boston area. The Events & Information Center has maps, illustrated booklets, and self-guided walking-tour directions, as well as a bulletin board where campus activities are publicized. You might want to check out the university's art and science museums (see chapter 14) and Web site (www.harvard.edu), too.

Events & Information Center: Holyoke Center, 1350 Mass. Ave. ☎ *617/495-1573.* **MBTA:** *Red Line to Harvard.* **Open:** *Mon–Sat 9am–5pm, Sun noon–5pm. Free guided tours twice a day on weekdays, once on Sat, during school year (except vacations), and during the summer four times a day Mon–Sat and twice on Sun. Call for exact times; reservations aren't necessary.*

175

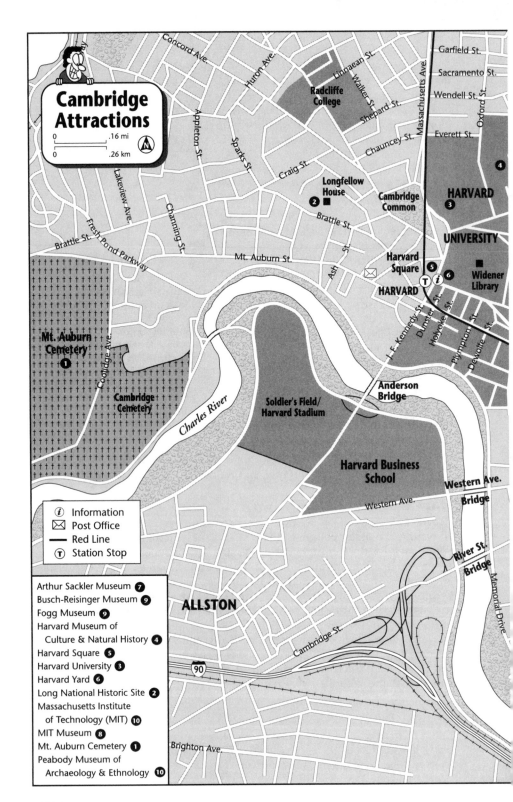

Cambridge Attractions

0 ——— .16 mi
0 ——— .26 km

Concord Ave.
Huron Ave.
Linnaean St.
Garfield St.
Sacramento St.
Walker St.
Radcliffe College
Wendell St.
Appleton St.
Sparks St.
Shepard St.
Chauncey St.
Everett St.
Massachusetts Ave.
Oxford St.
Craig St.
Longfellow House **2**
Cambridge Common
HARVARD **4**
3
Lakeview Ave.
Channing St.
Brattle St.
HARVARD UNIVERSITY
Brattle St.
Fresh Pond Parkway
Mt. Auburn St.
Ash St.
Harvard Square **5** **6**
HARVARD **T** *i*
Widener Library
Coolidge Ave.
Mt. Auburn Cemetery **1**
J. F. Kennedy St.
Dunster St.
Holyoke St.
Plympton St.
DeWolfe St.
Cambridge Cemetery
Charles River
Anderson Bridge
Soldier's Field/ Harvard Stadium
Harvard Business School
Western Ave.
Bridge
Western Ave.
River St.
Bridge
Memorial Drive

i Information
✉ Post Office
— Red Line
T Station Stop

ALLSTON
Cambridge St.
90

Brighton Ave.

Arthur Sackler Museum **7**
Busch-Reisinger Museum **9**
Fogg Museum **9**
Harvard Museum of Culture & Natural History **4**
Harvard Square **5**
Harvard University **3**
Harvard Yard **6**
Long National Historic Site **2**
Massachusetts Institute of Technology (MIT) **10**
MIT Museum **8**
Mt. Auburn Cemetery **1**
Peabody Museum of Archaeology & Ethnology **10**

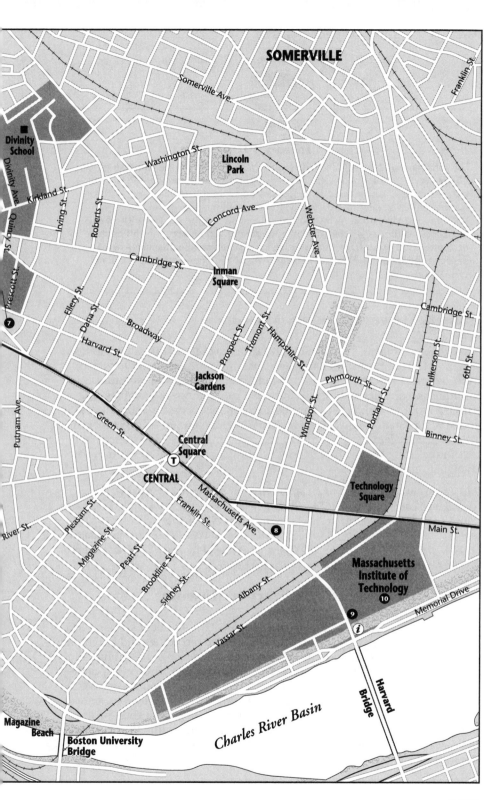

History 101

The John Harvard Statue (1884) in Harvard Yard is known as the **"Statue of Three Lies"** because the inscription reads "John Harvard—Founder—1638." In fact, the college was founded in 1636; Harvard (one of many involved in its formation) didn't establish the university, but donated money and his library; and this isn't John Harvard, anyway. No portraits survive, so the model for the benevolent-looking bronze gentleman was, according to various accounts, his nephew or a student. Sculptor Daniel Chester French's name may seem familiar—he also designed the statue of Abraham Lincoln that's at the presidential memorial in Washington.

Isabella Stewart Gardner Museum

Fenway

The exquisite home of Isabella Stewart Gardner (1840–1924), designed in the style of a 15th-century Venetian palace, became a museum after her death. It overflows with European, American, and Asian painting and sculpture, and furniture and architectural details imported from European churches and palaces. You'll see works by Titian, Botticelli, Raphael, Rembrandt, Matisse, and Mrs. Gardner's friends James McNeill Whistler and John Singer Sargent. Titian's magnificent *Europa* is one of the most important Renaissance paintings in the United States. The special exhibition gallery features two or three changing shows a year.

280 The Fenway, at Museum Rd., off Huntington Ave. ☎ ***617/566-1401.*** *www.boston.com/gardner.* **MBTA:** *Green Line E to Museum; walk 2 blocks straight ahead (away from Huntington Ave.).* **Admission:** *$11 adults weekends, $10 adults weekdays, $7 seniors, $5 college students with valid ID, $3 college students on Wed, free for children under 18.* **Open:** *Tues–Sun 11am–5pm and some Mon holidays. Closed Mon, Jan 1, Thanksgiving, Dec 25.*

Kids John F. Kennedy Library & Museum

Dorchester

The Kennedy era springs to life here, where the 35th president's accomplishments and legacy are captured in sound and video recordings and fascinating displays of memorabilia and photos. You begin by viewing a 17-minute film about Kennedy's early life, then move on to the exhibits. They incorporate campaign souvenirs, film of Kennedy debating Richard Nixon and delivering his inaugural address, a replica of the Oval Office, gifts from foreign dignitaries, letters, documents, and keepsakes. There's a film about the Cuban Missile Crisis and displays on the Civil Rights movement, the Peace Corps, the space program, the Kennedy family, and First Lady Jacqueline Bouvier Kennedy.

Columbia Pt., off Morrissey Blvd. ☎ *617/929-4523. www.cs.umb.edu/jfklibrary.*
MBTA: *Red Line to JFK/UMass, then take the free shuttle bus, which runs every 20
min.* **Admission:** *$8 adults, $6 seniors and students with ID, $4 children 13–17,
free for children under 13.* **Open:** *Daily 9am–5pm (last film begins at 3:55);
June–Aug Wed until 8pm. Closed Jan 1, Thanksgiving, Dec 25.* **By car:** *Take
I-93/Route 3 south to Exit 15 (Morrissey Blvd./JFK Library), turn left onto
Columbia Rd., and follow signs to free parking lot.*

More JFK

At the **John F. Kennedy National Historic Site,** the 35th president's birthplace is restored to its appearance in 1917, affording a fascinating look at domestic life of the period and the roots of the Kennedy family. The house is shown
only by guided National Park Service ranger tour, at 10:45 and 11:45am and at
1, 2, 3, and 4pm. Guided tours are $2 for adults and free for children under 16.
The house, at 83 Beals St., Brookline (☎ **617/566-7937**), is open from mid-
May to October, Wednesday to Sunday 10am to 4:30pm. **MBTA:** Green Line C
to Coolidge Corner, then walk 4 blocks north on Harvard Street.

John Hancock Observatory
Back Bay

This 60th-floor space would offer a good introduction to Boston even if it
didn't have a sensational view. The multimedia exhibits include a light-and-
sound show that chronicles the events leading to the Revolutionary War and
demonstrates how Boston's land mass has changed. There are several entertaining exhibits, including an interactive computer quiz about the city. Allow
at least 45 minutes.

200 Clarendon St., at St. James Ave. ☎ *617/572-6429.* **MBTA:** *Green Line to
Copley; walk diagonally across Copley Sq.* **Admission:** *$4.25 adults, $3.25
seniors and children 5–15.* **Open:** *9am–11pm Mon–Sat; Sun 10am–11pm
May–Oct; noon–11pm Nov–Apr. Ticket office closes at 10pm.*

Museum of Fine Arts
Fenway

At only a few museums in the country can you round a corner and suddenly
come upon a beloved piece of art that's almost as familiar as the face in the
mirror. Here, it happens all the time. The MFA is considered the second-best
art museum in the country (after New York's Metropolitan Museum of Art),
and there's something for everyone—classical art, a Buddhist temple,
medieval sculpture and tapestries, and American and European paintings and
sculpture, notably the impressionists, including 43 Monets. There are also

179

voluminous collections of Asian art, prints, photographs, furnishings, and decorative arts, and new permanent galleries for the art of Africa, Oceania, and the ancient Americas. And remember that what adults hear as "magnificent Old Kingdom Egyptian collections," kids hear as "mummies!"

Anyone with even a passing interest in art could happily spend a whole day here and only scratch the surface of the magnificent collections; allow at least half a day. Pick up a floor plan at the information desk or take a free guided tour (weekdays except Monday holidays at 10:30am and 1:30pm, Wednesday at 6:15pm, Saturday at 10:30am and 1pm). A family activity booklet is always available at the information desk, and many family and kid-only activities are scheduled throughout the year.

465 Huntington Ave., at Museum Rd. ☎ *617/267-9300. www.mfa.org.* **MBTA:** *Green Line E to Museum. Or Orange Line to Ruggles; walk 2 blocks on Ruggles St.* **Admission:** *Adults $10 entire museum, $8 when only West Wing is open. Students and senior citizens $8 entire museum, $6 when only West Wing is open. Children under 18 free when accompanied by an adult. Voluntary contribution ($5 suggested), Wed 4–9:45pm. No fee to visit only shop, library, or auditoriums.* **Open:** *Entire museum, Mon–Tues 10am–4:45pm, Wed 10am–9:45pm, Thurs–Fri 10am–5pm, Sat–Sun 10am–5:45pm; West Wing only, Thurs–Fri 5–9:45pm. Closed Thanksgiving, Dec 25.*

MFA FYI

The Huntington Avenue entrance to the Museum of Fine Arts is usually much less busy than the West Wing lobby—and farther from the T, gift shop, restaurants, parking garage, and access to special exhibits. If you're eager to get started on a lengthy visit (which generally involves lots of walking anyway), walk back along Huntington Avenue when you leave the T and enter from the curved driveway.

Museum of Science
Science Park (on bridge between Boston and East Cambridge)

For the ultimate fun, pain-free educational experience, head here. The demonstrations, experiments, and interactive displays introduce facts and concepts so effortlessly that everyone learns something. Take a couple of hours or a whole day to explore the more than 450 permanent and temporary exhibits, which are dedicated to improving "science literacy." They cover every field of science, and children and adults learn from them and (just as important) have a great time playing with them. There's even a Discovery Center for preschoolers.

The **Mugar Omni Theater** (separate admission) bombards you with images on a 4-story domed screen and sounds from 84 speakers. The engulfing sensations of the IMAX format and steep pitch of the seating area will have you hanging on for dear life. Films change every 4 to 6 months.

The **Charles Hayden Planetarium** (separate admission) takes you deep into space with daily star shows and shows on special topics that change several times a year. On weekends, rock-music laser shows (separate admission) take over.

Science Park, off Route 28. ☎ *617/723-2500. www.mos.org. **MBTA:** Green Line to Science Park; follow signs along elevated walkway onto bridge. **Admission:** To exhibit halls $9 adults, $7 seniors and children age 3–14, free for children under 3. To Mugar Omni Theater, Hayden Planetarium, or laser shows, $7.50 adults, $5.50 seniors and children age 3–14, free for children under 3. Discounted tickets to 2 or 3 parts of the complex available. **Open:** Museum Sat–Thurs 9am–5pm, Fri 9am–9pm; shows during museum hours and some evenings. Closed Thanksgiving, Dec 25.*

Scientific Method

The Museum of Science's separate-admission theaters are worth planning for. Even if you're skipping the exhibits, try to see a show. If you're making a day or half-day of it, buy all your tickets at once, not only because it's cheaper but because shows sometimes sell out. Tickets for daytime shows must be purchased in person. You can order evening show tickets over the phone using a credit card; there's a service charge for doing so, but it's worth doing if time is short.

 ## New England Aquarium
Waterfront

This entertaining complex is home to more than 7,000 fish and aquatic mammals. The main building's focal point is the aptly named Giant Ocean Tank, which contains 187,000 gallons of saltwater, a replica of a Caribbean coral reef, and a conglomeration of sea creatures that seem to coexist amazingly well. (You may recognize it from the 1998 movie *Next Stop Wonderland*.) The sharks may be so docile because they're fed five times a day by scuba divers who bring the food right to them. Other exhibits show off denizens of the waters around the world, and at the floating marine mammal pavilion, "Discovery," sea lions perform every 90 minutes throughout the day. Allow at least 2½ hours.

Central Wharf, off Atlantic Ave. at State St. ☎ *617/973-5200. www.neaq.org. **MBTA:** Blue Line to Aquarium. **Admission:** $11 adults, $10 seniors, $5.50 children 3–11, free for children under 3. $1 off all fees 4–8pm summer Wed and Thurs.*

No admission fee for those visiting only the outdoor exhibits, cafe, and gift shop.
Open: *July 1–Labor Day Mon–Tues and Fri 9am–6pm, Wed–Thurs 9am–8pm, Sat–Sun and holidays 9am–7pm; early Sept–June Mon–Fri 9am–5pm, Sat–Sun and holidays 9am–6pm. Closed Thanksgiving, Dec 25, and until noon Jan 1.*

North End

Boston's Italian-American neighborhood is so popular with the young professionals who walk to work downtown that it's now estimated to be less than half Italian. Nevertheless, this is the place for Italian restaurants, cafes, bakeries and pastry shops, food stores, and churches (the 10am Sunday Mass at Sacred Heart, on North Square, is in Italian). Hanover and Salem streets are the main thoroughfares, but do yourself a favor and detour onto some side streets, too.

Between I-93, Commercial St., and North Washington St. ***MBTA:*** *Green or Orange Line to Haymarket; cross under the elevated highway.*

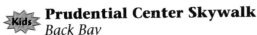 Prudential Center Skywalk
Back Bay

From the 50th floor of the Prudential Tower, you get the only 360° view of Boston—and way beyond. The panorama extends for miles, even as far as the mountains of southern New Hampshire and the beaches of Cape Cod when the sky is clear. The limited exhibits are less interesting than those at the John Hancock Observatory, but the view is a little better, especially at sunset.

800 Boylston St., at Fairfield St. ☎ ***617/236-3318.*** ***MBTA:*** *Green Line E to Prudential or B, C, or D to Copley; walk toward tower.* ***Admission:*** *$4 adults, $3 seniors and children 2–10.* ***Open:*** *Daily 10am–10pm.*

Public Garden
Back Bay

At the country's first botanical garden, something lovely is in bloom at least half the year, and the spring flowers are particularly impressive. The Public Garden is just 8 square blocks, but they're filled with flowers, ornamental greenery, flowering trees and shrubs, ducks, geese, and swans. You might even see a wedding. There's also a somewhat haphazard collection of statuary, including a commemoration of the first use of ether as an anesthetic and an equestrian rendering of George Washington.

Near the corner of Charles and Beacon streets is a 35-foot strip of cobblestones topped with the bronze figures that immortalize Robert McCloskey's book ***Make Way for Ducklings.*** Installed in 1987 and wildly popular since the moment they were unveiled, Nancy Schön's renderings of Mrs. Mallard and her eight babies are irresistible. If you don't know the whole story of the family's perilous trip across town to meet Mr. Mallard at the lagoon, ask one of the parents or children you'll certainly find here.

Between Arlington, Boylston, Charles, and Beacon sts. ***MBTA:*** *Green Line to Arlington. Or Red Line to Charles; follow Charles St. 5 blocks to Beacon St.*

History 101

Before the Back Bay was filled in, the Charles River flowed right up to Charles Street, which now separates the Public Garden from Boston Common. On the night of April 18, 1775, the British troops bound for Lexington and Concord boarded boats to Cambridge ("two if by sea") at the edge of the Common and set off across what's now the Public Garden.

 Swan Boats
Back Bay

Riding the swan boats has been a classic Boston experience since 1877. In those days, the boats were wooden swans; now, fiberglass birds on pedal boats (powered by iron-thighed attendants, not by you) take over the lagoon at the Public Garden every spring and offer an excellent break in the midst of a busy day. If you or your children have read *The Trumpet of the Swan*, by E. B. White, this is the place. Allow 30 minutes.

Public Garden Lagoon. ☎ *617/522-1966 or 617/624-7020.* **MBTA:** *Green Line to Arlington. Or Red Line to Charles; follow Charles St. 5 blocks to Beacon St.* **Admission:** *Adults $1.75, children under 13, 95¢.* **Open:** *Daily, third Mon of Apr through Sept; summer 10am–6pm; spring and fall 10am–4pm.*

Worksheet: Your Must-See Attractions

Enter the attractions you most would like to visit to see how they'll fit into your schedule. Then use the date book on the following pages to plan your itinerary.

Attraction and location	Amount of time you expect to spend there	Best day and time to go

DAY 1

Morning:

Lunch:

Afternoon:

Dinner:

Evening:

DAY 2

Morning:

Lunch:

Afternoon:

Dinner:

Evening:

DAY 3

Morning:

Lunch:

Afternoon:

Dinner:

Evening:

DAY 4

Morning:

Lunch:

Afternoon:

Dinner:

Evening:

DAY 5

Morning:

Lunch:

Afternoon:

Dinner:

Evening:

Chapter 14

More Fun Stuff to Do

In This Chapter

➤ More museums, sights, attractions, and activities

➤ Whale watching and island-hopping

➤ A look at spectator sports

The less-famous relatives of the sites and activities in chapter 13 can be equally interesting if you're drawn to a particular topic. In this chapter, you'll learn where to learn more, plus where to watch whales and where to watch athletes. Not all of the following attractions can be found on maps in chapter 13, but telephone numbers and nearest T-stops have been included to help you find them.

You Gotta Have Art (And History & Science): More Museums

On Beacon Hill, the **Museum of Afro-American History,** 46 Joy St. (☎617/742-1854; www.afroammuseum.org), has the most comprehensive information on the history and contributions of blacks in Boston and Massachusetts. Its chief artifact is the **African Meeting House** (1806), 8 Smith Court, the oldest standing black church in the United States. The building once known as the "Black Faneuil Hall" offers an informative audio-visual presentation, lectures, concerts, and church meetings. It's open 10am to 4pm, daily in the summer, weekdays only from Labor Day to Memorial Day. The suggested donation is $5 for adults, $3 for seniors, students, and children. **MBTA:** Red or Green line to Park Street; climb the hill, walk around the State House to the left, and follow Joy Street 3½ blocks.

In the Back Bay, across from the Hynes Convention Center, the **Institute of Contemporary Art,** 955 Boylston St. (☎ **617/266-5152;** www. primalpub.com/ica), hosts rotating exhibits of 20th-century art, including painting, sculpture, photography, and video and performance art. Admission is $5.25 for adults, $3.25 for students, $2.25 for seniors and children under 16, and free to all Thursday after 5pm. It's open Wednesday and Friday through Sunday noon to 5pm, and Thursday noon to 9pm. **MBTA:** Green Line B, C, or D to Hynes/ICA, Boylston Street exit.

In Cambridge, the **Harvard University Art Museums** house a total of about 150,000 works of art in three world-class collections. The **Fogg Art Museum** (32 Quincy St., near Broadway) shows something different in each of its 19 rooms, from 17th-century Dutch landscapes to contemporary sculpture. The **Busch-Reisinger Museum** (enter through the Fogg) is the only museum in North America devoted to the art of Northern and Central Europe—specifically Germany. The **Arthur M. Sackler Museum** (485 Broadway, at Quincy Street) houses the university's collections of Asian, ancient, and Islamic art. One admission charge covers all three museums (☎ **617/495-9400**). It's $5 for adults, $4 for seniors, $3 for students, and free for children under 18. They're free to all on Saturday before noon and all day Wednesday, and closed on major holidays. Open hours are Monday to Saturday 10am to 5pm, Sunday 1 to 5pm. **MBTA:** Red Line to Harvard. Cross Harvard Yard diagonally from the T station and cross Quincy Street, or turn your back on the Coop and follow Mass. Ave. to Quincy Street, then turn left.

Also on the Cambridge campus, the **Harvard Museum of Natural History** and the **Peabody Museum of Archaeology & Ethnology** house the university's collections of items and artifacts related to the natural world. The Peabody Museum has great displays on people and cultures from all over the globe, with particularly interesting Native American collections. The adjacent natural history museum incorporates botanical, zoological (from insects to dinosaurs), and mineralogical collections. The best-known is the **Glass Flowers,** 3,000 eerily lifelike models of more than 840 plant species.

One admission charge covers the Peabody Museum, at 11 Divinity Ave. (☎ **617/496-1027;** www.peabody.harvard.edu), and the Museum of Natural History, at 26 Oxford St. (☎ **617/495-3045;** www.hmnh.harvard.edu). It's $5 for adults, $4 for students and seniors, $3 for children 3 to 13, and free for children under 3. The museums are free to all on Saturday before noon, and closed January 1, July 4, Thanksgiving, and December 25. Open hours are Monday to Saturday 9am to 5pm, Sunday 1 to 5pm. **MBTA:** Red Line to Harvard. Cross Harvard Yard, keeping the John Harvard statue on your right, and turn right at the Science Center. Take the first left onto Oxford Street.

Out of Order

Two popular attractions were closed for building renovations at press time, and neither was expected to reopen before fall 1999. Both are worth a visit; call to see if they're open when you're in town.

➤ The **Longfellow National Historic Site** is at 105 Brattle St. in Cambridge. The books and furniture have remained intact since the poet Henry Wadsworth Longfellow died there in 1882. During the siege of Boston in 1775–76 the house served as the headquarters of Gen. George Washington, with whom Longfellow was fascinated. On a tour led by a National Park Service ranger—the only way to see the house—you'll learn about the history of the building and its famous occupants (☎ **617/876-4491;** www.nps.gov/long/index.htm). **MBTA:** Red Line to Harvard; walk 8½ blocks up Brattle Street.

➤ The 30-foot glass **Mapparium,** a hollow, walk-through globe, is at the world headquarters of the First Church of Christ, Scientist, 275 Huntington Ave. (entrance on Mass. Ave.). It shows the political divisions of the world from 1932 to 1935, when the globe was constructed (☎ **617/450-3790**). **MBTA:** Green Line E to Symphony.

Twin Powers: Copley Square's Treasures

No, the **Boston Public Library,** 700 Boylston St. (☎ **617/536-5400;** www.bpl.org), isn't a museum. It *is* an architectural monument packed with noteworthy art. The original 1895 building, a registered National Historic Landmark designed by Charles F. McKim, is an Italian Renaissance–style masterpiece. The lobby doors, murals, frescoes, sculptures, and paintings are magnificent. Pick up a brochure or take a free **Art & Architecture Tour** (Monday at 2:30pm, Tuesday and Wednesday at 6:30pm, Thursday and Saturday at 11am, and September through May on Sunday at 2pm). The library is open Monday through Thursday 9am to 9pm, Friday and Saturday till 5pm, and Sunday (October through May only) 1 to 5pm. **MBTA:** Green Line to Copley or Orange Line to Back Bay.

Across the square is **Trinity Church,** H. H. Richardson's Romanesque masterpiece. Completed in 1877, it was built on 4,502 pilings driven into the mud that was once the Back Bay. Should you happen to visit on a Friday, organ recitals are given at 12:15pm. Otherwise, brochures and guides are available to help you find your way around a building considered one of the finest examples of church architecture in the country. The church is at 545 Boylston St. (☎ **617/536-0944**). It's open daily 8am to 6pm; Sunday services (Episcopal) are at 8, 9, and 11am and 6pm.

Historic Houses

Fans of the **Paul Revere House** (see the Freedom Trail listings in chapter 13) might enjoy houses that are as interesting for their architecture as they are for their occupants. Excellent tours of two Beacon Hill houses focus on the late 18th and early 19th century. The homes are the work of Charles Bulfinch, also the architect of the nearby Massachusetts State House.

The **Harrison Gray Otis House,** 141 Cambridge St. (☎ 617/227-3956; www.spnea.org), was designed in 1796 for an up-and-coming young lawyer who later became mayor of Boston. The restored Federal-style mansion is furnished in the elegant style to which a wealthy family in the young United States would have been accustomed. Tours (the only way to see the house) start on the hour Wednesday through Sunday from 11am to 4pm. (This is the headquarters of the Society for the Preservation of New England Antiquities—if that's up your alley, ask about the society's other properties.) Admission is $4 for adults, $3.50 for seniors, $2 for children 12 and under. **MBTA:** Red Line to Charles/MGH.

The **Nichols House Museum,** 55 Mount Vernon St. (☎ 617/227-6993), is an 1804 Beacon Hill home with beautiful antique furnishings collected by several generations of the Nichols family. From May through October, it's open Tuesday through Saturday; November through April, Monday, Wednesday, and Saturday (open days may vary, so call ahead). Tours start at 12:15pm and continue every half hour on the quarter hour through 4:15pm. Admission is $5.

In the Back Bay, the **Gibson House Museum,** 137 Beacon St. (☎ 617/267-6338), is an 1859 brownstone decorated in the over-the-top style that embodies the word *Victorian.* The museum is open for tours at 1, 2, and 3pm Wednesday through Sunday from May to October, and weekends only from November to April. It's closed on major holidays. Admission is $5.

Gardener's Eden: The Arnold Arboretum

The most spectacular garden in Boston is the **Arnold Arboretum,** 125 Arborway, Jamaica Plain (☎ 617/524-1718; www.arboretum.harvard.edu). Founded in 1872, it's one of the oldest parks in the United States. Its 265 acres contain more than 15,000 ornamental trees, shrubs, and vines from all over the world. Admission is free. The grounds are open daily from sunrise to sunset. The Visitor Center is open weekdays 9am to 4pm, and weekends noon to 4pm. **MBTA:** Orange Line to Forest Hills; follow signs to the entrance.

More Reasons to Visit Cambridge

The public is welcome at the **Massachusetts Institute of Technology** (**MIT**) campus, a mile or so down Mass. Ave. from Harvard Square, across the Charles River from Beacon Hill and the Back Bay. Visit the **Information Center,** 77 Mass. Ave. (☎ 617/253-4795), to take a free guided tour (weekdays, 10am and 2pm) or pick up a copy of the *Walk Around MIT* map and brochure. The school has an excellent outdoor sculpture collection, which includes works by Picasso and Alexander Calder, and notable modern architecture by Eero Saarinen and I. M. Pei. Even more modern are the holography displays at the **MIT Museum,** 265 Mass. Ave. (☎ 617/253-4444), where you'll also find works in more conventional media. The museum is open Tuesday through Friday 10am to 5pm, weekends noon to 5pm, and closed on major holidays. Admission is $3 for adults, $1 for students, seniors, and children under 12. **MBTA:** No. 1 (Dudley-Harvard) bus; exit at first stop across bridge. Or Red Line to Kendall/MIT, and use the campus map at street level on the outbound side.

Death Takes a Holiday: A Celebrity Cemetery

Three important colonial burying grounds—Old Granary, King's Chapel, and Copp's Hill—are in Boston on the Freedom Trail (see chapter 13). The most famous cemetery in the area is in Cambridge. **Mount Auburn Cemetery,** 580 Mount Auburn St. (☎ **617/547-7105**), the final resting place of many well-known people, is also famous simply for existing. Dedicated in 1831, it was the first of America's rural, or garden, cemeteries. The graves of Henry Wadsworth Longfellow, Oliver Wendell Holmes, Julia Ward Howe, and Mary Baker Eddy are here, as are those of Charles Bulfinch, James Russell Lowell, Winslow Homer, Transcendentalist leader Margaret Fuller, and abolitionist Charles Sumner. In season, you'll see gorgeous flowering trees and shrubs. Stop at the office or front gate to pick up brochures and a map or to rent the 60-minute audiotape tour ($5; a $12 deposit is required), which you can listen to in your car or on a portable tape player. The Friends of Mount Auburn Cemetery (☎ **617/864-9646**) conduct workshops and lectures, and coordinate walking tours. Call for topics, schedules, and fees. The cemetery is open daily from 8am to dusk; there is no admission charge. Animals and recreational activities such as jogging and picnicking are not allowed. MBTA bus routes no. 71 and 73 start at Harvard station and stop near the cemetery gates; they run frequently on weekdays, less often on weekends. By car (5 minutes) or on foot (30 minutes), take Mount Auburn Street or Brattle Street west from Harvard Square; just after they intersect, the gate is on the left.

Take a Walk (And Maybe Take in a Movie)

The **Esplanade** is the wide strip of public parkland on the south bank of the Charles River Basin, across Storrow Drive from the Back Bay. It makes a great place to stroll, watch ducks and sailboats, and absorb some culture. The **Hatch Shell,** an amphitheater best known for Fourth of July performances by the Boston Pops, is on the Esplanade (see chapter 19 for more information). **MBTA:** Red Line to Charles.

The Esplanade is part of the **Dr. Paul Dudley White Charles River Bike Path,** a 17.7-mile circuit (used by pedestrians, joggers, and in-line skaters as well as bikers) that begins near the Museum of Science and loops along both sides of the river to Watertown and back. You can enter and exit at many points along the way. Especially pleasant stretches are on the Cambridge side of the river near Harvard Square (**MBTA:** Red Line to Harvard) and Kendall Square (**MBTA:** Red Line to Kendall/MIT or Green Line to Lechmere).

Harborwalk, a theoretical loop of public waterfront property, is slowly becoming a reality as new development on the downtown waterfront includes legally mandated public access. From anywhere downtown or in the North End (the plan goes), you'll eventually be able to walk to and along the edge of the sea. Comfortable spots with seating and great views are on Long Wharf, on the other side of the Aquarium entrance, and off Commercial Street at the foot of Fleet Street. **MBTA:** Blue Line to Aquarium.

A Day at the Zoo

Kids The **Franklin Park Zoo** (☎ 617/541-LION; www.zoonewengland. com) is making a strong push to be included on any list of the country's best. Its population constantly becomes more diverse, and visitors get the gratifying feeling that the animals are as comfortable in their habitats as the humans are in theirs. If you're traveling with animal-mad youngsters, the Children's Zoo is both entertaining and educational. The big problem is that the northeast corner of Franklin Park isn't exactly downtown, so even if you're driving, expect to spend at least half a day. Admission is $6 for adults, $5 for seniors, $3 for children 2 to 15, free for children under 2. It's open April to September weekdays 10am to 5pm, weekends and holidays 10am to 6pm; October to March daily 10am to 4pm, and closed Thanksgiving and December 25. **MBTA:** Orange Line to Forest Hills, then bus no. 16 to the main entrance.

Thar She Blows! Whale Watching

Kids The waters off the coast of Massachusetts are prime whale-watching territory. **Stellwagen Bank,** which runs from Gloucester to Provincetown about 27 miles east of Boston, is a rich feeding ground. The most commonly sighted species in this area are baleen whales, the finback and the humpback, and you might also see minke whales and rare right whales. They often perform for their audience by jumping out of the water, and dolphins occasionally join the show. Trained naturalists come along to narrate and explain.

Once the novelty of putting out to sea is behind them, children tend not to be thrilled with the time it takes to reach the bank, which makes their reaction to a sighting all the more gratifying. This is not the most time- or cost-effective way to spend half a day, but it is an "only in New England" experience kids (and adults) will remember for a long time.

The New England Aquarium sponsors whale-watching expeditions (☎ 617/973-5277 or 617/973-5281 for reservations; www.neaq.org) daily from May through mid-October and on weekends in April and late October. Tickets (cash only) are $24 for adults, $19 for senior citizens and college students, $17.50 for children age 12 to 18, and $16.50 for children age 3 to 11. Children must be 3 years old and at least 30 inches tall. Reservations are recommended and can be held with a MasterCard or Visa.

Boston Harbor Whale Watch (☎ 617/345-9866; www.bostonwhale. com) promises more time watching whales than trying to find them. Tours depart from Rowes Wharf beginning in mid-June and operate Friday, Saturday, and Sunday only through June. From July through early September there's daily service. Departure times are 10am on weekdays, 9am and 2pm on weekends. Expect to spend about $4\frac{1}{2}$ hours at sea. Tickets are $20 for adults, $18 for seniors and children under 13. Reservations are suggested.

The following cruise companies also offer whale watches: **A.C. Cruise Line** (☎ 800/422-8419 or 617/261-6633); **Boston Harbor Cruises** (☎ 617/227-4321); and **Massachusetts Bay Lines** (☎ 617/542-8000).

The A-B-Seas

Whale-watchers should dress warmly, because it's much cooler at sea than in town, and wear rubber-soled shoes. Take sunglasses, sunscreen, a hat, and a camera with plenty of film. If you're prone to motion sickness, take appropriate precautions (ginger, crystallized or in ginger ale, can help alleviate nausea), because you'll be out on the open water.

A Vacation in the Islands

Majestic ocean views, hiking trails, historic sites, rocky beaches, nature walks, campsites, and picnic areas abound in New England. To find them all together, take a 45-minute trip east (yes, *east*) of Boston to the **Boston Harbor Islands** (☎ 617/727-7676). There are 30 islands in the Outer Harbor, and at least a half dozen are open for exploring, camping, or swimming. Bring a sweater or jacket. You can investigate on your own or take a ranger-led tour. Note that fresh water is not available on any of the islands.

Boston Harbor Cruises (☎ 617/227-4321) serves Georges Island from Long Wharf; the trip takes 45 minutes and tickets are $8 for adults, $7 for seniors, $6 for children under 12. Cruises depart at 10am, noon, and 2pm in the spring and fall, and daily on the hour from 10am to 4pm in the summer. Water taxis and admission to the islands are free. On **Georges Island** you'll find Fort Warren (1834), where Confederate prisoners were kept during the Civil War. The island has a visitor center, refreshment area, fishing pier, picnic area, and a wonderful view of Boston's skyline. From there, water taxis run to **Lovell, Gallops, Peddocks, Bumpkin,** and **Grape islands,** which have picnic areas and campsites. Lovell Island also has the remains of Fort Standish. For more information, stop at the **kiosk on Long Wharf** or try:

➤ The **Boston Harbor Islands National Recreation Area** Web site (www.nps.gov/boha/index.htm).

➤ The **Metropolitan District Commission** (☎ 617/727-5290; www.magnet.state.ma.us/mdc/harbor.htm), which administers Georges, Lovell, and Peddocks islands.

➤ The state **Department of Environmental Management** (☎ 617/740-1605), which oversees Gallops, Grape, and Bumpkin islands.

➤ The **Friends of the Boston Harbor Islands** (☎ 617/740-4290; www.tiac.net/users/fbhi).

On the Rocks: Ice-Skating

The skating rink at the Boston Common **Frog Pond** (☎ 617/635-2197), off Beacon Street, is a popular cold-weather destination. It's an open surface with an ice-making system and a clubhouse where you can rent skates for $5; admission is $3 for adults, free for children under 14. There's also skating at the lagoon at the **Public Garden,** but the surface depends on New England's capricious weather.

Wide World of Sports

Fans interested in Boston's well-deserved reputation as a great sports town may want to check out the **Sports Museum of New England** (☎ 617/624-1234; www. sportsmuseum.org), on the fifth and sixth levels of the **FleetCenter,** 150 Causeway St. The museum's collection of memorabilia, art, and interactive displays highlights the region's storied sports legacy. Admission is $5 for adults, $4 for seniors, students, and children 6 to 17. Hours (subject

Extra! Extra!

Check the calendar in chapter 1 for information on the Boston Marathon and the Head of the Charles rowing regatta.

to change during events) are Tuesday to Saturday 10am to 5pm and Sunday noon to 5pm. (**MBTA:** Green or Orange line to North Station.)

Take Me Out to the Ball Game

Kids No other experience in sports matches watching the **Red Sox** play at **Fenway Park,** which they do from April to early October (and later if they make the playoffs). The quirkiness of the oldest park in the major leagues (1912) and the fact that the team last won the World Series in 1918 only add to the mystique. If you're a baseball fan, you have to visit at least once.

Tickets go on sale in early December for the following season, and the earlier you order, the better chance you'll have of landing seats during your visit. Forced to choose between tickets for a low-numbered grandstand section (say, 10 or below) and less-expensive bleacher seats, go for the bleachers and the better view. The ticket office (☎ 617/267-8661 for information, or 617/267-1700 for tickets; www.redsox.com) is at 24 Yawkey Way, near the corner of Brookline Avenue. Games usually begin at 6 or 7pm on weeknights and 1pm on weekends. **MBTA:** Green Line B, C, or D to Kenmore or D to Fenway.

You can also take a **tour of Fenway Park,** which includes a walk on the warning track. From May to September, tours begin on weekdays only at 10am, 11am, noon, and 1pm, plus 2pm when the team is away. There are no tours on holidays or before day games. Admission is $5 for adults, $4 for seniors, $3 for children under 16. Call ☎ 617/236-6666 for more information.

Extra! Extra!

What if you didn't order Red Sox tickets in advance? Arrests for scalping tickets around Fenway Park are not unheard of, so watch out. Throughout the season, a limited number of standing-room tickets go on sale the day of the game, and there's always the possibility that tickets will be returned. It can't hurt to check, especially if the team isn't playing well. And this is another area where your concierge may be able to lend a hand.

Best of the Rest

The **Celtics** (www.bostonceltics.com) play at the FleetCenter from early October to April or May. Prices are as low as $10 for some games and top out at $70. If the team is playing terribly, you can sometimes buy a ticket or two for face value by asking around at one of the many bars in the area. **Bruins** (www.bostonbruins.com) tickets often sell out early despite being among the priciest in the league ($43 to $70).

For Celtics and Bruins information, call the FleetCenter (☎ **617/624-1000;** www.fleetcenter.com); for tickets, call Ticketmaster (☎ **617/931-2000;** www.ticketmaster.com).

The **New England Patriots** (☎ **800/543-1776;** www.patriots.com) play from August through December (or January if they make the playoffs) at Foxboro Stadium on Route 1, south of the city. You can catch a bus from South Station or the Green Line Riverside T station (call ☎ **800/23-LOGAN** for information). Tickets ($23 to $60) almost always sell out. Plan as far in advance as you can.

The **New England Revolution** (☎ **508/543-0350**) of Major League Soccer plays at Foxboro Stadium from April through July. Tickets are available through Ticketmaster.

Dollars & Sense

Kids College sports in Boston, especially hockey, are great fun and (usually) cheap. If you want to see a game, check the papers when you arrive and call to see if tickets are still available. Except for BC football and the occasional big rivalry or playoff race, there probably will be available tickets. The Division I schools are **Boston College** (☎ **617/552-3000**); **Boston University** (☎ **617/353-3838**); **Harvard University** (☎ **617/495-2211**); and **Northeastern University** (☎ **617/373-4700**).

Chapter 15

Charge It!
A Shopper's
Guide to
Boston

In This Chapter

➤ The biggest name and the other big names

➤ The top shopping areas

➤ Where to go for just the right thing

Boston the city represents a great blend of tradition and the cutting edge, and Boston the shopping destination does the same. Fine old names and mom-and-pop shops coexist, usually peacefully, with the big national and international chains. In this chapter, I'll assume that you have plenty of generic clothing, gift, and music stores in the mall at home—and that you'll recognize them if you see them here. The places you can only find in Boston and Cambridge will be in the spotlight. But don't worry about missing out on the big names, because I'll point you toward those, too.

Good News About Taxes

When was the last time you saw those words together? The Massachusetts sales tax is 5%, but it does not apply to clothing priced below $175 or to food. If you do buy something for $175 or more, only the amount over $175 is subject to sales tax.

How Soon Can I Start?

Most stores open at 9:30 or 10am and close at around 6 or 7pm (on Sunday, noon to 5 or 6pm). There are many exceptions, though: Shopping malls are open later, many art galleries open at 11am and are closed on Monday, and smaller, quirkier shops may keep odd hours. When in doubt, call ahead.

You Take the High Road: Shopping Strategies

This chapter directs you toward streets and neighborhoods, singling out particularly agreeable destinations, but that doesn't mean those are the only places worth checking out. Follow your nose (eyes, instincts, whatever). And please don't let me catch you saying anything like, "I don't know, honey. It says it's a GAP, but it's not in the book." Live a little—looking around is free.

Extra! Extra!

Most of the attractions listed in chapters 13 and 14 have excellent gift shops that sell unique items. Although they have a captive audience, that doesn't mean prices are inflated—most are pretty reasonable.

Discount Me In: Filene's Basement

This world-famous New England institution has kept savvy shoppers from paying retail since 1908. Far from passing off their finds as pricey indulgences, true devotees boast about their bargains. Here's how it works: After 2 weeks on the selling floor, merchandise is automatically marked down 25% from its already discounted price. The boards hanging from the ceiling tell the crucial dates; the original sale date is on the back of the price tag. Prices fall until, after 35 days, anything that hasn't sold, for 75% off, goes to charity. If just reading about it gets your juices flowing, you haven't lived until (true story) you've clipped the original $225 price tag off a silk dress and responded to the first person who offers a compliment by saying, "Oh, do you like it? It was $17."

Filene's Basement (which is no longer part of the Filene's department store chain) has branches throughout the Northeast and Midwest, but the automatic markdown policy applies only at the original store, which attracts 15,000 to 20,000 shoppers a day. The men's, women's, and children's merchandise ranges from head to toe, from utilitarian store-brand basics to designer evening wear, from bathing suits to business suits to anything else that looks promising to the store's eagle-eyed buyers.

Try to beat the lunchtime and weekend crowds, but if you can't, don't despair—just be patient. Filene's Basement (☎ 617/542-2011) is at 426 Washington St., at Summer Street. It's open weekdays 9:30am to 7:30pm, Saturday 9am to 7:30pm, and Sunday 11am to 7pm, with earlier opening times for some special sales; check newspaper ads for details. You can enter directly from the Downtown Crossing stop on the MBTA Red and Orange lines.

The Other Big Names

Maybe you have them at home, maybe you don't. They're all famous for a reason.

Brooks Brothers, 46 Newbury St., Back Bay (☎ 617/267-2600), and 75 State St., near Faneuil Hall Marketplace (☎ 617/261-9990). Beautifully made, traditional men's and women's clothing for preppies and would-be preppies.

Crate & Barrel, South Market Building, Faneuil Hall Marketplace (☎ 617/742-6025); Copley Place (☎ 617/536-9400); and 48 Brattle St., Harvard Square (☎ 617/876-6300). Contemporary and classic housewares and home accessories—this is wedding present central. The store at 1045 Mass. Ave., Cambridge (☎ 617/547-3994), carries only furniture and home accessories.

Kids **The Disney Store,** North Market Building, Faneuil Hall Marketplace (☎ 617/248-3900); Copley Place (☎ 617/266-5200); and CambridgeSide Galleria, Cambridge (☎ 617/577-8833). The walls have ears. And T-shirts, and knickknacks . . .

Kids **FAO Schwarz,** 440 Boylston St., at Berkeley Street, Back Bay (☎ 617/262-5900). A delightful branch of the legendary New York toy emporium.

Filene's, 426 Washington St., at Summer Street, Downtown Crossing (☎ 617/357-2100), and CambridgeSide Galleria, Cambridge (☎ 617/621-3800). Not Filene's Basement—a full-service department store, with all the usual offerings.

Lord & Taylor, 760 Boylston St., adjacent to the Prudential Center, Back Bay (☎ 617/262-6000). Another big New York name, with especially good end-of-season sales on men's and women's clothing and accessories.

Macy's, 450 Washington St., at Summer Street, Downtown Crossing (☎ 617/357-3000). *The* big New York name.

Neiman Marcus, Copley Place (☎ 617/536-3660). Texas-size prices for the trappings of true luxury. Great cosmetics department.

Kids **Newbury Comics,** 332 Newbury St., Back Bay (☎ 617/236-4930); 1 Washington Mall, Washington Street off State Street, Downtown Crossing (☎ 617/248-9992); and 36 John F. Kennedy St., in the Garage mall, Harvard Square (☎ 617/491-0337). The latest CDs (with lots of independent labels and imports), tapes, posters, T-shirts, and, of course, comics.

Saks Fifth Avenue, Shops at Prudential Center, Back Bay (☎ 617/262-8500). The high end of the high-end New York department stores.

Tiffany & Co., Copley Place (☎ 617/353-0222). Beautiful window displays, impeccable service, and cool boxes.

Kids **Tower Records,** 360 Newbury St., at Mass. Ave., Back Bay (☎ 617/247-5900), and 95 Mount Auburn St., at John F. Kennedy Street, Harvard Square (☎ 617/876-3377). Records, tapes, CDs, videos, periodicals, and books of every description. The Back Bay location is one of the largest record stores in the country.

Kids **Urban Outfitters,** 361 Newbury St., at Mass. Ave., Back Bay (☎ 617/236-0088), and 11 John F. Kennedy St., Harvard Square (☎ 617/864-0070). Funky, trendy clothing and home accessories. Just the thing if you are a teenager or want to dress like one.

Boston Shopping

0 _____ .5 mi
0 _____ .8 km

Caswell-Massey **19**
Chanel **34**
Copley Place **19**
Crate & Barrel **19**
Dairy Fresh Candies **21**
Disney Store **19**
Faneuil Hall Marketplace **22**
FAO Schwartz **35**
Filene's **32**
Filene's Basement **32**
Gargoyles, Grotesques
  & Chimeras **6**
Globe Corner Bookstore **13**
Gucci **19**
Haley & Steele **11**
Helen's Leather Shop **25**
Hermès of Paris **38**
J. Oliver's **26**
J. Pace & Son **20**
John Lewis, Inc. **10**

Koo De Kir **27**
La Ruche **9**
Loehmann's **31**
Lord & Taylor **14**
Macy's **33**
Museum of Fine Arts
  Gift Shop **19**
Neiman Marcus **17**
Newbury Comics **4**
Saks Fifth Avenue **15**
Shop at the Union **36**
Shops at Prudential Center **16**
Shreve, Crump & Low **37**
Society of Arts & Crafts **7**
Tiffany & Co. **18**
Tower Records **3**
Treasured Legacy **19**
Urban Outfitters **1**
Waterstone's Booksellers **8**

Avenue Victor Hugo
  Bookshop **5**
Barnes & Noble **29**
Beadworks **2**
Borders **28**
Boston Antiques Cooperative
  I&II **24**
Boston City Store **23**
Brattle Book Store **30**
Brooks Brothers **12**

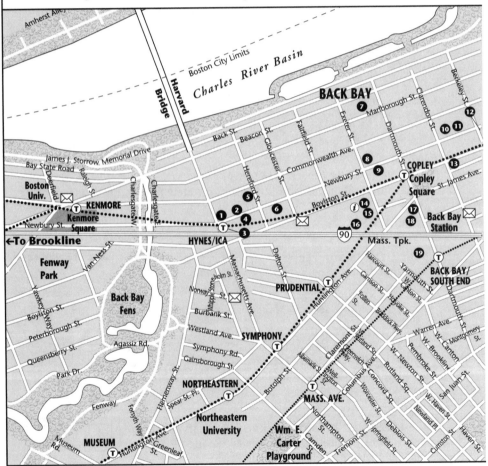

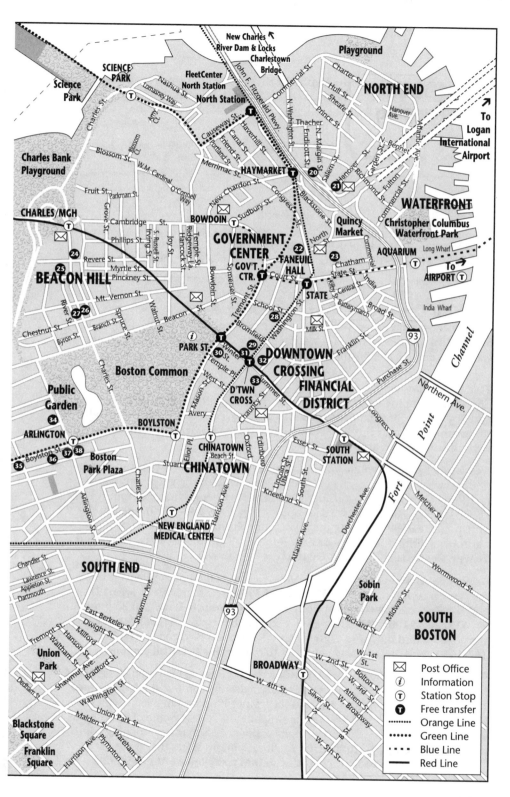

Kids **Warner Bros. Studio Store,** North Market Building, Faneuil Hall Marketplace (☎ **617/227-1101**), and the Shops at Prudential Center (☎ **617/859-3770**). Like the Disney Store, with different cartoons.

Art Beat

The **Museum of Fine Arts** has well-stocked off-premises gift shops at Copley Place (☎ **617/536-8818**) and in the South Market Building at Faneuil Hall Marketplace (☎ **617/720-1266**). Maybe you'll even be inspired to see the real thing.

Till You Drop: The Top Shopping Areas

Make sure you have your wallet (or a checkbook and two forms of ID). The areas below are all excellent for walking around, window-shopping, people-watching, and budget-busting.

The Back Bay

The main shopping streets are Newbury from Arlington Street to Mass. Ave., and Boylston from Charles Street south to Gloucester Street. A (very rough) rule of thumb is that the closer you are to the Public Garden, the more expensive the stores are.

Newbury Street is where you'll find many of the city's best art galleries (see below), often above street level. To get a sense of the geography of this boutique-intensive strip, consider the shops at either end: across from the Public Garden, **Burberrys,** 2 Newbury St. (☎ **617/236-1000**), the posh British raincoat and clothing purveyor, and **Chanel,** in the lobby of the Ritz-Carlton, 15 Arlington St. (☎ **617/859-0055**). Eight blocks away, you'll find **Tower Records** and **Urban Outfitters** (see above).

On **Boylston Street** opposite the Public Garden is the upscale Heritage on the Garden complex, home to **Hermès of Paris,** 22 Arlington St. (☎ **617/ 482-8707**). It's across the street from **Shreve, Crump & Low,** 330 Boylston St. (☎ **617/267-9100**), the oldest jewelry store in the country (1796). Six blocks along, you'll find the **Mass. Army Navy Store,** 895 Boylston St. (☎ **617/ 267-1559**), and one of many entrances to a sprawling two-mall complex.

Skybridges connect the **Shops at Prudential Center,** 800 Boylston St. (☎ **800/ SHOP-PRU** or 617/267-1002; www.prudentialcenter.com), and **Copley Place,** 100 Huntington Ave. (☎ **617/375-4400**). Since it opened in 1985, Copley Place has set the standard for upscale shopping in Boston. Some of its 100-plus shops will be familiar, but this is emphatically not a suburban shopping complex that happens to be in the city. You'll see famous stores that don't have another branch in Boston, such as **Caswell-Massey** (☎ **617/437-9292**),

Gucci (☎ 617/247-3000), **Joan & David** (☎ 617/536-0600), **Liz Claiborne** (☎ 617/859-3787), **Louis Vuitton** (☎ 617/437-6519), and **Polo Ralph Lauren** (☎ 617/266-4121). On ground level at Dartmouth Street is **Treasured Legacy** (☎ 617/424-8717), a small store packed with African American art, African sculpture and textiles, art books, and general-interest titles. The complex also has a handful of restaurants, including a branch of **Legal Sea Foods** (☎ 617/266-7775), but no food court. (**MBTA:** Orange Line to Back Bay, or Green Line to Copley and walk 2 blocks.)

The **Shops at Prudential Center** have a food court, a "fashion court," pushcarts loaded with souvenirs and accessories, a post office, more than 40 shops and boutiques, and five restaurants, including another **Legal Sea Foods** (☎ 617/266-6800). There's outdoor space in front and back if you need some fresh air. (**MBTA:** Green Line E to Prudential, or Green Line to Copley and walk 3 blocks.)

Faneuil Hall Marketplace

The busiest attraction in Boston is consumer catnip, packed with shops, boutiques, and pushcarts that sell everything from rubber stamps to costume jewelry, flowers to souvenirs. It has plenty of chain stores (see above), but be sure to browse the pushcarts and shops on the second floor for the quirky items that say you actually went somewhere on your vacation. The **Marketplace** (☎ 617/338-2323) is between North, Congress, and State streets and I-93. (**MBTA:** Green or Blue line to Government Center or Orange Line to Haymarket.)

City Planning

Possibly the wackiest shop in town (a crowded category) is the **Boston City Store** (☎ 617/635-2911), on the lower level of Faneuil Hall. It sells the equivalent of the contents of the municipal attic and basement, from old street signs (look for your name) to used office equipment and furniture. The selection changes regularly according to what's outlived its usefulness or been declared surplus, but you'll always find lucky horseshoes from the mounted police for $5

Charles Street

This is one of Beacon Hill's two commercial streets (Cambridge is the other). The picturesque stretch from Cambridge Street to Beacon Street has many antique shops, gift shops, and cafes. Because it's a landmark district, it also has entertaining zoning laws—you've never seen a 7-Eleven that looks this classy. Antique fanciers who are short on time will at least want to peruse the wide-ranging stock at **Boston Antique Cooperative I & II,** 119 Charles St.

(☎ 617/227-9810 or 617/227-9811). Real antique hounds will want to spend a couple of hours prowling around. And if you really like cowboy boots (go figure), **Helen's Leather Shop,** 110 Charles St. (☎ **617/742-2077**), is the place to go.

Downtown Crossing
The heart of Downtown Crossing is the traffic-free (more or less) pedestrian mall along Washington, Winter, and Summer streets. It's home to **Filene's Basement** and two major department stores: **Filene's** and **Macy's** (see above). This area is also packed with smaller clothing and shoe stores, food and merchandise pushcarts, and two big chain bookstores (**Barnes & Noble** and **Borders**). And if Filene's Basement doesn't do it for you, there's a branch of the New York discount legend **Loehmann's** at 387 Washington St. (☎ **617/338-7177**).

The North End
The North End is *the* place for Italian groceries, and it has a retail surprise in store, too. There's an especially good selection of imported olive oils and other foodstuffs at **J. Pace & Son,** 42 Cross St. (☎ **617/227-9673**). Around the corner, satisfy your sweet tooth at **Dairy Fresh Candies,** 57 Salem St. (☎ **800/336-5536** or 617/742-2639). Then go left on Cooper Street and take the first right to reach the **Nostalgia Factory,** 51 North Margin St. (☎ **800/479-8754** or 617/720-2211; www.nostalgia.com). Its collection of old advertising, original movie posters, vintage war and travel posters, and political memorabilia must be seen to be believed.

Cambridge
Harvard Square, with its bookstores, boutiques, and T-shirt shops, has a mix of national and regional outlets as well as independent retailers. It has an especially good selection of bookstores (see below) and innumerable specialty shops. Be sure to check out the window displays at **Kids Calliope,** 33 Brattle St. (☎ **617/876-4149**), an excellent children's clothing and toy store. And if your favorite fragrance is hard to find, **Colonial Drug,** 49 Brattle St. (☎ **617/864-2222**), carries an encyclopedic selection of perfume.

A walk along shop-lined **Mass. Ave.** in either direction to the next T stop will take a well-spent hour or so. The stretch from Harvard Square north to **Porter Square** is more upscale; southeast toward **Central Square,** funkier and less commercially dense.

In East Cambridge, the **CambridgeSide Galleria** (100 CambridgeSide Place; ☎ **617/621-8666**) is a three-level mall with more than 100 specialty stores. You'll find the usual suspects, plus catalog titan **J. Crew** (☎ **617/225-2739**), three restaurants, and a food court that opens onto an outdoor plaza next to a canal. It's convenient if your brain hurts after a few hours at the Museum of Science, 3 blocks away. (**MBTA:** Green Line to Lechmere and walk 2 blocks, or Red Line to Kendall/MIT, then the free shuttle bus, which runs every 10 to 20 minutes Monday to Saturday from 10am to 9:30pm and Sunday from 11am to 7pm).

Unselfish Shellfish

The following businesses will ship a top-quality live lobster overnight (and make someone at home very happy):

➤ Bay State Lobster, 379–395 Commercial St. ☎ **617/523-7960.**

➤ James Hook & Co., 15 Northern Ave., at Atlantic Avenue. ☎ **617/423-5500.**

➤ Legal Sea Foods Fresh by Mail, Logan Airport Terminal C. ☎ **800/477-5342** or 617/569-4622.

But I Only Want . . .

Here's where to go for that one special whatchamacallit that will make your vacation (if not your life) complete.

. . . A Piece of Art

Newbury Street is art central. You'll find an infinite variety of styles and media in its dozens of galleries, where browsers and questions are welcome. I'll tip you off to a few of my favorites if you promise to walk around and explore.

Working east to west: **Barbara Krakow Gallery,** 10 Newbury St., fifth floor (☎ **617/262-4490**); **Alpha Gallery,** 14 Newbury St., second floor (☎ **617/536-4465**); **Robert Klein Gallery,** 38 Newbury St., fourth floor (☎ **617/267-7997**); **Gallery NAGA,** 67 Newbury St. (☎ **617/267-9060**); **Haley & Steele,** 91 Newbury St. (☎ **617/536-6339**); **Pucker Gallery,** 171 Newbury St. (☎ **617/267-9473**); **Nielsen Gallery,** 179 Newbury St. (☎ **617/266-4835**); and **Vose Galleries of Boston**, 238 Newbury St. (☎ **617/536-6176**).

Not really a gallery but not to be missed is **Gargoyles, Grotesques & Chimeras,** 262 Newbury St. (☎ **617/536-2362**), which stocks home accessories, photographs, and, yes, gargoyles.

. . . The Perfect Book

Wow, have you ever come to the right place. **Harvard Square** is to books as Newbury Street is to art, and several stores in Boston are so good you may not feel the need to cross the river. At all of these stores, budget browsing time and stick to it, or you may never go anywhere else.

Near Downtown Crossing you'll find the **Brattle Book Store,** 9 West St., off Washington Street (☎ **800/447-9595** or 617/542-0210). It buys and sells used, rare, and out-of-print titles. Be sure to check the outdoor carts. In the Back Bay, **Avenue Victor Hugo Bookshop,** 339 Newbury St., near Hereford Street (☎ **617/266-7746**), buys, sells, and trades new and used books and estate libraries. The selections of periodicals and general fiction are immense. **Waterstone's Booksellers** is a British chain, with large branches off Newbury Street at 26 Exeter St. (☎ 617/859-7300) and in the Upper Rotunda of Quincy Market (☎ 617/589-0930). A small local chain with a huge selection is the **Globe Corner Bookstore** (offspring of the dear departed original on the Freedom Trail). It sells travel guides and essays, atlases, globes, maps, and nautical charts in the Back Bay at 500 Boylston St., at Clarendon Street (☎ 617/859-8008), and at 28 Church St. (☎ 617/497-6277) in Harvard Square.

Ah, Harvard Square. Walk in any direction and you'll find somebody specializing in something. For example, **Grolier Poetry Book Shop**, at 6 Plympton St., off Mass. Ave. (☎ 617/547-4648), sells only poetry; **Revolution Books**, 1156 Mass. Ave. (☎ 617/492-5443), will raise your political consciousness; and **Schoenhof's Foreign Books**, 76A Mt. Auburn St. (☎ 617/547-8855; www.schoenhofs.com) is a veritable United Nations of books and dictionaries.

There are also two world-class general-interest bookstores:

WordsWorth Books, 30 Brattle St. (☎ 800/899-2202 or 617/354-5201; www.wordsworth.com), where everything except textbooks is discounted at least 10%; and the **Harvard Book Store**, 1256 Mass. Ave., at Plympton Street (☎ 800/542-READ outside 617, or 617/661-1515; www.harvard.com), which has a basement full of remainders and used books.

🧒 WordsWorth's excellent children's selection is up the street at **Curious George Goes to WordsWorth**, 1 John F. Kennedy St. (☎ 617/498-0062).

. . . One Perfect Piece of Jewelry

My favorite jewelry boutique is **John Lewis, Inc.,** 97 Newbury St. (☎ 617/266-6665), a museumlike shop with beautifully crafted (on the premises, no less) pieces to suit both traditional and trendy tastes. Also in the Back Bay, visit the **Society of Arts and Crafts**, 175 Newbury St. (☎ 617/266-1810), and the **Artful Hand Gallery**, Copley Place (☎ 617/262-9601). On the Freedom Trail in the North End, **High Gear**, 139 Richmond St. (☎ 617/523-5804), sells costume jewelry at wholesale prices. The jewelry at 🧒 **Beadworks** will suit you exactly—you make it yourself using your choice of the dazzling variety of raw materials. There are shops at 349 Newbury St. (☎ 617/247-7227) and in Harvard Square at 23 Church St. (☎ 617/868-9777).

. . . A Housewarming Gift

This is a tiny selection of the knickknack emporia you'll find in every neighborhood already mentioned:

In the Back Bay, the **Shop at the Union**, 356 Boylston St., off Arlington Street (☎ 617/536-5651); **La Ruche**, 168 Newbury St., off Exeter Street (☎ 617/536-6366); and **Restoration Hardware**, 711 Boylston St., at Exeter Street (☎ 617/578-0088; www.restorationhardware.com).

On Beacon Hill, **Koo De Kir,** 34 Charles St. (☎ **617/723-8111**), and **J. Oliver's,** 38 Charles St. (☎ **617/723-3388**).

In Cambridge, **Joie de Vivre,** 1792 Mass. Ave., outside Porter Square (☎ **617/864-8188**); and **Bowl & Board,** 1063 Mass. Ave. (☎ **617/661-0350**); and ~~Kids~~ **The Games People Play,** 1100 Mass. Ave. (☎ **800/696-0711** or 617/492-0711), both outside Harvard Square.

. . . A College Sweatshirt

Or T-shirt, or key chain, or stuffed animal, or bumper sticker. Harvard is the big name, but why do the obvious? Most of the following also sell course books, if you're curious.

The **Boston University Bookstore,** 660 Beacon St., Kenmore Square (☎ **617/267-8484**); the **Emerson College Book Store,** 80 Boylston St., near Downtown Crossing (☎ **617/728-7700**); the **MIT Coop,** 3 Cambridge Center, Kendall Square (☎ **617/499-3200**) and 84 Mass. Ave. (☎ **617/499-2000**); the **Northeastern University Bookstore,** 360 Huntington Ave., between Symphony Hall and the Museum of Fine Arts (☎ **617/373-2286**); and the **Suffolk University Bookstore,** 148 Cambridge St., Beacon Hill (☎ **617/227-4085**). For Harvard merchandise, try the **Harvard Coop,** 1400 Mass. Ave. (☎ **617/499-2000**); the **Harvard Shop,** 52 John F. Kennedy St. (☎ **617/864-3000**); and **J. August & Co.,** 1320 Mass. Ave. (☎ **617/864-6650**).

Chapter 16

Battle Plans for Seeing the Sights: Six Great Itineraries

In This Chapter

➤ Six easy-to-follow itineraries

➤ Tips on when to go, what to see, and where to eat

Whew! That was a lot of information. If you're like a lot of people, you've been flipping through the last four chapters and wondering how you'll ever fit in everything you want to see and do. That's the feeling that prompts many people to join guided tours. If you don't want to go that route, or if you already have and you want to learn more, this chapter and the next are for you.

The attitude *not* to take is the one that makes people list every little thing they've ever read about, then set out to see it all, in alphabetical order. Equally unfulfilling is seeing things just because you think you should. Yes, you can shuffle along the Freedom Trail in lockstep, never lifting your head from your map. The vacation that starts like that ends with you back at the office and the kids back at school saying, "It was okay, I guess."

After all my preaching about being flexible and taking time to explore, I'm certainly not about to suggest that you race through every itinerary with no regard for what's going on around you. If you stumble upon a street fair but you're supposed to be at the Old North Church before it closes, chat with yourself (not out loud, please) or your companions. Just the fact that you're using the word *supposed* will probably help you decide what to do.

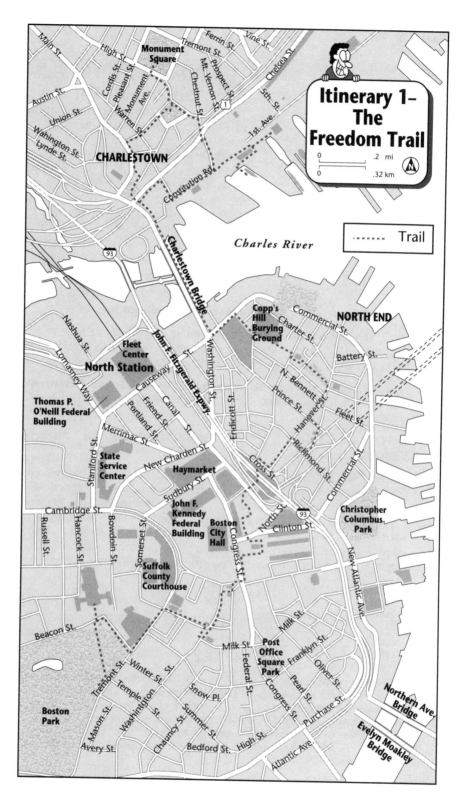

Itinerary 1–
The
Freedom Trail

0 .... .2 mi
0 .... .32 km

⋯⋯⋯ Trail

Charles River

CHARLESTOWN

NORTH END

Copp's
Hill
Burying
Ground

Fleet
Center
North Station

Thomas P.
O'Neill Federal
Building

State
Service
Center

Haymarket

John F.
Kennedy
Federal
Building

Boston
City
Hall

Christopher
Columbus
Park

Suffolk
County
Courthouse

Post
Office
Square
Park

Boston
Park

Monument
Square

Dollars & Sense

Depending on what you schedule, an **Arts/Boston coupon book** or a **CityPass** can save a ton of money. See chapter 12.

Itinerary 1: The Full-Out Freedom Trail

You've probably already noticed that the first half of chapter 13 is an itinerary in itself. At the risk of getting us both struck by lightning, I'll say again: You don't have to go in order, you don't have to scrutinize every little thing, you don't even have to (gasp!) go everywhere. But, it's fun and informative, it's efficient, and just about every stop is chock-full of thought-provoking conversation pieces. The whole trail takes at least 2 hours, and that's if you don't linger anywhere. Some pointers:

1. You can't tour the **Massachusetts State House** on Sunday.

2. **Park Street Church** is open to the public only from late June to August (but the plaques at the entrance offer a billboard's worth of information).

3. The **Old South Meeting House** is a block from **Filene's Basement.** Don't buy more than you can carry comfortably unless your hotel is close by.

4. The **Old State House** is opposite the National Park Service's excellent Visitor Center at 15 State St.

5. **Faneuil Hall Marketplace** makes a convenient place to pause or even to break the Freedom Trail into two chunks. You can buy take-out food at any time of day, and there are many sit-down restaurants, too. **Durgin-Park** is the logical choice for classic New England fare. The Marketplace makes a good jumping-off point for a visit to the Waterfront (see below). Just a reminder: If you're continuing on the Freedom Trail from here, use the rest rooms before you set out.

Take Five

From Faneuil Hall Marketplace, it's a short walk to **Christopher Columbus Park** and the **plaza at the end of Long Wharf.** Both are pleasant places to bring a snack or sandwich and watch the boats that keep the harbor hopping. Cross Atlantic Avenue toward the New England Aquarium and the Marriott Long Wharf. The wharf (between the two) ends in a well-situated brick plaza. The park, to the left of the hotel, offers plenty of shade, playground equipment, and benches.

6. **Hanover Street**'s plethora of cafes makes it another fine stopping place. In case you missed them in chapter 11, my favorite spots for coffee and a sweet include **Caffè Graffiti,** 307 Hanover St.; **Caffè dello Sport,** 308 Hanover St.; **Caffè Vittoria,** 296 Hanover St.; and **Mike's Pastry,** 300 Hanover St.

7. Across Charter Street from **Copp's Hill Burying Ground** is a small park—another good place to rest your feet before the trip to Charlestown.

8. The MBTA runs a ferry that will return you to Long Wharf from the Charlestown Navy Yard and give you a great view of the Inner Harbor.

History 101

From the Old State House, State Street runs about half a mile down to the end of Long Wharf. Block out the office towers and try to picture it 200 or so years ago. It was even longer, jam-packed on either side with wharves and warehouses, merchants and mariners—the backbone of colonial and postrevolutionary Boston.

Itinerary 2: On the Waterfront

The Big Dig is nobody's idea of attractive, but its final goal is important: to reunite downtown Boston with the harbor. Meanwhile, if you or anyone else in your group had (or has) a childhood fixation on Tonka trucks, welcome to paradise. Build some extra time into your schedule to check out the equipment. Once you cross the construction site, you'll find at least half a day's (and as much as a full day's) worth of attractions in an easily manageable area.

If you're splitting up the Freedom Trail, this itinerary fits neatly after the first half and lunch at Faneuil Hall Marketplace. With the second half, it can go before or after (take the MBTA ferry from the Charlestown Navy Yard to Long Wharf). Or work backward through the second half (beginning in Charlestown), then visit the Waterfront.

1. Start at the **New England Aquarium.** It opens at 9am, if this is your morning agenda. Early risers will find plenty of seating in the surrounding harbor-front areas—perfect places to relax with a cup of coffee before plunging in.

2. If you want to take a **sightseeing cruise,** you can do so from Long Wharf (turn right as you leave the Aquarium) or Rowes Wharf (turn left and walk about 5 minutes along the shoreline). Or skip the cruise and head for Museum Wharf.

3. From Rowes Wharf, **Museum Wharf** is about 10 minutes away. Continue along the water, cross the Fort Point Channel on the New Northern Avenue Bridge, and turn right; or follow Atlantic Avenue another block to Congress Street and turn left. You'll soon come to:

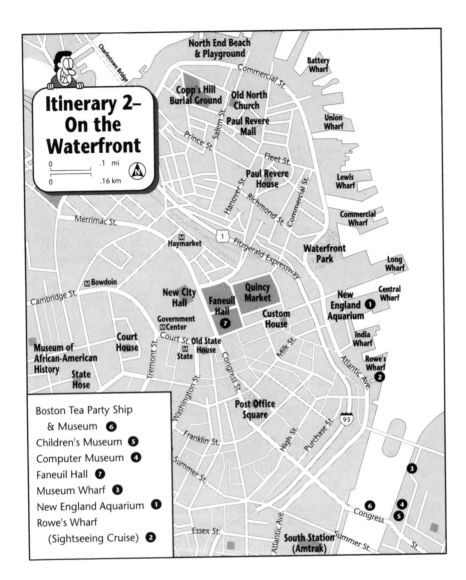

Itinerary 2—
On the Waterfront

0   .1 mi
0   .16 km

North End Beach
& Playground

Charlestown Bridge

Commercial St.

Battery
Wharf

Copp's Hill
Burial Ground

Old North
Church

Union
Wharf

Salem St.

Paul Revere
Mall

Prince St.

Fleet St.

Lewis
Wharf

Paul Revere
House

Hanover St.

Richmond St.

Commercial St.

Commercial
Wharf

Merrimac St.

M Haymarket

1

Fitzgerald Expressway

Waterfront
Park

Long
Wharf

M Bowdoin

New City
Hall

Quincy
Market

New
England
Aquarium ❶

Central
Wharf

Cambridge St.

Faneuil
Hall
❼

Custom
House

Government
M Center

Court
House

Court St.

Old State
House

India
Wharf

Tremont St.

M State

Congress St.

Milk St.

Atlantic Ave.

Rowe's
Wharf
❷

Museum of
African-American
History

State
Hose

Washington St.

Post Office
Square

93

Boston Tea Party Ship
& Museum ❻

Children's Museum ❺

Computer Museum ❹

Faneuil Hall ❼

Museum Wharf ❸

New England Aquarium ❶

Rowe's Wharf
(Sightseeing Cruise) ❷

Franklin St.

Summer St.

Essex St.

High St.

Purchase St.

Atlantic Ave.

South Station
(Amtrak)

Summer St.

St.

❸

❻

❹

❺

Congress

4. The **Computer Museum.**

5. The **Children's Museum.**

6. The **Boston Tea Party Ship & Museum.**

   (These are mix-and-match attractions; you probably won't have the time (or the patience) to do justice to all three. Work this out with your group in advance.)

7. From Museum Wharf, your inclination might be to head back toward downtown. **Faneuil Hall Marketplace** makes a good place to regroup, and don't forget that there's a little restaurant row on Northern Avenue just past the World Trade Center. It's about a 15-minute walk past uninspired scenery, but the **Daily Catch** and **Jimbo's Fish Shanty** are worth a trek.

214

Kids **Itinerary 3: Kidding Around**

You know your kids, and I don't, but we both know what travel and unfamiliar surroundings can lead to: that winning combination of overwhelmed and "I'm bored." This 1-day itinerary allows you to combine attractions with down time in whatever proportions work for your family. Hang on to the leftover breakfast bagels; you'll need them later. And note that the full itinerary works only when the Boston Duck Tours (April to November) and the swan boats (late April to September) are operating.

1. Start with a **Boston Duck Tour.** The ticket booth, in the Prudential Center, opens no later than 9am. (If you're *really* organized, a limited

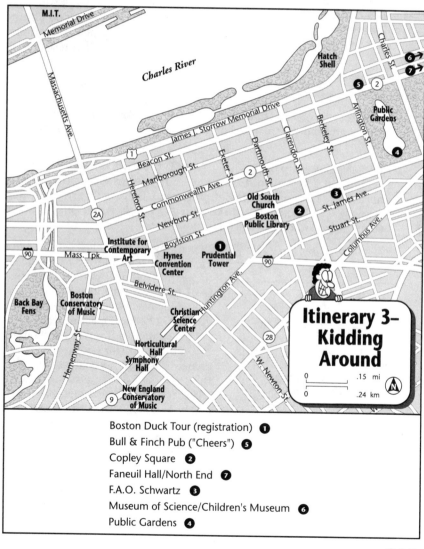

Boston Duck Tour (registration) **1**

Bull & Finch Pub ("Cheers") **5**

Copley Square **2**

Faneuil Hall/North End **7**

F.A.O. Schwartz **3**

Museum of Science/Children's Museum **6**

Public Gardens **4**

Take Five

If you have just a little time to kill before your Duck Tour, the Prudential Center offers lots to look at. If you'd rather get outdoors (and away from the consumerism), the **Christian Science Center reflecting pool** is across the street from the Duck Tour pick-up area.

number of tickets go on sale 2 days in advance.) Tickets are timed; if your tour isn't leaving right away, you can explore a bit of the Back Bay (see stops 2 through 4). Or take the Duck Tour, then head out.

2. Exit the Prudential Center onto Boylston Street and turn right. Three blocks up is Copley Square, where you'll find ***The Tortoise and Hare at Copley Square,*** a two-piece sculpture by Nancy Schön. It's not as prominent as another Schön work we'll get to shortly, but it makes a good photo backdrop and resting place. Continue on Boylston Street until you see a giant teddy bear (2 blocks).

3. **F.A.O. Schwarz** is great for window-shopping. You might try telling the kids this toy store is actually a toy museum, but agreeing on a budget (of time and money) beforehand is probably a better way to keep the peace.

4. Another 2 blocks up on Boylston Street is the **Public Garden.** Here you'll find the **swan boats,** along with live swans, ducks, and geese. This is why you brought that leftover bread. Diagonally across the park from where you entered is ***Make Way for Ducklings,*** Nancy Schön's better-known kid-oriented sculpture.

Tourist Traps

A 1-day tour, whether on a trolley or a bus, is a deal only if it covers everything you want to do and not too much that you don't. If you're not using the tour to cover a lot of ground in 1 day, it's probably cheaper to walk or take public transportation (or even cabs) from place to place.

5. Depending on your kids' ages and how much TV they're allowed to watch, they (and you) may want to visit the **Bull & Finch Pub,** better known as the *Cheers* bar. It's at 84 Beacon St. (☎ **617/227-9605**), across from the Public Garden, and serves good burgers in a rather tourist-intensive atmosphere. It does *not* look like the set of the TV show. You can also backtrack 2 blocks on Boylston Street, turn left and walk 2½ blocks to the **Hard Rock Cafe,** 131 Clarendon St. (☎ **617/424-ROCK**), which offers above-average food and souvenirs.

6. The next step depends on the ages of the children. If the **Children's Museum** sounded like just the thing, ride the MBTA Green Line to Park

Street, transfer to the Red Line, and head to South Station. If the kids are older, take the Green Line to Science Park and spend most of the afternoon at the **Museum of Science.** You can also see a show at the Mugar Omni Theatre.

7. Let the kids decide where to have dinner. A trip to the **North End** might be fun, or they may prefer to check out the cornucopia of offerings at **Faneuil Hall Marketplace.** Both are convenient to the afternoon museums, and both involve a fair amount of the walking that makes bedtime so much less of a struggle.

Itinerary 4: Art Appreciation

Boston is a great art destination, whether you want to look at it or buy it. This 1-day itinerary combines opportunities to do both. Depending on what's going on at the museums, you may want to spend more time at one or the other, and if a special exhibit is up, you may have a timed ticket. Remember that these pieces fit together in several ways. *Note:* To locate the stops on this tour, refer to the "Boston Attractions" map on page 172.

1. Start at the **Museum of Fine Arts (MFA).** It opens at 10am, and you can take a tour at 10:30am. Or just grab a floor plan and explore on your own. There's no way for me to enumerate or exaggerate the pleasures of this museum; if you have the time, you can easily spend a day here. But you probably don't, so try to go in with some idea of what you want to concentrate on.

2. The **Isabella Stuart Gardner Museum** is about 2 blocks away. The Gardner is to the MFA as a boutique is to a department store, and the architecture and greenery are as enjoyable as the art. But it's not for everyone (I have a friend who doesn't care for representational art and won't visit with me even if I pay). If you think it's not for you, spend more time at the MFA.

3. Both museums serve food. The Gardner has a small **cafe;** the MFA has a **cafeteria,** a **cafe,** and a fine **restaurant** (you'll probably need a reservation). If you can hold off for a couple of hours, **afternoon tea** at a downtown hotel makes a mood-setting prelude for stop 4. (You can also skip stop 4.)

4. **Newbury Street** is art gallery central. Take the MBTA Green Line from Museum to Arlington or Copley, walk 1 block over, and feast your eyes. Don't forget to look above the first floor. And don't forget that the antique shops of **Charles Street** are just across the Public Garden.

Performing Arts

A possible detour: On Friday afternoon during the season, the Boston Symphony Orchestra performs at Symphony Hall, 10 minutes from the MFA on Huntington Avenue. A limited number of rush (same-day, one per person) tickets go on sale at 9am.

5. If you have the time or inclination, any one of the **historic houses** listed in chapter 14 allows you to make good use of an hour or so. And all are close enough to Newbury and Charles streets that if you change your mind about that limited-edition print, you can swing by afterward and pick it up.

Itinerary 5: Cambridge for Beginners

You'll barely scratch the surface of Cambridge in half a day, but don't kid yourself: You haven't exactly seen every corner of Boston, either. You can start the day in Harvard Square and spend the morning before heading to Lexington or Concord (see part 7). This itinerary easily stretches to fill a day.

1. Start in Harvard Square.

2. It's adjacent to Harvard Yard. You can stop in at the university's Events & Information Center for a tour or a pamphlet, or just wander through on your way to the museums. The area surrounding the John Harvard Statue is the original campus, known as the "Old Yard." On the other side of University Hall (the building behind the statue), still in the Yard, is Tercentenary Theater, which got its name from the 300th-anniversary celebration in 1936.

Pssst!

With your back to Memorial Church and Widener Library in front of you, turn left and mount the steps of Sever Hall. The work of architect H. H. Richardson (who's better known for Boston's Trinity Church), it has a "whispering gallery." Stand on one side of the entrance arch, station a friend or willing passerby on the opposite side, and speak softly. Someone standing next to you can't hear what you say, but the person at the other side of the arch can.

3. On the far side of the Yard, Quincy Street is where you'll find the **university art museums.**

4. The **natural history museums** are nearby. Turn left when you leave the Yard, and cross Broadway, Cambridge Street, and Kirkland Street. Turn left, the right for the Peabody Museum; right, then left to reach Oxford Street and the Museum of Natural History.

5. Harvard Square offers more dining options than you could sample in a month. **Bartley's Burger Cottage** is always a fun choice. A good stop for takeout is **Stuff-Its**, 8½ Eliot St. (☎ **617/497-2220**), which has been making what are now known as "wraps" for years.

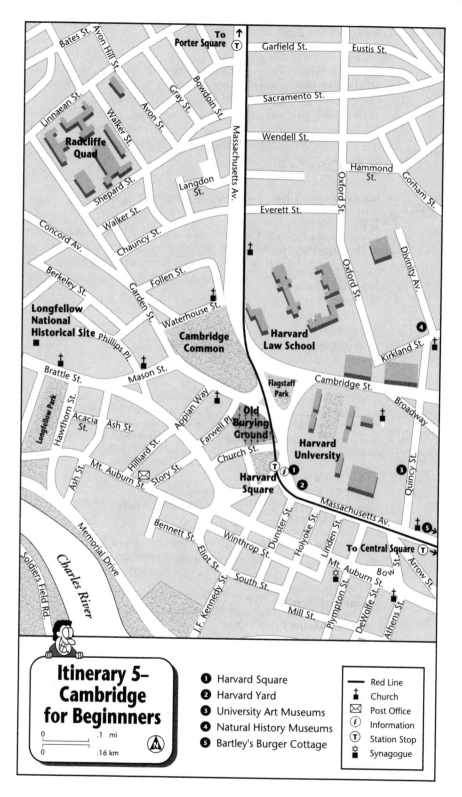

Bates St.   Avon Hill St.   Linnaean St.

To Porter Square (T)

Garfield St.   Eustis St.

Bowdoin St.   Gray St.   Avon St.   Walker St.

Sacramento St.

Wendell St.

Radcliffe Quad

Shepard St.

Langdon St.

Massachusetts Av.

Hammond St.   Oxford St.   Corham St.

Walker St.

Everett St.

Concord Av.   Chauncy St.

Oxford St.   Divinity Av.

Berkeley St.   Garden St.   Follen St.

Longfellow National Historical Site

Phillips Pl.   Waterhouse St.

Cambridge Common

Harvard Law School

(4)

Kirkland St.

Brattle St.   Mason St.

Longfellow Park   Hawthorn St.   Acacia St.   Ash St.

Appian Way   Farwell Pl.

Flagstaff Park

Cambridge St.

Broadway

Old Burying Ground

Harvard University

Ash St.   Hilliard St.   Story St.

Mt. Auburn St.

Church St.

(T) (i) (1)

Harvard Square

(2)

(3)

Quincy St.

Bennett St.   Winthrop St.   Dunster St.   Holyoke St.   Linden St.

Massachusetts Av.

To Central Square (T)

Memorial Drive   Eliot St.   South St.   Mt. Auburn St.   Bow St.   Arrow St.

(5)

Charles River

Soldiers Field Rd.   J.F. Kennedy St.   Mill St.   Plympton St.   DeWolfe St.   Athens St.

Itinerary 5– Cambridge for Beginnners

0   .1 mi
0   .16 km

(1) Harvard Square
(2) Harvard Yard
(3) University Art Museums
(4) Natural History Museums
(5) Bartley's Burger Cottage

— Red Line
✝ Church
✉ Post Office
(i) Information
(T) Station Stop
✡ Synagogue

219

6. From here, you can move on to **Lexington** or **Concord,** or head into Boston for more sightseeing. The **MIT** campus is on the way, if you want to stop off there. Or stay put; especially on weekends, Harvard Square offers enough diversions to fill an afternoon. If shopping and hanging out don't sound fulfilling, consider visiting **Mount Auburn Cemetery** or (if it's open) the **Longfellow National Historic Site.** Both are in beautiful West Cambridge.

Itinerary 6: The 1-Day, Super-Duper Express Tour

Twenty-four hours will only whet your appetite for more of whatever you decide to do. This itinerary begins in the morning, but it's circular—you can pick it up anywhere along the way and continue till you're back where you started. All stops on this itinerary can be found on maps throughout chapters 13 and 15.

Time-Savers

Having only a day can be quite liberating. If you *know* you can't do everything you want to, the pressure is off. You're free to spend the whole day on one thing—communing with sharks or Impressionists or revolutionaries—and you don't need to explain why you never got around to anything else.

1. If **Filene's Basement** is on your list, be there when it opens (usually at 9:30am). Spend no more than an hour.

2. Follow part of the **Freedom Trail** on your own from Boston Common to **Faneuil Hall Marketplace,** or take a 90-minute National Park Service ranger tour from the Visitor Center at 15 State St.

3. Have lunch at **Durgin-Park** or pick up take-out food at Faneuil Hall Marketplace. Cross Atlantic Avenue and picnic in Christopher Columbus Park or on Long Wharf.

4. Complete the Freedom Trail and ride the MBTA ferry back to Long Wharf.

5. Pick one of these four: Take a **sightseeing cruise** from Long Wharf or Rowes Wharf. Or explore the **New England Aquarium.** Or head to Museum Wharf and visit the **Computer Museum** or the **Children's Museum.**

6. Head to the Back Bay for dinner and a show, the view from the **John Hancock Observatory** or the **Prudential Center Skywalk.** Let

the time of year and how hungry you are determine which you do first. Sunset is the perfect hour to visit either tower, though timing your visit to catch it may mean you wait a while to get a table for dinner. Three branches of **Legal Sea Foods** are within easy walking distance; the stroll to the Boston Park Plaza Hotel runs past or through gorgeous Copley Square. If you'd rather eat first, finish up at one of the observatories, then fall asleep planning a longer visit for next time.

Chapter 17

Designing Your Own Itinerary

In This Chapter

➤ Budgeting your time

➤ Pacing yourself

➤ Making tough choices

The itineraries in chapter 16 might need a tuck here or some extra room there to match your schedule and taste—or they might not fit at all. If you've been paying attention, there are check marks all over the margins of the five previous chapters. Those check marks form the pattern for your customized itinerary.

If you're moving to Boston, welcome. Everyone else, you have some prioritizing to do. There simply aren't enough hours in the day—or at least in your visit—for you to do everything that has caught your attention so far. The worksheets in this chapter will help you make the most of the hours you do have.

Back to the Drawing Board: Your Top Attractions

Turn back to chapter 13, where you and your fellow travelers assigned a number (from one to five) to your top attractions and listed them on the worksheet. Enter them here according to number.

#1 Picks

➤ _____

➤ _____

➤ _____

➤ _____

➤ _____

➤ _____

➤ _____

➤ _____

➤ _____

➤ _____

#2 Picks

➤ _____

➤ _____

➤ _____

➤ _____

➤ _____

➤ _____

➤ _____

➤ _____

➤ _____

➤ _____

#3 Picks

➤ _____

➤ _____

➤ _____

➤ _____

➤ _____

➤ _____

➤ _____

➤ _____

➤ _____

➤ _____

#4 Picks

➤ _____

➤ _____

➤ _____

➤ _____

➤ _____

➤ _____

➤ _____

➤ _____

➤ _____

➤ _____

Now go back to chapter 14 and find the other activities and attractions that fit your interests. Assign each one a number, and add them to the lists above. Then flip through chapters 12 and 15, and add anything else that's littered with check marks to the appropriate list. (You're probably wondering why there are no spaces for number five. If you're a typical visitor, you've already listed a week's worth of activities without including them, that's why.)

Suppose your number one list says "Museum of Fine Arts, Filene's Basement, Museum of Science, swan boats, John Hancock Observatory, Paul Revere House, whale watch." That would easily fill 2 days to overflowing. You might start the first day at the MFA, have lunch in or near the Public Garden (home of the swan boats), and spend the afternoon at the Museum of Science. The next day, you'd concentrate on downtown, starting at Filene's Basement, moving on to the Paul Revere House (about 15 minutes away), then over to the Waterfront to set out for whale watching. At the end of either day, the John Hancock Observatory would make a great evening excursion.

Time-Savers

If all this planning seems like a drag, remember that you can cannibalize the itineraries in chapter 16. Mix and match, work backward, or substitute activities in the same neighborhood while keeping the same basic structure.

Notice that the sample itinerary didn't include the whole Freedom Trail or the New England Aquarium, and the world didn't immediately come to an end. *See what you want to see, not what you think you should see.*

Budgeting Your Time

Sights take an average of about 2 hours to visit. Some, like the Boston Tea Party Ship & Museum and the swan boats, will probably take less; others, such as the Museum of Fine Arts and the New England Aquarium, take longer. Add travel and meal time, plus some mental relaxation, and that means you have time for three to four sights per day.

Add the number of entries on your number one and two lists, and divide by the number of full days in your trip. (Don't include days earmarked for out-of-town trips, no matter how organized you think you are.) If you get a number larger than four and all of the sights are time-consuming, you have a bit of a problem. Of course, it is physically possible to see six or eight big sights in a day. Like a lot of other physically possible things, that's a terrible idea. You're better off reducing the number of sights per day, but how?

➤ **Lengthen your visit.** But that may not be possible.

➤ **Split up.** More than one person will probably have more than one list of number ones. Half a day or even a day apart may make more people happier.

➤ **Skip the number threes.** You'll have more fun and make better use of your hard-earned money. Rather than jumping from museum to museum, snapping pictures of sculptures from the window of a speeding cab, immerse yourself in fewer experiences and enjoy them more.

Getting All Your Ducks in a Row

Visualize, visualize, visualize. Grab a map and mark your must-see attractions, then mark your hotel. Now find activities that naturally group together, and plan to visit them on the same day. Most of Boston's attractions are neatly arranged, but watch out for the catch-as-catch-can approach that leads to too much backtracking. If you absolutely can't leave town without seeing the Aquarium and Faneuil Hall Marketplace, the route from one to the other doesn't run through the Kennedy Library. Think strategically.

Time-Savers

Be sure you're prepared for the whims of New England's notorious weather. You already know (I hope) about seasonal closings. You also need to have Plan B ready in case sweltering heat or hip-deep snow keeps you from pursuing that full-day walking tour.

Fill-Ins

These are things you do on the way to something else. Shopping is a natural; go back to chapter 15 and list stores and neighborhoods you want to visit. List them here.

Shopping

➤ _____

➤ _____

➤ _____

➤ _____

➤ _____

➤ _____

➤ _____

➤ _____

➤ _____

➤ _____

Plot these on the map, and match them with sights you already know you want to see. Be realistic about time—storming the ramparts at Filene's Basement takes a lot longer than staring into every window on Newbury Street.

Dining is another fill-in. For now, don't worry about dinner. If there are specific places where you want to have lunch, plot them on the map and note them here. If nothing jumps out at you, look through chapters 10 and 11 for places in or near your clusters of attractions. Note those below.

Lunch

➤ _____

➤ _____

➤ _____

➤ _____

➤ _____

➤ _____

➤ _____

➤ _____

➤ _____

➤ _____

Sketching Out Your Itineraries

Finally, you're ready to outline some itineraries. A basic one should go something like this:

Breakfast at (*hotel/place/neighborhood*). See (*attraction*) in the morning. Lunch at (*place/neighborhood*) or (*alternate place*). Walk or take the T to (*attraction*) and spend the afternoon.

Don't forget to include other attractions and shopping: "Pass through the Public Garden on the way to the Prudential Center"; "stop at the Harvard Square Newbury Comics on the way to Mount Auburn Cemetery."

Itinerary #1

➤ _____

➤ _____

➤ _____

➤ _____

➤ _____

Itinerary #2

➤ _____

➤ _____

➤ _____

➤ _____

➤ _____

Itinerary #3

➤ _____

➤ _____

➤ _____

➤ _____

➤ _____

Itinerary #4

➤ _____

➤ _____

➤ _____

➤ _____

➤ _____

Bring on the Night

The clued-in wags in the audience are saying, "This shouldn't take long." It's true that Boston lags far behind some—okay, a lot of—other cities in the all-night-party department. It's also true that the wealth of cultural offerings will keep you off the street all evening and leave you rested and refreshed for early morning sightseeing. (I'm valiantly seeing the nightlife glass as half-full. Please play along.)

One thing you can't do in Boston is dine at a fine restaurant as late as you want, then go dancing till the sun comes up. You just can't. You can go club-hopping in several neighborhoods, but clubs close at 2am, bars at 1am or earlier. By the time you figure out that Central Square is beat, anywhere you might have gone on Lansdowne Street is already full or closed. On the plus side, as in any city with so many neighborhoods, the bar scene is great. In short, the attitude you need is not "What else is there?" but "Let's make the most of this."

For some activities, including the Symphony or the Pops, the theater, the ballet, and many sporting events, you need to plan ahead. If you know you have an 8pm curtain, work backward from that: dinner reservations at 6pm, napping and primping from 4:30pm on—you don't want to schedule more than one big thing for that afternoon.

Check the nightlife recommendations in the chapters that follow, and don't forget to include dinner reservations you might already have made as you fill in the spaces below.

Night #1
➤ _____

➤ _____

Night #2
➤ _____

➤ _____

Night#3
➤ _____

➤ _____

Night#4
➤ _____

➤ _____

Finally, get out the map and the colored markers again, and make sure you know where those dinner reservations are in relation to that afternoon's sightseeing. You don't want to emerge from the Museum of Science in jeans and sneakers an hour before your reservation at Rialto.

Part 6

On the Town: Nightlife & Entertainment

Boston is more famous for culture than for carousing, and deservedly so. You can take in the work of a world-class performing arts company, have a drink, and be home in bed while your friends in New York are still deciding which shoes to wear. If "world-class" is more than your vacationing mind can deal with, other options run from jazz and comedy clubs to alfresco movies. You can also hit the dance clubs—for all of 4 hours or so, before the city's puritanical history closes in on you. The trick is making the best of the opportunities you have.

In this section you'll learn about the Boston area's abundant cultural offerings. They suit every audience and any budget—from free films to expensive comedy headliners to pay-what-you-wish experimental theater, it's all here. You'll also find a guide to bars and to the limited but hopping club scene.

Chapter 18

We've Got Tonight: An Overview

In This Chapter

➤ How to find out what's on

➤ How to get tickets and how to get a deal

➤ What to wear and how to get there

Nightlife is the only aspect of a visit to Boston with an A/B switch: Either you're really compulsive and plan months in advance, or you go with the flow. There's something to be said for both approaches, and the one you choose will depend on your interests and the circumstances of your visit.

Laying the Groundwork

IN ADVANCE: As you learned when you were tying up loose ends back in chapter 4, you can find out what's planned and who's performing months (and occasionally even years) ahead of your visit. Most of the information sources in chapter 1 have good entertainment sections; the best are on the *Boston Globe*'s Web site, Boston.com (www.boston.com), which includes *Boston* magazine's listings, too. If you already know what you want to see—say, Boston Ballet's *Nutcracker,* or a particular symphony or Pops performance—contact individual organizations for information. Major pop and rock artists come to the FleetCenter (☎ **617/624-1000;** www.fleetcenter.com). If you're enamored of a particular performer or group, see if he, she, or it has a Web site or bulletin board with advance schedules.

ON THE FLY: For up-to-date entertainment listings, consult the "Calendar" section of the Thursday *Boston Globe*, the "Scene" section of the Friday *Boston Herald*, and the Sunday arts sections of both papers. The weekly *Boston Phoenix* (published on Thursday) has especially good club listings, and the biweekly *Improper Bostonian* (free at newspaper boxes around town) offers extensive live music listings.

Time-Savers

Some hotel packages—the best-known are *Nutcracker* weekends—include tickets to a cultural event. Find a deal that offers what you want to see and you won't have to worry about whether you can get tickets.

That's the Ticket

IN ADVANCE: Some companies and venues will sell you tickets over the phone; many will refer you to a ticket agency. The major agencies that serve Boston are **TicketMaster** (☎ 617/931-2000; www.ticketmaster.com), **Next Ticketing** (☎ 617/423-NEXT; www.boston.com/next), and **Tele-Charge** (☎ 800/447-7400). They calculate service charges per ticket, not per order, but the extra money is well spent if you have your heart set on seeing something in particular. If there's any chance that your plans will change, be sure you understand the refund policy before you pay.

ON THE FLY: For many events, you can just show up—call the box office to ask if what you're interested in is expected to sell out. Or visit a **BosTix** booth (see below) and check out what's available. If you have some extra time and discover that a concert or play that you hadn't planned for is sold out, visit the venue in person. By waiting until the day before or the day of a performance, you'll sometimes have access to tickets that were held back for one reason or another and have just gone on sale.

"Well, That Seems Like a Lot of Money!"

Not to worry. In exchange for not knowing what you'll see until a few hours before, you can sometimes get a great deal on tickets. There are three **BosTix** booths—at Faneuil Hall Marketplace (on the south side of Faneuil Hall), in Copley Square (at the corner of Boylston and Dartmouth streets), and in Harvard Square (in the Holyoke Center arcade at 1350 Mass. Ave.). They sell same-day tickets to musical and theatrical performances for half price, subject to availability. Credit cards are not accepted, and there are no refunds or exchanges. Check the board for the day's offerings.

BosTix (☎ 617/723-5181; www.boston.com/artsboston) also offers full-price advance ticket sales, and discounts on theater, music, and dance events. The Boston locations are TicketMaster outlets. The booths are open Tuesday through Saturday 10am to 6pm (half-price tickets go on sale at 11am), and Sunday 11am to 4pm. The Copley Square and Harvard Square locations are also open Monday 10am to 6pm.

Extra! Extra!

Just what you've been waiting for: a chance to test your theory that your concierge is actually a magician. If he or she comes through with the tickets you want, a tip is in order.

Do We Look Okay?

As with most other situations, if you're neat and clean, you can pretty much go anywhere. I'll take this opportunity to renew my one-person campaign against attending the theater dressed like a baseball manager, but I don't know how much good it'll do. I do suggest that you pack some clothing without writing on it in case you wind up at the symphony, ballet, or theater. (And if you manage to score tickets to opening night of anything or to a big benefit, formal wear might be in order—ask the person who hooks you up.)

Extra! Extra!

The late-night dining scene is, to put it mildly, sketchy. Most restaurants won't even take a reservation for a posttheater meal because they're not open that late. You can get bar snacks and dessert at some places, though, so at least you won't go hungry.

Traveling & Timing

Do not, under any circumstances, attempt to save time by driving to the Theater District. You have to arrive at least an hour in advance to have a prayer of parking within walking distance. Shows start on time, which means that jumping in a cab at Faneuil Hall Marketplace at 7:45pm and expecting to make an 8pm curtain is a fool's errand. Leave extra time, take the T, or both.

➤ The closest T stops to the **Theater District** are Boylston and Arlington on the Green Line, New England Medical and Chinatown on the Orange Line, and (with about a 15-minute walk) South Station on the Red Line.

➤ **Symphony Hall** has its own stop on the Green Line E; the other branches stop at Hynes Convention Center/ICA, a 10-minute walk away on Mass. Ave.

➤ **Harvard Square** also has a stop, on the Red Line. If you're coming from the Back Bay, you can walk to Mass. Ave. and take the no. 1 (Dudley-Harvard) bus to the end of the line.

➤ The **FleetCenter** is at North Station, on the Orange and Green lines.

The Performing Arts

Everyone from the internationally acclaimed professional to the enthusiastic amateur can use Boston's arts scene to engage (or indulge) in self-expression. For visitors, that means there's almost always something interesting afoot. I can't guarantee the quality of the entertainment, but it's generally pretty high, whether you're at a student recital or a bar with a live band. To cut out the middleman and amuse yourself, grab some friends and head to a bar or dance club.

Curtain Up: The Performing Arts

The biggest names in classical music, dance, theater, jazz, and world music often appear as part of the **BankBoston Celebrity Series,** 20 Park Plaza, Boston, MA 02116 (☎ **617/482-2595,** or 617/482-6661 for Celebrity Charge; www.celebrityseries.org). It's a subscription series that also offers tickets to individual events.

Classical Music

The **Boston Symphony Orchestra (BSO)** and the **Boston Pops** (and other companies that work around their schedules) perform at acoustically perfect **Symphony Hall,** 301 Mass. Ave., at Huntington Avenue. The BSO's season runs from September to April, the Pops's from May to early July. Call ☎ **617/266-1492** (617/CONCERT) for program information, or 617/266-1200 for SymphonyCharge; or check www.bso.org. **MBTA:** Green Line E to Symphony.

If you weren't able to buy tickets in advance, check at the box office 2 hours before show time, when returns from sub-scribers go on sale (at full price). A limited number of inexpensive symphony "rush" tickets (one per person, same day only) go on sale at 9am Friday and 5pm on Tuesday and Thursday. Wednesday evening and Thursday morning rehearsals are some-times open to the public; call to see if tickets are available.

Dollars & Sense

The **Hatch Shell** on the Esplanade (☎ **617/ 727-9547**, ext. 555) is an amphitheater best known as the home of the Boston Pops' Fourth of July con-certs. Almost every night in the summer, it plays host to free music and dance perfor-mances and films. Bring a blanket: Seating is on the lawn in front of the stage.

More Music

The **Handel & Haydn Society** (☎ **617/266-3605;** www.handelandhaydn. org) is the oldest continuously performing arts organization in the country. Its cutting-edge "historically informed" concerts take place year-round.

Students and faculty members at two prestigious institutions perform fre-quently during the academic year; admission is usually free. Contact the **New England Conservatory of Music,** 290 Huntington Ave. (☎ **617/ 262-1120,** ext. 700), and Cambridge's **Longy School of Music,** 1 Follen St. (☎ **617/876-0956,** ext. 120).

Time-Savers

The Boston Pops ends its season with a week of free outdoor concerts at the Hatch Shell on the Charles River Esplanade. They include the traditional Fourth of July concert, which features fireworks and draws enormous crowds. The other concerts that week are smaller—relative to the half million people on the big day, that is—which makes reaching and leaving the Hatch Shell much quicker.

Several museums offer concert series. Performances at the **Isabella Stewart Gardner Museum** (☎ **617/734-1359**) are on weekend afternoons from September through April. The **Museum of Fine Arts** (☎ **617/267-9300** or 617/369-3300) stages concerts in the courtyard on Wednesday evening from

June through September. If you're visiting Lexington or Concord, see if your trip coincides with a concert at the **DeCordova Museum and Sculpture Park** (☎ 617/259-8355), on Sandy Pond Road in nearby Lincoln.

Major Concert & Theater Venues

Note: The Boston venues mentioned here can be found on the map on page 240, "Boston After Dark."

➤ **Berklee Performance Center,** 136 Mass. Ave., at Boylston Street. ☎ **617/266-7455** (concert line), or 617/266-1400, ext. 261. **MBTA:** Green Line B, C or D to Hynes/ICA.

➤ **Boston Center for the Arts,** 539 Tremont St., between Berkeley and Clarendon streets. ☎ **617/426-7700** (events line), or 617/426-0320 (box office). **MBTA:** Orange Line to Back Bay.

➤ The New England Conservatory of Music's **Jordan Hall,** 30 Gainsborough St., at Huntington Avenue. ☎ **617/536-2412** or 617/262-1120, ext. 700 (concert line). **MBTA:** Green Line E to Symphony.

➤ Harvard University's **Sanders Theatre,** 45 Quincy St., at Cambridge Street, Cambridge. ☎ **617/496-2222**; www.fas.harvard.edu/~memhall. **MBTA:** Red Line to Harvard.

The Theater Scene

One of the last cities where pre-Broadway tryouts are held, Boston also is a popular destination for touring companies of established Broadway hits. Add two accomplished repertory companies and too many colleges to mention, and you get yet another area where there's something for everyone. Once again, the Boston theaters mentioned here can be found on the map on page 240.

You'll find most of the shows headed to or coming from Broadway in the Theater District, at the **Colonial Theatre** (106 Boylston St.; ☎ **617/426-9366**), the **Shubert Theatre** (265 Tremont St.; ☎ **617/482-9393**), the **Wang Theatre** (270 Tremont St.; ☎ **617/482-9393**), and the **Wilbur Theater** (246 Tremont St.; ☎ **617/423-4008**). The Shubert and the Wang make up the Wang Center for the Performing Arts (www.boston.com/wangcenter).

The **Huntington Theatre Company** performs at the Boston University Theatre, 264 Huntington Ave. (☎ **617/266-0800**; www.bu.edu/huntington). The **American Repertory Theatre** (ART) makes its home at Harvard University's Loeb Drama Center, 64 Brattle St., Cambridge (☎ **617/547-8300**; www.amrep.org).

The **Lyric Stage,** 140 Clarendon St. (☎ **617/437-7172**) mounts contemporary and modern works in an intimate second-floor setting. The **Emerson Majestic Theatre,** 219 Tremont St. (☎ **617/824-8000**), offers dance and music performances and Emerson College student productions. The **57 Theatre,** 200 Stuart St., in the Radisson Hotel Boston (☎ **800/233-3123**), often books one-person shows. Some ART projects and independent productions are at the **Hasty Pudding Theatre,** 12 Holyoke St., Cambridge (☎ **617/496-8400**). The Loeb and the Hasty Pudding also feature student productions. Other college venues include Suffolk University's **C. Walsh Theatre,** 55 Temple St., Beacon Hill (☎ **617/573-8680**), and various performance spaces at **MIT** (☎ **617/253-4720,** Theater Arts Hotline).

Theater for Beginners (And Willing Veterans)

Adults and children alike relish the antics at these long-running shows. Both take place at the Charles Playhouse, 74 Warrenton St., off Stuart Street, in the Theater District. Tickets are available at the box office and through TicketMaster.

I'm not a big believer in wasting time and money on bringing kids younger than 10 or so to the theater, but that's up to you, and them. Take into account the willingness of your fellow audience members to hear yet another explanation of why being quiet is a good idea.

The off-Broadway sensation ***Blue Man Group*** (☎ **617/426-6912**)—three cobalt-colored performance artists backed by a rock band—creates organized mayhem using wacky props, music, and willing audience members. ***Shear Madness*** (☎ **617/426-5225;** www.shearmadness.com) is a "comic murder mystery" set in a hair salon. One of the original audience-participation productions, it has run since 1980, and the show's never the same twice.

Shall We Dance?

Boston Ballet is definitely not just *The Nutcracker*—it's the country's fourth-largest dance company, and an extremely good one. The season runs from October through May. For information, call ☎ **800/447-7400** (Tele-charge) or 617/695-6955; www.boston.com/bostonballet. Most performances are at the Wang Theatre, 270 Tremont St., and the Shubert Theatre, 265 Tremont St.

For contemporary dance, check the offerings of **Dance Umbrella** (☎ **617/ 482-7570;** www.danceumbrella.org).

Tourist Traps

If you're taking children to their first *Nutcracker,* consider the tickets an investment and spend as much as you can. The Wang Theatre was built as a 1920s movie palace, and it's so tall that, from the balconies, the dancers appear to be about the size of a real nutcracker (the metal kind). If breaking the bank isn't an option, be sure to pack your opera glasses or binoculars.

Performances take place at venues in Boston and Cambridge, most often at the Emerson Majestic Theatre, 219 Tremont St.

Major Pop & Rock Concert Venues

Harborlights, a giant white tent with intimate single-level seating, closed in 1998 when its lease on the South Boston waterfront expired. To see if it has been reopened, call ☎ 617/374-9000 or check www.harborlights.com.

➤ **FleetCenter,** 150 Causeway St. ☎ **617/624-1000** (events line), or 617/931-2000 (TicketMaster). www.fleetcenter.com. **MBTA:** Orange or Green Line to North Station.

➤ **Orpheum Theater,** 1 Hamilton Pl. ☎ **617/679-0810** or 617/ 423-NEXT. **MBTA:** Red or Green Line to Park Street.

➤ **The Paradise,** 967 Commonwealth Ave. ☎ **617/562-8804** or 617/423-NEXT. www.tparty.com/tpc/paradise.html. **MBTA:** Green Line B to Pleasant St.

Chapter 20

Where Everybody Knows . . . Something: The Bar & Club Scene

In This Chapter

➤ Where to go for a drink

➤ Dancing till dawn (yeah, right)

➤ Gay and lesbian bars and clubs

Bostonians had some quibbles with the TV show *Cheers,* but no one ever complained that the concept of a neighborhood bar where the regulars practically lived was implausible. The typical watering hole tends to be fairly insular—you won't be confronted, but don't expect to be welcomed with open arms, either. This is one area where you can and probably should judge a book by its cover. If you poke your head in the door and see people who look like you and your friends, give it a whirl. Have your ID ready.

Identity Crisis

The drinking age in Massachusetts is 21; a valid driver's license or passport is required as proof of age. The law is strictly enforced, especially near college campuses (in other words, practically everywhere)—periodic "sting" operations make bar and club operators quite jumpy. Be prepared to show ID if you appear to be younger than 35 or so, and try to be patient while the amazed 30-year-old ahead of you fishes out a license.

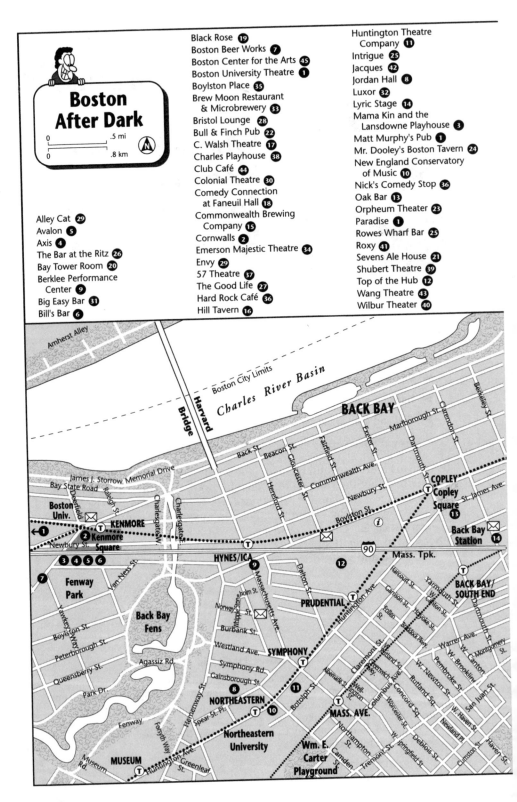

Boston After Dark

0   .5 mi

0   .8 km

Alley Cat **29**
Avalon **5**
Axis **4**
The Bar at the Ritz **26**
Bay Tower Room **20**
Berklee Performance
  Center **9**
Big Easy Bar **31**
Bill's Bar **6**

Black Rose **19**
Boston Beer Works **7**
Boston Center for the Arts **45**
Boston University Theatre **1**
Boylston Place **35**
Brew Moon Restaurant
  & Microbrewery **33**
Bristol Lounge **28**
Bull & Finch Pub **22**
C. Walsh Theatre **17**
Charles Playhouse **38**
Club Café **44**
Colonial Theatre **30**
Comedy Connection
  at Faneuil Hall **18**
Commonwealth Brewing
  Company **15**
Cornwalls **2**
Emerson Majestic Theatre **34**
Envy **29**
57 Theatre **37**
The Good Life **27**
Hard Rock Café **36**
Hill Tavern **16**

Huntington Theatre
  Company **11**
Intrigue **25**
Jacques **42**
Jordan Hall **8**
Luxor **32**
Lyric Stage **14**
Mama Kin and the
  Lansdowne Playhouse **3**
Matt Murphy's Pub **1**
Mr. Dooley's Boston Tavern **24**
New England Conservatory
  of Music **10**
Nick's Comedy Stop **36**
Oak Bar **13**
Orpheum Theater **23**
Paradise **1**
Rowes Wharf Bar **25**
Roxy **41**
Sevens Ale House **21**
Shubert Theatre **39**
Top of the Hub **12**
Wang Theatre **43**
Wilbur Theater **40**

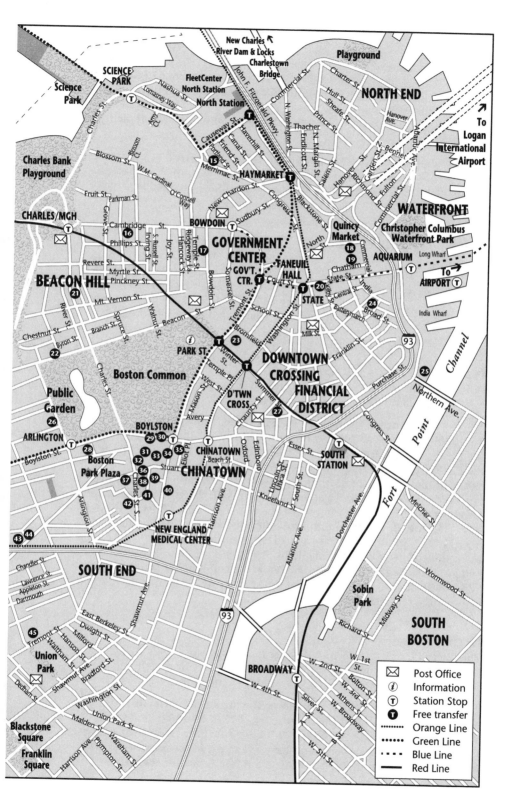

New Charles River Dam & Locks
Charlestown Bridge
Playground

SCIENCE PARK
Science Park

FleetCenter
North Station
North Station

NORTH END

To Logan International Airport

Charles Bank Playground

Blossom St.
W.M. Cardinal
O'Connell Way
Fruit St.
Parkman St.

Causeway St.
Haverhill St.
Canal St.
Friend St.
Portland St.
Merrimac St.
New Chardon St.

Hull St.
Sheafe St.
Charter St.
Prince St.
Snowhill St.
N. Margin St.
Salem St.
Thacher St.
Endicott St.
Hanover St.
Richmond St.
N. Bennet
Hanover Ave.
Garden Ct.
Fulton
Commercial St.
Atlantic Ave.

WATERFRONT

Christopher Columbus Waterfront Park

CHARLES/MGH

Cambridge St.
Revere St.
Myrtle St.
Phillips St.
Pinckney St.

BOWDOIN

Sudbury St.
GOVERNMENT CENTER
GOV'T. CTR.

Quincy Market

FANEUIL HALL

AQUARIUM

Long Wharf

To AIRPORT

BEACON HILL

Mt. Vernon St.
Chestnut St.
Byron St.
River St.
Branch St.
Spruce St.
Walnut St.
Beacon St.
Bowdoin St.
Tremont St.
Somerset St.
Court St.
School St.
Washington St.

STATE

Chatham
State St.
Central St.
India
Broad St.
Battery St.
Battery march
Milk St.
Franklin St.

India Wharf

PARK ST.

Boston Common

Public Garden

ARLINGTON

Boylston St.

BOYLSTON

Boston Park Plaza

CHINATOWN
Beach St.

DOWNTOWN CROSSING
FINANCIAL DISTRICT

D'TWN CROSS.

Avery
West St.
Mason St.
Temple Pl.
Winter St.
Bromfield
Chauncy St.
Summer St.
Essex St.
Oxford
Edinboro
Lincoln St.
Utica St.
Kneeland St.
South St.
Tyler St.
Hudson St.

SOUTH STATION

Purchase St.
Congress St.

Point
Fort
Northern Ave.
Melcher St.

Channel

NEW ENGLAND MEDICAL CENTER

Arlington St.
Harrison Ave.
Charles St. S.
Stuart
Eliot Pl.

SOUTH END
Chandler St.
Lawrence St.
Appleton St.
Dartmouth

East Berkeley St.
Dwight St.
Milford
Waltham St.
Hanson St.
Tremont St.
Bradford St.
Shawmut Ave.
Washington St.
Union Park St.
Malden St.
Wareham St.
Plympton St.
Harrison Ave.
Dedham St.

Union Park

Blackstone Square

Franklin Square

SOUTH BOSTON

Sobin Park
Richard St.
Midway St.
Wormwood St.
Congress St.
Dorchester Ave.
Atlantic Ave.

BROADWAY
W. 1st St.
W. 2nd St.
W. 3rd St.
W. 4th St.
W. 5th St.
W. Broadway
Bolton St.
Athens St.
Silver St.
Dorchester Ave.

⊠ Post Office
ⓘ Information
Ⓣ Station Stop
🅣 Free transfer
·········· Orange Line
•••••••• Green Line
· · · · Blue Line
—— Red Line

241

The *Cheers* bar is the **Bull & Finch Pub**, 84 Beacon St. (☎ **617/227-9605;** www.cheersbos.com). It looks nothing like the bar on *Cheers* (the outside does, though). The Bull & Finch really is a neighborhood bar, but today it attracts mostly legions of out-of-towners with good pub grub and plenty of souvenirs.

Another fun place to see lots of other tourists is the **Hard Rock Cafe**, 131 Clarendon St. (☎ **617/424-ROCK;** www.bostondine.com). The bar is shaped like a guitar, the room is decorated with memorabilia, the food is pretty good, and, yes, you can buy a T-shirt.

Drinks with a View

The **Bay Tower Room** is an elegant lounge on the 33rd floor of 60 State St. (☎ **617/723-1666**) that has live music and dancing Monday through Saturday. No jeans or athletic shoes are allowed. **Top of the Hub** is on the 52nd floor of the Prudential Tower (☎ **617/536-1775**). The view is especially beautiful at sunset. There is music and dancing nightly, and dress is casual but neat.

Notable Hotel Bars

Hotel bars can be particularly agreeable, albeit pricey, places to while away an hour or three. And the people-watching is great.

The **Bristol Lounge,** in the Four Seasons Hotel, 200 Boylston St. (☎ **617/ 351-2000**), is the city's premier hotel bar, and especially convenient for after the theater. There's live piano music every night. The **Bar at the Ritz** is in the Ritz-Carlton, 15 Arlington St. (☎ **617/536-5700**). It's famous for its perfect martinis. The Boston Harbor Hotel, 70 Rowes Wharf, at Atlantic Avenue (☎ **617/439-7000**), has two appealing options on the ground floor: **Intrigue,** a cafe with a harbor view; and the businesslike **Rowes Wharf Bar.** The **Oak Bar** at the Fairmont Copley Plaza Hotel, 138 St. James Ave. (☎ **617/267-5300**), is a wood-paneled cigar-smoker's haven with an oyster bar and nightly live entertainment. Proper dress is required. The ground-floor lounge at the **Regal Bostonian Hotel,** at Faneuil Hall Marketplace (☎ **617/ 523-3600**), offers a sensational view of the scene at the marketplace, and live piano music on weeknights.

Brew Pubs

The microbrewery craze is in full swing in Boston. Most don't charge a cover, but the beer will set you back at least $3 a mug, more if something fancy is involved. Brew pubs are also popular dining destinations.

The two local branches of **Brew Moon Restaurant & Microbrewery** are at 115 Stuart St., in the Theater District (☎ **617/523-6467**), and in Harvard Square at 50 Church St. (☎ **617/499-2739**). They serve award-winning beers (and house-brewed root beer!) and have live music at the **Sunday jazz brunch,** 11am to 3pm. Near North Station, the **Commonwealth**

Brewing Company, 138 Portland St. (☎ **617/523-8383**), was Boston's first brew pub—it opened in 1986. There's live music and dancing downstairs Thursday through Saturday nights; the cover is waived if you've been eating upstairs. Near Kenmore Square, **Boston Beer Works,** 61 Brookline Ave. (☎ **617/536-2337**), is large and extremely loud, especially before and after Red Sox games. In Harvard Square, **John Harvard's Brew House,** 33 Dunster St. (☎ **617/868-3585**), serves reasonably priced food that's as good as the excellent beers.

Irish Bars

Sometimes you just need an expertly poured Guinness and the sound of a brogue. Most of these places have a cover charge ($5 or less) at night. The jam-packed **Black Rose,** 160 State St. at Faneuil Hall Marketplace (☎ **617/742-2286**), makes up for its touristy location with authentic entertainment. In Cambridge, head to **The Field** (☎ **617/354-7345**) at 20 Prospect St. in Central Square for some genuine pub atmosphere. **Mr. Dooley's Boston Tavern,** 77 Broad St. (☎ **617/338-5656**), is a popular Financial District hangout. In Somerville's Davis Square, the **Burren,** 247 Elm St. (☎ **617/776-6896;** MBTA: Red Line to Davis), offers live entertainment and movie-backdrop cachet—unless you were asleep, you saw it in *Next Stop Wonderland.* In Brookline, **Matt Murphy's Pub,** 14 Harvard St. (☎ **617/232-0188;** MBTA: Green Line D to Brookline Village), has great bartenders, excellent food, live music on weekend nights, and, best of all, no smoking.

Do You Know of Any Plain Bars?

Sure. Every neighborhood has one; I especially like places where you can hear yourself think and the person next to you speak. (Don't count on either of those on weekend nights or immediately after work, though.) Extremely unscientific research has led me to prefer bars in Cambridge over those in Boston, so I'll mention those first.

In Harvard Square, **Casablanca,** 40 Brattle St. (☎ **617/876-0999**), and **Grendel's Den,** 89 Winthrop St. (☎ **617/491-1160**) are deservedly legendary**.** In Central Square, the **Green Street Grill,** 280 Green St. (☎ **617/876-1655**), has perhaps the best blues and jazz jukebox on the planet. In Boston, on Beacon Hill, you'll find a postcollegiate crowd at the **Sevens Ale House,** 77 Charles St. (☎ **617/523-9074**), and the **Hill Tavern,** 228 Cambridge St. (☎ **617/742-6192**). Near Downtown Crossing, **The Good Life,** 28 Kingston St., off Summer Street (☎ **617/451-2622**), is a relatively new, extremely popular retro lounge. In Kenmore Square, **Cornwalls,** 510 Commonwealth Ave. (☎ **617/262-3749**), is an entertaining dash of England in a city noted for its Irish bars.

The Club Scene

Check the "Calendar" section of the Thursday *Globe,* the *Phoenix,* the *Improper Bostonian,* or the "Scene" section of the Friday *Herald* while you're making plans.

The original **House of Blues** is at 96 Winthrop St. in Harvard Square (☎ 617/491-BLUE, or 617/497-2229 for tickets; www.hob.com). It offers evening and weekend matinee shows, big names, and hordes of fans. Advance tickets are highly recommended.

Time-Savers

Eat and primp till midnight, and you might as well go right to bed: Most bars close by 1am, clubs close at 2, and the T shuts down between 12:30 and 1am. Get your act together by 11 or risk winding up at Dunkin' Donuts in your party clothes.

That's a Laugh: Comedy Clubs

The city's premier comedy club is the **Comedy Connection at Faneuil Hall,** on the upper level of Quincy Market (☎ 617/248-9700). A large room with a clear view from every seat, it draws top-notch talent from near and far. In the Theater District, **Nick's Comedy Stop,** 100 Warrenton St. off Stuart Street (☎ 617/482-0930), doesn't have the same cachet, but it's still a good time. In Harvard Square, you'll find generally younger comics and more experimental material at the **Comedy Studio,** in the Hong Kong, 1236 Mass. Ave. (☎ 617/661-6507).

Live Music & Dance Clubs

Boston and Cambridge each have a neighborhood suited to club-hopping, and Boston has another street where you can bounce from place to place without springing for cab fare. That makes club-hopping easy, but on Friday and Saturday it means huge crowds of loud teenagers and recent college graduates.

Dance clubs that usually feature DJs sometimes book live acts, and live-music clubs rarely restrict themselves to one genre. "Twenty-one and over" means just that; "18 and over" means 18-, 19-, and 20-year-olds are admitted but aren't allowed to drink alcohol.

Boston's primo nightlife destination is Kenmore Square, specifically **Lansdowne Street,** just outside the square off Brookline Avenue. The city's best dance club, **Avalon,** is at 15 Lansdowne St. (☎ 617/262-2424). The multilevel space (with a full concert stage) attracts chic 20-somethings. The dress code calls for jackets, shirts with collars, and no jeans or athletic wear. Next door is **Axis,** 13 Lansdowne St. (☎ 617/262-2437), which generally draws a younger crowd for progressive rock at bone-rattling volume. **Mama Kin** and the **Lansdowne Playhouse,** 36 Lansdowne St. (☎ 617/536-2100), book live rock acts—usually not including the co-owners, who are members of Aerosmith. **Bill's Bar,** 5½ Lansdowne St. (☎ 617/421-9678), books live music by less-prominent but promising artists.

Boylston Place is a tarted-up alley off Boylston Street near Tremont Street. It holds, among other clubs, the **Alley Cat** (☎ 617/351-2510), an unpretentious lounge that caters to a collegiate and postcollegiate crowd; the **Big Easy Bar** (☎ 617/351-7000), with a slightly older clientele and a New Orleans theme; and **Envy** (☎ 617/542-3689), a new lounge and club valiantly courting an even older crowd.

Cambridge's **Central Square** pulls in a diverse, enthusiastic crowd more interested in aptitude than attitude. You'll find lots of 18-plus shows and not much elbow room. The **Middle East**, 472–480 Mass. Ave. (☎ 617/ 492-9181), fills two rooms nightly for progressive and alternative rock. **T.T. the Bear's Place**, 10 Brookline St. (☎ 617/492-0082, or concert line 617/492-BEAR; www.tiac.net/users/ttbears), books everything—rock, roots, ska, funk, pop, even poetry. On the other side of the square, the **Cantab Lounge**, 738 Mass. Ave. (☎ 617/354-2685), is a friendly, very loud neighborhood bar that attracts a three-generation crowd, usually for R&B or rock, sometimes for jazz. South of the square at 343 Western Ave. is the **Western Front** (☎ 617/492-7772), a deceptively unadorned place that's known internationally for its reggae bookings.

Off the Beaten Track

Just about anything goes at **Johnny D's**, 17 Holland St., Somerville (☎ 617/ 776-2004, or concert line 617/776-9667; www.johnnyds.com). The family-owned and -operated restaurant and music club is one of the best in the area (MBTA: Red Line to Davis).

In the Theater District, the **Roxy** is a ballroom-turned-club on the second floor of the Tremont Hotel (☎ 617/338-7699). It books excellent DJs and live music and occasional concerts (and once in a while a boxing match). No jeans or athletic shoes are allowed.

Harvard Square's reputation as a folk-music proving ground stems almost entirely from the presence of **Club Passim**, 47 Palmer St. (☎ 617/492-7679). It's a coffeehouse known for nurturing new talent and showcasing established musicians.

All That Jazz

Two elegant clubs book the biggest names in jazz. Depending on whom you ask, either is the best in the Boston area, with the other a close second. The **Regattabar** is in the Charles Hotel, 1 Bennett St., Harvard Square (☎ 617/661-5000, or 617/876-7777 for Concertix). The large room sometimes gets a little noisy. **Scullers Jazz Club** is in the Doubletree Guest Suites Hotel, 400 Soldiers Field Rd. (☎ 617/562-4111; www.scullersjazz.com). Patrons tend to be more hard-core and quieter than the

Dollars & Sense

On summer Fridays at 6:30pm, the free Waterfront Jazz Series (☎ 617/635-3911) brings amateurs and professionals to Christopher Columbus Park, on the Waterfront, for a refreshing interlude of music and cool breezes.

crowds at the Regattabar, but it really depends on who's performing. Ask about dinner packages, which include preferred seating.

Gay & Lesbian Bars & Clubs

In addition to the clubs here, 1 night a week is gay night at some mainstream clubs. On Sunday, **Avalon** and **Axis** play host to the largest gathering of gay men in town, and possibly in New England. For listings, check *Bay Windows* and the monthly *Phoenix* supplement "One in 10."

Club Café, at 209 Columbus Ave. in the South End (☎ **617/536-0966**), draws men and women for conversation (the noise level is reasonable), dining, live music in the front room, and video entertainment in the back room. Thursday is see-and-be-seen night. **Jacques,** 79 Broadway, in the Theater District (☎ **617/426-8902**), is the only drag venue in town. The friendly crowd of gay and straight patrons sometimes engages in a shocking activity—that's right, disco dancing. **Luxor,** 69 Church St., near the Theater District (☎ **617/423-6969**), is a video bar that shows the latest music clips and compilations of snippets from movies and old TV shows concocted by the veejays.

Screen Gems

Free Friday Flicks at the Hatch Shell (☎ **617/727-9547,** ext. 550) are family films shown on a large screen in the amphitheater on the Esplanade usually used for concerts. This is one of Boston's most enjoyable summertime activities. The lawn in front of the Hatch Shell turns into a giant, car-less drive-in as hundreds of people picnic while the sky grows dark, then watch a classic crowd-pleaser (*The Wizard of Oz* and *Raiders of the Lost Ark* are favorites). Bring sweaters in case the breeze off the river grows chilly.

Classic films are shown in series at the **Boston Public Library** (☎ **617/536-5400;** www.bpl.org) and the **Museum of Fine Arts** (☎ **617/267-9300;** www.mfa.org). The area theaters closest to revival houses—they feature lectures and live performances in addition to foreign and classic films—are the **Brattle Theater,** 40 Brattle St., Cambridge (☎ **617/876-6837;** www.beaconcinema.com/brattle), and the **Coolidge Corner Theater,** 290 Harvard St., Brookline (☎ **617/734-2500;** www.coolidge.org/Coolidge). Classic and foreign films are the tip of the iceberg at the quirky **Harvard Film Archive,** 24 Quincy St., Cambridge (☎ **617/495-4700**), which also shows student films.

Part 7

Side Trips from Boston

Besides being the mythical "hub of the solar system," Boston is the hub of a net-work of fascinating day trips. The historical and literary legacy of Lexington and Concord, the rugged coast and maritime tradition of the North Shore, the Pilgrim heritage of Plymouth, and the many delights of Cape Cod are all within easy traveling distance, and well worth exploring.

In this section you'll find suggestions to help you decide which trip or trips to take, travel pointers, and ideas for sightseeing, dining, and staying overnight.

Chapter 21 introduces the destinations and tells you how to get information before leaving the city, and chapter 22 suggests a few attractions, hotels and restaurants for each side trip.

Getting There & Getting Around

In This Chapter

➤ Seven areas (and 10 towns) to investigate

➤ Getting information in advance and in person

➤ When to go and how to get there

You know where Paul Revere's ride started, but not where it ended. You know the Pilgrims landed on Plymouth Rock, but not what it looks like. You watched *Bewitched* and dreamed of visiting Salem. Well, these last two chapters are for you. They outline the "greatest hits" of destinations that make manageable day trips from Boston: Lexington and Concord, Salem and Marblehead, Gloucester and Rockport, Plymouth, and three Cape Cod towns: Sandwich, Chatham, and Provincetown. Check chapter 1 for information about contacting the **Massachusetts Office of Travel & Tourism,** which can be a great help as you plan. And if you're on a long trip and want more complete listings, you need a book like *Frommer's New England.*

In this chapter I'll briefly describe each destination, tell you how to get information before you go and once you get there, and summarize transportation options. You can reach most of these places by public transit. For maximum flexibility—a big consideration everywhere except Plymouth—seriously consider renting a car and making your own schedule. As of right now, I'm lifting the ban on driving in Boston and Cambridge.

When Is the Best Time to Go?

You can be sure that everything is open on summer weekends, and you can be sure of finding tons of other people. To beat the largest crowds, try to schedule your day trip for a weekday. If you can swing a spring or fall visit, you'll find shorter or nonexistent lines, some lower prices, and less stressed-out merchants and residents. In the winter, some businesses and attractions may be closed, but you'll have the open ones almost all to yourself. Depending on the community, the off-season starts and ends at different times. For example, in Plymouth it begins the Monday after Thanksgiving; in Lexington and Concord, it ends Patriots Day weekend. Cape Cod is racing to the point of having no off-season at all, but is usually less frantic between Labor Day and Memorial Day, especially on weekdays.

Extra! Extra!

Unless otherwise indicated, the **MBTA** operates the public transportation lines mentioned in this chapter. Call ☎ **617/222-3200** or check www.mbta.com for specific schedules and fare information.

Lexington & Concord

The first fighting of the Revolutionary War took place in the quiet country villages of Lexington and Concord. Now thriving suburbs, they make excellent places to get in touch with history—and not just the history of April 1775. In Lexington you'll see the first battlefield of the revolution, the town common. Six miles away in Concord, the colonial legacy coexists with artifacts of the 19th-century intellectual "flowering of New England."

Lexington and Concord together make a manageable day trip; if you're especially interested in the Concord attractions, they can fill a day by themselves. Some attractions close from November through March or mid-April. They reopen after Patriots Day, celebrated on the Monday closest to April 19.

Extra! Extra!

To leave the decision-making and the hassle of driving entirely to someone else, you might want to take a guided half- or full-day bus trip. For a good selection and fair prices, contact Gray Line's **Brush Hill Tours,** 435 High St., Randolph, MA 02368 (☎ **800/343-1328** or 781/986-6100; fax 781/986-0167; www.grayline.com).

Lexington Essentials

To drive to Lexington from Boston (9 miles) or Cambridge (6 miles), take Soldiers Field Road or Memorial Drive west and pick up Route 2. Use the exit for Route 4/225, and follow signs into the center of town. Or take Route 128 (I-95) to Exit 31, and proceed into town. There's parking on Mass. Ave. (the

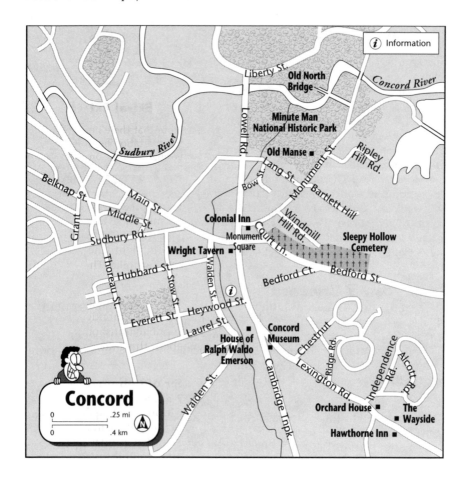

same one you saw in Boston and Cambridge), and a public metered lot near the corner of Mass. Ave. and Waltham Street.

By public transportation, take the Red Line to the end of the line, Alewife. Bus routes no. 62 (Bedford) and no. 76 (Hanscom) run from there to Lexington every hour during the day and every half hour during rush periods, Monday through Saturday. There is no service on Sunday, and no public transportation between Lexington and Concord.

Sketch maps and information are available from the **Chamber of Commerce Visitor Center,** 1875 Mass. Ave., Lexington, MA 02173 (☎ **781/862-1450**). It's open daily 9am to 5pm (9:30am to 3:30pm October through June). There is a community Web site (www.lexingtonweb.com). At the Lexington end of the National Park Service's Minute Man National Historical Park, the **Battle Road Visitor Center** is off Route 2A, one-half mile west of I-95 Exit 33B (☎ **781/862-7753;** www.nps.gov/mima/).

Concord Essentials

First of all, it's pronounced "conquered."
Not being a linguist, I can't say why, but if
you call it "*con*-cored," you're announcing
yourself as an out-of-towner.

To drive from Lexington, take Mass. Ave.
west, across Route 128, and pick up Route
2A. Pass through Lincoln and bear right
onto Lexington Road in Concord. HISTORIC
CONCORD signs lead to the center of town.
If you miss the turnoff, continue about a
half mile and take the next right onto Cambridge Turnpike. To go straight to
Walden Pond, take what's now Route 2/2A another mile or so and turn left
onto Route 126. From Boston and Cambridge, take Soldiers Field Road or
Memorial Drive west to Route 2. In Lincoln, stay in the right lane. Where the
road makes a sharp left, go straight onto Cambridge Turnpike. There's parking throughout town and at the attractions.

Extra! Extra!

Note that there's no public
transportation between
Lexington and Concord.

By public transportation, the commuter rail takes about 45 minutes from
North Station in Boston, with a stop at Porter Square in Cambridge. There
is no bus service from Boston to Concord, and no public transportation
between Lexington and Concord. The station is about three-quarters of a
mile from the town center.

Visitor information is available from the **Chamber of Commerce,** 2
Lexington Rd., Concord, MA 01742 (☎ **978/369-3120**). Its information
booth is on Heywood Street, 1 block southeast of Monument Square. It's
open weekends in April and daily May through October, 9:30am to 4:30pm.
One-hour tours are available starting in May on Saturday, Sunday, and
Monday holidays, or on weekdays by appointment. Group tours are available
by appointment. Concord also has a Web site (www.concordma.com), which
has an area with visitor information. Part of the National Park Service's
Minute Man National Historical Park, the **North Bridge Visitor Center** is
north of the town center at 174 Liberty St., off Monument Street (☎ **978/
369-6993;** www.nps.gov/mima/).

Salem & Marblehead

The postrevolutionary China trade brought great prosperity to the North
Shore, but Salem was already internationally famous. The witch trials of 1692
led to 20 deaths, centuries of lessons on the evils of prejudice, and countless
bad puns ("Stop by for a spell" is a favorite slogan). Today you'll see plenty
of witch-associated attractions as well as reminders of the area's rich maritime legacy. Adjacent Marblehead is a simply gorgeous little town. It boasts
just the right mix of scenery, history, architecture, and shopping for a fun
day trip.

Much like Lexington and Concord, Salem and Marblehead together make a
busy day trip. Either one can also fill a day.

Salem Essentials

To drive to Salem from Boston (17 miles), take the Callahan Tunnel to Route 1A north past the airport and into downtown Salem. Be careful in Lynn, where the road turns left and immediately right. Or take I-93 or Route 1 to Route 128, then Route 114 into downtown Salem. From Marblehead, follow Route 114 (Pleasant Street) west. There's plenty of on-street parking, and a reasonably priced municipal garage across from the National Park Service Visitor Center.

Bus route no. 450 runs from Haymarket (Orange or Green line), and commuter trains operate from North Station. The bus takes an hour, the train 30 to 35 minutes. An experimental program that started in 1998 instituted ferry service from Boston. It runs from July through October and takes about an hour. For more information, contact **Massport** (☎ **800/23-LOGAN;** www.massport.com) or **Harbor Express** (☎ **978/741-3442**).

The **Salem Office of Tourism & Cultural Affairs,** 93 Washington St., Salem, MA 01970 (☎ **800/777-6848;** e-mail SalemMA@cove.com), publishes a free visitor's guide with the **Salem Chamber of Commerce.** The chamber is in Old Town Hall, 32 Derby Sq., Salem, MA 01970 (☎ **978/744-0004**), where it maintains an information booth (weekdays, 9am to 5pm). Salem has an excellent community Web site (www.salemweb.com). The **National Park Service Visitor Center,** 2 New Liberty St. (☎ **978/740-1650;** www.nps.gov/sama/), distributes brochures and pamphlets, including one that describes a walking tour of the historic district. It's open daily, 9am to 5pm.

Marblehead Essentials

To drive straight to Marblehead from Boston, take the Callahan Tunnel and follow Route 1A past the airport north through Revere and Lynn. Bear right where you see signs for Swampscott and Marblehead. Follow Lynn Shore Drive into Swampscott, bear left onto Route 129, and follow it into Marblehead. Or take I-93 or Route 1 to Route 128, then Route 114 through Salem into Marblehead. Parking is limited, so don't be picky, and be sure you know your time limit.

Bus route no. 441/442 runs from Haymarket (Orange or Green line) in Boston to downtown Marblehead. During rush periods on weekdays, the no. 448/449 connects Marblehead to Downtown Crossing. The trip takes about an hour. The 441 and 448 buses detour to Vinnin Square shopping center in Swampscott; otherwise, the routes are the same.

The **Marblehead Chamber of Commerce,** 62 Pleasant St., P.O. Box 76, Marblehead, MA 01945 (☎ **781/631-2868;** www.marbleheadchamber.org), publishes a visitor's guide. It also distributes individual pamphlets that list dining,

Newport, Schmooport

Marblehead's magnificent harbor helps make it the self-proclaimed "Yachting Capital of America." There is sailboat racing in the outer harbor all summer, and "Race Week" in July attracts enthusiasts from all over the country.

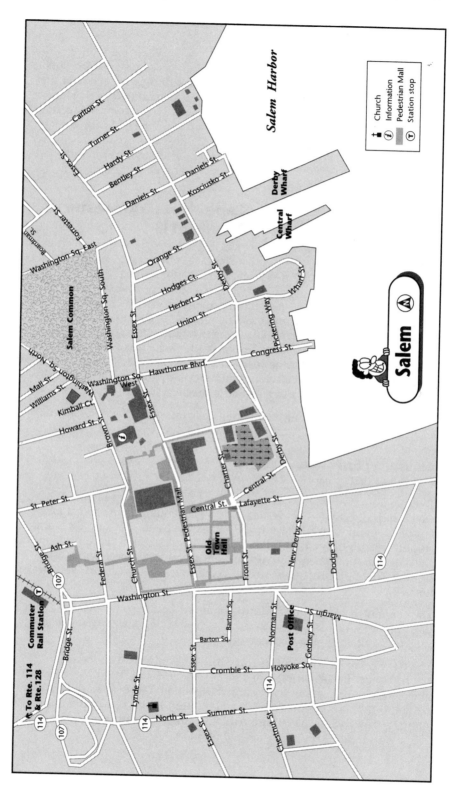

Salem

Salem Harbor

Derby Wharf

Central Wharf

Salem Common

Old Town Hall

Post Office

Commuter Rail Station

To Rte. 114 & Rte. 128

Legend
- ✝ Church
- ⓘ Information
- ▦ Pedestrian Mall
- Ⓣ Station stop

253

Get Out of Town

Before you hit the road, be absolutely sure you know where to go. Downtown Boston's traffic patterns change regularly because of the Big Dig, so ask at the front desk for specific directions to the route you need.

shopping, and accommodations options and marine services; and a map of the historic district with two well-plotted walking tours. The **information booth** on Pleasant Street near Spring Street is open daily in season, 10am to 5:30pm. Marblehead also has a community Web site (www.marblehead.com).

Cape Ann (Gloucester & Rockport)

New England's rocky shore and crashing waves take center stage on Cape Ann, a beautiful peninsula made up of Gloucester, Rockport, Essex, and Manchester-by-the-Sea. Gloucester (as in the Gorton's fisherman) is one of the state's few remaining commercial fishing ports. The inhabitants have made their living from the sea since long before the first European settlement, in 1623. Just to the north, Rockport sits at the tip of the cape. It's a lovely little town that over the years has been an active fishing port, a center of granite excavation, and a thriving summer community whose specialty seems to be selling fudge and refrigerator magnets to out-of-towners.

The contrast of urban Gloucester and bucolic Rockport makes for an enjoyable 1-day trip; exploring either can also fill a day.

Gloucester Essentials

First things first: *Gloucester* rhymes with *roster*.

To drive from Boston, the quickest path is I-93 or Route 1 to Route 128, which runs directly to Gloucester. Exit 14 puts you on Route 133, a longer but prettier approach to downtown than exits 11 and 9. Route 128 is almost entirely inland; the exits for Manchester (16 and 15) allow access to Route 127—near, not on, the water—if you want to combine speed and a little scenery. There's plenty of on-street parking, and a free lot on the causeway to Rocky Neck.

The commuter rail runs from North Station in Boston to Gloucester. The trip takes about an hour. The station is across town from downtown, so allow time for getting to the waterfront area.

The **Gloucester Tourism Commission,** 22 Poplar St., Gloucester, MA 01930 (☎ **800/649-6839** or 978/281-8865; www1.shore.net/~nya/gloucester.html), operates the Visitors Welcoming Center at Stage Fort Park, off Route 127 near the intersection with Route 133. It's open daily during the summer, 9am to 5pm. The **Cape Ann Chamber of Commerce** (see box "Cape Ann Info") is another excellent resource.

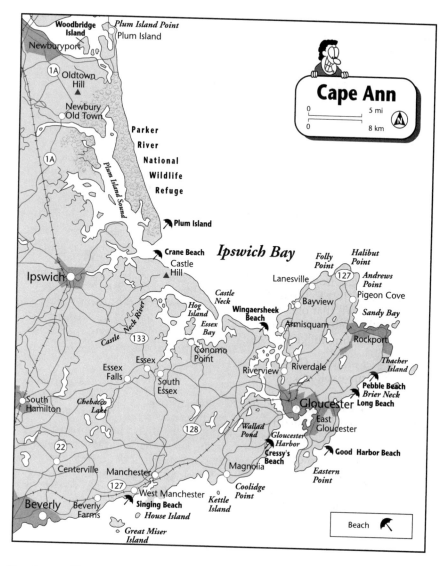

Rockport Essentials

By car from Boston, take I-93 or Route 1 to Route 128. Just before it ends, you'll see signs pointing left to Route 127. Or continue to the very end (Exit 9), turn left onto Bass Avenue, and go about a half mile to Route 127A north. From Gloucester, follow Main Street to Eastern Avenue (Route 127) or Bass Avenue. Route 127A is more scenic but a bit longer than Route 127. In downtown Rockport, circle once to look for parking (mind the limits on many meters), then try the back streets. Or use the parking lot on Upper Main Street (Route 127) on weekends. Parking from 11am to 6pm costs $6 to $7, and a free shuttle takes you downtown and back.

The commuter rail runs from North Station in Boston to Rockport. The trip takes 60 to 70 minutes. The station is off Upper Main Street, about a mile from the center of town.

Cape Ann Info

The Cape Ann Transportation Authority, or CATA (☎ **978/283-7916**), runs buses from town to town on Cape Ann. For more information on all four communities, contact the **Cape Ann Chamber of Commerce,** 33 Commercial St., Gloucester, MA 01930 (☎ **800/321-0133** or 978/283-1601; www. cape-ann.com/cacc). Its information center is open year-round.

The **Rockport Chamber of Commerce and Board of Trade,** 3 Main St. (☎ **978/546-6575;** www.rockportusa.com), is open daily in summer 9am to 5pm, and winter weekdays 10am to 4pm. The chamber also operates an information booth seasonally (mid-May to mid-October) on Upper Main Street (Route 127), about a mile from downtown—look for the WELCOME TO ROCKPORT sign. At either location, ask for the pamphlet *Rockport: A Walking Guide,* which has a good map and describes three short walking tours.

Plymouth

Everyone educated in the United States knows at least a little about Plymouth and the Pilgrims. No matter how many elementary school Thanksgiving pageants you've suffered through, you'll find something interesting to see or do. Plymouth Rock sits near a replica of the *Mayflower,* and there are several museums and historic houses. One of the best things about downtown Plymouth is that very little is prefabricated—it's a real community, coming up on the 400th anniversary of its establishment, where 17th-century relics fit into the 21st-century landscape.

Time-Savers

Although it's a year-round community, Rockport is most enjoyable during the summer season, which runs from mid-May to mid-October. Many businesses close for the winter; from January to mid-April, the town is pretty but somewhat desolate. If you can schedule only 1 weekday trip, make it this one. For traffic and congestion, downtown Boston has nothing on Rockport on a summer Saturday afternoon.

Plymouth is a manageable day-trip destination particularly suited to families traveling with children. It also makes a good stop between Boston and Cape Cod.

Plymouth Essentials

Plymouth is enormous; the section you want is the small area between Route 3 and the harbor. By car from Boston, follow I-93 south about 9 miles and bear left onto Route 3. Proceed to Exit 6 and take Route 44 east, then follow signs to the historic attractions. The 40-mile trip takes about 45 minutes if it's not rush hour. Or continue on Route 3 to the Regional Information Complex at Exit 5 for maps, brochures, and information. To go directly to Plimoth Plantation, take Exit 4. The downtown area is fairly compact, so park where you can. The waterfront meters are particularly convenient.

The commuter rail serves Plymouth from South Station, a 1-hour trip, during the day on weekdays and all day on weekends (at peak commuting times service is to nearby Kingston). **Plymouth & Brockton** buses (☎ 617/773-9401 or 508/746-0378) leave from South Station and take about the same time. The bus is more expensive than the commuter rail but runs more often. A pilot local bus program instituted in 1997 connects the stations with downtown and other destinations in a loop. Plymouth & Brockton operates the service, which costs 75¢ for adults and 35¢ for seniors and students.

While you're planning, contact **Plymouth Visitor Information,** P.O. Box ROCK, Plymouth, MA 02361 (☎ 800/USA-1620 or 508/747-7525; www.visit-plymouth.com). In town, if you haven't visited the Regional Information Complex, you'll want to at least pick up a map at the **Visitor Center** (☎ 508/747-7525), 130 Water St., across from the town pier.

Cape Cod

As Boston's suburbs expand, Cape Cod—especially the communities closest to the mainland—becomes less and less seasonal. The gorgeous scenery, picturesque little towns, and sandy beaches that make the famous peninsula a summer wonderland also make it incredibly popular year-round, particularly with retirees.

The three towns spotlighted here (on the grossly unscientific basis that I like them) are Sandwich, not far from the Sagamore Bridge; Chatham, at the elbow of the Cape; and Provincetown, at the tip. Sandwich and Chatham are easy to reach by car. You can drive to Provincetown, too, but the ferry from Boston is more fun and much less exasperating. For more in-depth coverage of the Cape, you'll want a more specific resource, such as *Frommer's Cape Cod, Nantucket & Martha's Vineyard.*

For general information, consult the **Cape Cod Chamber of Commerce,** Routes 6 and 132, Hyannis, MA 02601 (☎ 508/362-3225; fax 508/362-3698; www.capecod.com). Addresses of individual chambers of commerce appear below, but there may not be another 70 miles on earth with more sources of information. Just about anywhere you stop—the Regional Information Complex at Route 3 Exit 5 is one good place—you'll see piles of pamphlets, booklets, and souvenir maps.

History 101

The *Mayflower* first landed in the New World on November 11, 1620, but not in Plymouth. The Pilgrims had booked passage to northern Virginia, and were *way* off course when rough weather and high seas forced them to make for Cape Cod Bay. They found a safe harbor there—at Provincetown.

How Will I Get There?

To reach Cape Cod from Boston, take I-93 south about 9 miles. Bear left onto Route 3, which ends at the Sagamore Bridge over the Cape Cod Canal. It feeds into Route 6, the Cape's main east-west route, which has no scenery other than trees and traffic.

Sandwich Essentials

Just an hour or so from Boston, Sandwich makes a good introduction to the Cape if time is short. It's also worth a visit if you're on a longer trip. Founded in 1637, Sandwich is one of the oldest communities on the Cape. It has just about every element of a New England picture postcard.

To get there, cross the bridge and immediately turn onto Route 6A east. It's only 3 miles, so if you miss the turnoff, don't fret—take Route 6 to exit 2 and follow Route 130 north a mile or so. The **Cape Cod Canal Region Chamber of Commerce,** 70 Main St., Buzzards Bay, MA 02532 (☎ **508/759-6000;** www.capecodcanalchamber.org), operates an information booth (☎ **508/833-1632**) on Route 130.

Chatham Essentials

The prettiest village on the Cape, Chatham (which rhymes with "madam") boasts enormous civic pride and great shopping to go with its dizzying scenery. Contact the **Chatham Chamber of Commerce,** P.O. Box 793, Chatham, MA 02633 (☎ **800/715-5567** or 508/945-5199). It operates a little information booth at 533 Main St. in the summer.

The fastest way to Chatham is to take Route 6 to Exit 11. Follow Route 137 south to Route 28 east and go 2 miles. It's about 2 hours from Boston, but what's your rush? Routes 6A and 28 also run east-west, and either is far more interesting (though a lot slower) than Route 6.

Provincetown Essentials

A world-famous artists' colony, Provincetown is perhaps best known for its role in the gay community. In the summer it's a cornucopia of tourism and self-expression in approximately equal measure, and the community is known for being one of the most tolerant in New England. Contact the **Provincetown Chamber of Commerce,** 307 Commercial St., P.O. Box 1017, Provincetown, MA 02657 (☎ **508/487-3424;** www.capecodaccess.com/provincetownchamber), or the gay-oriented **Provincetown Business Guild,** P.O. Box 421-94, 115 Bradford St., Provincetown, MA 02657 (☎ **800/637-8696** or 508/487-2313; www.provincetown.com/pbg/index.html). The chamber is at the head of MacMillan Wharf, where the ferry docks.

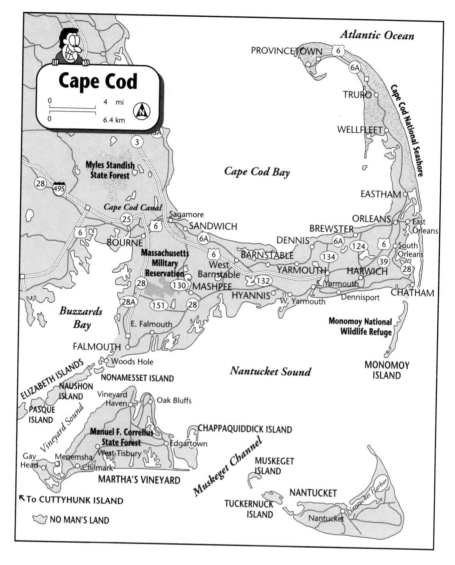

Provincetown is only about 60 miles from the Sagamore Bridge. The last 25 or so miles—Route 6 is the only road that runs all the way from Orleans to P-town—take approximately forever in the summer when the weather is good. **Bay State Cruises** (☎ **617/457-1428**) runs a ferry from Commonwealth Pier, on the South Boston waterfront, daily in the summer and on weekends in the spring and fall. It takes 3 hours and leaves Boston at 9am and Provincetown's MacMillan Wharf at 3:30pm. You'll have time for world-class people-watching, strolling around the novelty shops and art galleries, and sightseeing, although not enough to check out the famous beaches or the hopping gay nightlife scene. The same-day round-trip fare is $30 for adults, $23 for seniors, and $21 for children.

Chapter 22

On the Road Again: More Details on the Side Trips

In This Chapter

➤ The ins and outs of our 10 towns

➤ What to see, where to eat, and where to stay

Now you know where you're going and how to get there, but not what you'll be doing. This chapter offers brief descriptions of attractions, restaurants, and lodgings. In every case, choosing just a few was like picking a favorite letter—tough. If a destination sounds particularly agreeable, you'll certainly find a lot more to see and do than we have space for here.

Here are a few things *not* to do: Race from place to place as though the car will blow up if you go less than 50 miles per hour. Glance at everything, but don't look hard at any of it. Say *should, must,* and *ought* a lot. Complain because the 300-year-old buildings aren't part of a theme park. Especially if children are along, any of those is a surefire way to have a terrible time. If colonial artifacts are flying by faster than images on MTV, eyes of all ages will quickly glaze over. Take your time, and see what you want to see, not what you think you should see. Chat up the guides, guards, and attendants at the places you visit (but not if it keeps them from doing their jobs, of course). Would you rather have a dozen snapshots of the kids in front of old statues, or the memory of a fascinating conversation with the great-great-great-granddaughter of a Minuteman or a sea captain? Thought so.

Exploring Lexington

Start with the displays at the Chamber of Commerce's **Visitor Center,** 1875 Mass. Ave. Outside, on the Battle Green, you'll have a new perspective on the events of April 19, 1775. The landmark **Minuteman Statue** (1900) is of Capt. John Parker, who commanded the militia. A stop at the Visitor Center and a walk around the monuments and memorials won't take more than about half an hour, and you'll get a good sense of the battle here and of why the participants are still held in such high esteem.

History 101

European settlers had just reached what is now central Kentucky in 1775 when news came of the uprisings in Massachusetts. That's how Lexington, Kentucky, got its name.

If you prefer not to walk to the Munroe Tavern and the Museum of Our National Heritage, the nos. 62 and 76 buses pass by on Mass. Ave.

Lexington Historical Society Houses

Three important destinations were among the country's first "historic houses" when their restoration began in the 1920s. The **Buckman Tavern,** 1 Bedford St. (☎ 781/862-5598), is the only building still on the Green that was there on April 19, 1775. In the excellent tour, costumed guides describe the history of the building and its inhabitants, explain the battle, and discuss colonial life. If time is short and you have to pick one house to visit, this is the one.

About one-third of a mile away, the **Hancock-Clarke House,** 36 Hancock St. (☎ 781/861-0928), is restored and furnished in colonial style. It houses the Historical Society's museum of the Revolution. About a mile from the Green in the other direction is the **Munroe Tavern,** 1332 Mass. Ave. The British seized it to use as their headquarters and, after the battle, field hospital. The building (1690) is packed with fascinating artifacts and furniture.

Lexington Historical Society, 1332 Mass. Ave. ☎ *781/862-1703. link.ci.lexington.ma.us/ LexHistSoc/lhspage.htm.* **Guided tours:** *Mon–Sat 10am–5pm, Sun 1–5pm, Apr–Oct.* **Admission:** *Adults $4 per house, $10 for all three; children 6–16 $1 per house, $2 for all three. Last tour starts at 4:30pm; tours take 30–45 minutes. Group tours by appointment only.*

Two's Company

Many of the lodgings listed in this chapter require a minimum stay of 2 (sometimes 3) nights in the summer and on weekends. Be sure you understand what you're agreeing to before you make a reservation.

Kids Museum of Our National Heritage

The permanent exhibit "Lexington Alarm'd" makes a good overview, and the fascinating temporary exhibits explore history through popular culture—jigsaw puzzles, buffalo soldiers, quilts, George Washington. The museum is sponsored by the Scottish Rite of Freemasonry.

33 Marrett Rd. (Route 2A) at Mass. Ave. ☎ *781/861-6559 or 781/861-9638. www.mnh.org.* **Admission:** *Free.* **Open:** *Mon–Sat 10am–5pm, Sun noon–5pm. Closed Jan 1, Thanksgiving, Dec 25.*

Snacking & Sleeping

Lemon Grass, 1710 Mass. Ave. (☎ 781/862-3530), serves good, inexpensive-to-moderate Thai food. **Bertucci's,** 1777 Mass. Ave. (☎ 781/860-9000), is a branch of the family-friendly pizzeria chain. At **Aesop's Bagels,** 1666 Massachusetts Ave. (☎ 781/674-2990), you can pick up a light meal.

Lexington has no B&Bs (Concord has country inns to spare, if that's what you want). The **Sheraton Lexington Inn,** 727 Marrett Rd. (☎ 781/862-8700), is at Exit 30B off I-95, 5 to 10 minutes from the center of town by car. It has a seasonal outdoor pool and the usual business-chain amenities. Doubles run $129 to $234.

En Route from Lexington to Concord

Minute Man National Historical Park

This 900-acre national park (www.nps.gov/mima) is in Lexington, Concord, and Lincoln. It preserves the scene of the first Revolutionary War battle, on April 19, 1775. A visit can take as little as half an hour, for a jaunt to Concord's North Bridge, to half a day or more, for stops at both visitor centers and perhaps a ranger-led program. The park is open daily, year-round. At the Lexington end, the **Battle Road Visitor Center,** off Route 2A, one-half mile west of I-95 (☎ 781/862-7753), is open mid-April through October, 9am to 5pm daily. Concord's **North Bridge Visitor Center,** 174 Liberty St., off Monument Street (☎ 978/369-6993), overlooks the Concord River and the bridge. It's open daily in summer 9am to 5:30pm and in winter 9:30am to 4pm.

Walden Pond

A pile of stones at the **Walden Pond State Reservation,** Route 126 (☎ 978/369-3254), marks the site of the cabin where Henry David Thoreau lived from 1845 to 1847. Today the picturesque park is an extremely popular destination for hiking (a path circles the pond), picnicking, swimming, and fishing. It's a great place to see fall foliage. From Memorial Day to Labor Day, a daily parking fee is charged and the lot fills early every day—call first to make sure there's room.

To get there from Lexington, take Mass. Ave. west to Route 2A, bear left onto Route 2, and turn left onto Route 126. From Concord, take Walden Street (Route 126) south, away from Concord Center, cross Route 2 and look for signs pointing to the parking lot.

Exploring Concord

The **North Bridge Visitor Center** (see above) makes a fine introduction to the town. Audio stations and plaques near the bridge (a replica) and Daniel Chester French's *Minute Man* statue tell the story of the battle, and the riverbank is a great place to stroll or picnic. "Author's Ridge" at **Sleepy Hollow Cemetery** (entrance on Route 62 west) holds the graves of some of the town's literary lights, including the Alcotts, Emerson, Hawthorne, and Thoreau.

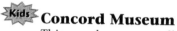 ## Concord Museum

This superb museum tells the story of the town through artifacts, murals, films, maps, documents, and other presentations, all expertly arranged and interpreted. One example: A lantern that signaled Paul Revere from the steeple of the Old North Church is on display, with enough explanatory material to show why it's a big deal but not enough to overwhelm you.

Lexington Rd. and Cambridge Turnpike. ☎ **978/369-9763.** *www.concordmuseum. org. Follow Lexington Rd. out of Concord Center and bear right at museum onto Cambridge Turnpike; entrance is on left. Parking on road is allowed.* **Admission:** *$6 adults, $5 seniors, $4 students, $3 children under 16, $12 families.* **Open:** *Apr–Dec, Mon–Sat 9am–5pm, Sun noon–5pm; Jan–Mar, Mon–Sat 11am–4pm, Sun 1–4pm.*

The Old Manse

Built in 1770 by the Rev. William Emerson (Ralph Waldo's grandfather), this house was occupied for almost 170 years by his widow, her second husband, their descendants, and briefly by newlyweds Nathaniel and Sophia Peabody Hawthorne. Mementos and memorabilia of the Emerson, Ripley, and Hawthorne families fill the house.

269 Monument St. (at North Bridge). ☎ **978/369-3909.** *From Concord Center, follow Monument St. until you see North Bridge parking lot on right; the Old Manse is on left.* **Guided tour:** *$5 adults, $4 students and seniors, $3.50 ages 6–12, $13 families (3–5 people).* **Open:** *Mid-Apr–Oct, Mon–Sat 10am–5pm and Sun and holidays noon–5pm. Closed Nov–mid-Apr.*

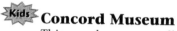 ## Orchard House

Little Women (1868), Louisa May Alcott's best-known and most popular work, was written and set at Orchard House. (Most of the events took place earlier, and the 1994 movie was filmed elsewhere.) Fans won't want to miss the excellent tour, copiously illustrated with family heirlooms.

399 Lexington Rd. ☎ **978/369-4118.** *www.louisamayalcott.org. Follow Lexington Rd. out of Concord Center past Concord Museum; house is on left. Overflow parking lot is across street.* **Guided tour:** *$6 adults, $5 seniors and students, $4 ages 6–17, $16.50 families (up to 2 adults and 4 children).* **Open:** *Apr–Oct, Mon–Sat 10am–4:30pm, Sun 1–4:30pm; Nov–Mar, Mon–Fri 11am–3pm, Sat 10am–4:30pm, Sun 1–4:30pm. Closed Jan 1–15, Easter, Thanksgiving, Dec 25.*

Ralph Waldo Emerson House

The philosopher, essayist, and poet moved here in 1835 and remained until his death in 1882. The tour gives a good look at the personal side of the great man and at the fashionably ornate interior decoration of the time.

28 Cambridge Turnpike. ☎ *978/369-2236. Follow Cambridge Turnpike out of Concord Center; just before Concord Museum, house is on right.* **Guided tour:** *$4.50 adults, $3 seniors and ages 7–17. Call to arrange group tours (10 people or more).* **Open:** *Mid-Apr–Oct, Thurs–Sat 10am–4:30pm, Sun 2–4:30pm. Closed Nov–mid-Apr.*

The Wayside

Part of Minute Man National Historical Park, the Wayside was Nathaniel Hawthorne's home from 1852 until his death in 1864. The Alcott family also lived here, as did Harriett Lothrop, who wrote the *Five Little Peppers* books (under the pen name Margaret Sidney). The fascinating tour illuminates the lives of the occupants and the house's crazy-quilt architecture.

455 Lexington Rd. ☎ *978/369-6975. www.nps.gov/mima. Follow Lexington Rd. out of Concord Center past Concord Museum and Orchard House; the Wayside is on left.* **Guided tour:** *$4 adults; children under 17 free.* **Open:** *Mid-Apr–Oct, Thurs–Tues 10:30am–4:30pm. Closed Nov–mid-Apr.*

Snacking & Sleeping

For basic-to-lavish picnic provisions, stop in downtown Concord at the **Cheese Shop,** 25–31 Walden St. (☎ **978/369-5778**), before setting out.

The 1716 **Colonial Inn,** 48 Monument Sq. (☎ **800/370-9200** or 978/ 369-9200), offers food and lodging in the center of town. There are two casual lounges that serve drinks and bar food, and a fancier restaurant that offers salads, sandwiches, and pasta at lunch and traditional American fare at dinner. From April to October, doubles in the historic main inn run $169 to $175; in the newer Prescott wing, $109 to $169.

Exploring Salem

In the immediate downtown area, walking is the way to go. To ride around, board the **Salem Trolley** (☎ **978/744-5469**; daily 10am to 5pm, April through October, weekends March and November) at the Essex Street side of the Visitor Center for a 1-hour narrated tour. Tickets ($8 adults, $7 students, $4 children 5 to 12, family $20) are good all day, and you can reboard as many times as you like at any of the 15 stops.

Kids Salem Maritime National Historic Site

Explanatory markers and several renovated and historic buildings dot the 9 acres that make up this waterfront site. Ranger-led tours vary according to seasonal schedules, and you can explore on your own. The newest exhibit is a full-size replica of a 1797 East Indian merchant vessel. The *Friendship* is a three-masted 171-footer docked alongside the site.

*174 Derby St. ☎ **978/740-1660**. www.nps.gov/sama. Take Derby St. east; just past Pickering Wharf, the orientation center is on the right. **Admission:** Free. **Guided tour:** $3 adults, $2 seniors and ages 6–16, $10 family. **Open:** Daily 9am–5pm. Closed Thanksgiving, Christmas, and New Year's Day.*

Kids The House of the Seven Gables

A cousin of Nathaniel Hawthorne's occupied this building, and stories and legends of the house and its inhabitants inspired his 1851 novel of the same name (an audiovisual program tells the story). The six rooms of period furniture include pieces referred to in the book, and a narrow, twisting secret staircase. The costumed guides can get a little silly as they mug for young visitors, but they're well versed in the history of the buildings and artifacts.

*54 Turner St. ☎ **978/744-0991**. www.7gables.org. From downtown, follow Derby St. east 3 blocks past Derby Wharf. **Guided tour:** $7 adults, $4 ages 6–17, free for children under 6. **Open:** May–Nov daily 10am–5pm; Dec–Apr Mon–Sat 10am–5pm, Sun noon–5pm. Closed Jan 1, Thanksgiving, Dec 25.*

Kids Peabody Essex Museum

This might be the best museum you've never heard of. The 1992 merger of the Peabody Museum and the Essex Institute combined fascinating collections that illustrate Salem's international adventures and its domestic development. Sign up for a tour of one or more historic houses or a gallery tour, or select from about a dozen pamphlets for self-guided tours on various topics.

*East India Square. ☎ **800/745-4054** or 978/745-9500. www.pem.org. Take Hawthorne Blvd. to Essex St., following signs for Visitor Center. Enter on Essex St. or New Liberty St. **Admission** (good on 2 consecutive days): $8.50 adults, $7.50 seniors and students with ID, $5 ages 6–16, $20 family. **Open:** Mon–Sat 10am–5pm, Sun noon–5pm. Closed Jan 1, Thanksgiving, Dec 25, Mon Nov–Memorial Day.*

Kids Salem Witch Museum

This is one of the most memorable attractions in eastern Massachusetts—it's both interesting and scary. It's a three-dimensional audiovisual presentation with life-size figures. The 30-minute narration dramatically but accurately tells the story of the witchcraft trials and the accompanying hysteria. (One man is pressed to death by rocks piled on a board on his chest—smaller children may need a reminder that he's not real.)

*$19\frac{1}{2}$ Washington Sq. ☎ **978/744-1692**. www.salemwitchmuseum.com. Follow Hawthorne Blvd. to the northwest corner of Salem Common. **Admission:** $6 adults, $5.50 seniors, $3.75 ages 6–14. **Open:** Sept–June, daily 10am–5pm; July–Aug, daily 10am–7pm. Closed Jan 1, Thanksgiving, Dec 25.*

Snacking & Sleeping

For a quick bite, seek out the dinerlike **Red's Sandwich Shop,** 15 Central St. (☎ 978/745-3527). It's cheap, good, and fast, and doesn't take credit cards. **In a Pig's Eye,** 148 Derby St. (☎ 978/741-4436), is a neighborhood tavern on the way to the House of the Seven Gables that serves great Mexican food and bar fare. One of the best restaurants on the North Shore is the moderate- to-expensive **Lyceum Bar & Grill,** 43 Church St. at Washington Street (☎ 978/745-7665). It serves creative American fare at lunch weekdays and dinner daily, and reservations are recommended.

History 101

On the traffic island across from the Salem Witch Museum is a statue that's easily mistaken for a witch. It's really Roger Conant, who founded Salem in 1626.

In the center of town, the **Hawthorne Hotel** overlooks Salem Common at 18 Washington Sq. (☎ 800/729-7829 or 978/744-4080; www.hawthornehotel. com). It dates from 1925 and is pleasantly appointed, though the rooms aren't huge. Doubles run about $99 to $182.

Exploring Marblehead

Marblehead is a wonderful place for aimless wandering, especially around "Old Town," the historic district. To add some structure, consult the Chamber of Commerce's walking tour pamphlet. Whatever else you do, be sure to spend some time enjoying the view from **Crocker Park** and **Fort Sewall,** on the harbor at opposite ends of Front Street.

Marblehead is a legendary (or notorious, if you're on a budget) shopping destination. All along Washington and Front streets, and scattered on Atlantic Avenue, shops and boutiques beckon.

Abbot Hall

Archibald M. Willard's famous painting *The Spirit of '76* is on display in the Selectmen's Meeting Room. The thrill of recognizing the ubiquitous drummer, drummer boy, and fife player is the main reason to stop here. The cases in the halls contain objects and artifacts from the collections of the Marblehead Historical Society.

Washington Sq. ☎ *781/631-0528. From the historic district, follow Washington St. up the hill toward the clock tower.* **Admission:** *Free.* **Open:** *Year-round, Mon, Tues, Thurs 8am–5pm, Wed 7:30am–7:30pm, Fri 8am–1pm; May–Oct, Fri 8am–5pm, Sat 9am–6pm, Sun 11am–6pm.*

Jeremiah Lee Mansion

Built in 1768 for a wealthy merchant, this is an outstanding example of pre-revolutionary Georgian architecture and worth a visit just to see the original hand-painted wallpaper. The Marblehead Historical Society's friendly guides are well versed in the history of the home and its renovations. The society occasionally offers walking tours of Marblehead and candlelight tours of the house. Call ahead to see if your schedules match.

161 Washington St. ☎ *781/631-1069. Follow Washington St. until it curves right and heads uphill toward Abbot Hall; house is on right.* **Guided tour:** *$4 adults, $3.50 students, free for children under 11.* **Open:** *Mid-May–Oct, Mon–Sat 10am–4pm, Sun 1–4pm. Closed Nov–mid-May.*

King Hooper Mansion

Shipping tycoon Robert Hooper lived well in this 1728 mansion, which gained a Georgian addition in 1747. The period furnishings, though not original, give a sense of the life of an 18th-century merchant prince. The building houses the Marblehead Arts Association, which stages monthly exhibits. The mansion also has a lovely garden; enter through the gate at the right of the house.

8 Hooper St. ☎ *781/631-2608. Look for the colorful sign where Washington St. curves at the foot of the hill near the Lee Mansion.* **Guided tour:** *Free; donation requested.* **Open:** *Mon–Sat 10am–4pm, Sun 1–5pm. Call ahead; no tours during private parties.*

Snacking & Sleeping

Consider a picnic or snack along the water. **Iggy's Bread of the World,** 5 Pleasant St. (☎ 781/639-4717), has fabulous gourmet baked goods and coffee. **Frostbiter's,** 78 Front St. (☎ 781/631-6222), serves sandwiches and all the trimmings; name notwithstanding, it closes in the winter. Both have small seating areas, but really, go outside. Almost as good as outside is the dining room at the **Barnacle,** 141 Front St. (☎ 781/631-4236), which serves lunch and dinner daily. It's moderately priced and doesn't take reservations or credit cards, but the view is amazing and the food tasty, plentiful, and fresh.

This is B&B heaven; the Chamber of Commerce accommodations listings include many of the town's innumerable inns and bed-and-breakfasts. Call or write for a pamphlet. The 21-unit **Harbor Light Inn,** 58 Washington St. (☎ 781/631-2186), is the largest in town and has a heated outdoor pool. The double rate of $105 to $155 includes continental breakfast.

A Tasty Detour en Route to Cape Ann

If you approach or leave Cape Ann on Route 128, turn away from Gloucester on Route 133 and head west to **Essex.** It's a beautiful little town known for Essex clams, salt marshes, shipbuilding, antique shops, and one celebrated restaurant. Legend has it that **Woodman's of Essex,** Main Street (☎ 800/649-1773 or 978/768-6451), was the birthplace of the fried clam in 1916. Today the thriving family business is a great spot to join legions of locals and visitors from around the world for lobster "in the rough," steamers, corn on the cob, onion rings, and (you guessed it) fried clams. Expect the line to be long, even in the winter, but it moves quickly and offers a good view of the regimented commotion in the food-preparation area. Eat in a booth, upstairs on the deck, or out back at a picnic table. Credit cards aren't accepted, but there's an ATM on the premises.

Exploring Gloucester

On Stacy Boulevard, west of downtown, one of the area's best-known pieces of art stands as a reminder of the sea's danger. Leonard Craske's bronze statue of the Gloucester Fisherman, known as "The Man at the Wheel," bears the inscription "They That Go Down to the Sea in Ships 1623–1923." More than 10,000 fishermen lost their lives during the city's first 300 years.

To reach East Gloucester, follow signs as you leave downtown or go directly from Route 128, Exit 9. On East Main Street, you'll see signs for the world-famous **Rocky Neck Art Colony,** the oldest continuously operating art colony in the country. Park in the lot on the tiny causeway and head west along Rocky Neck Avenue, which abounds with studios, galleries, restaurants, and people. The draw is the presence of working artists, not just shops that happen to sell art. Most galleries are open daily in the summer, 10am to 10pm.

Whale-Force Winds

The listings in chapter 14 include a full description of whale watching. If you didn't have a chance in Boston, Gloucester is a center for the cruises. Downtown you'll find **Cape Ann Whale Watch** (☎ 800/877-5110 or 978/283-5110; www.caww.com), **Capt. Bill's Whale Watch** (☎ 800/ 33-WHALE or 978/283-6995; www.cape-ann.com/captbill.html), and **Seven Seas Whale Watch** (☎ 800/238-1776 or 978/283-1776; www.cape-ann. com/whalewatch.html). At the Cape Ann Marina, off Route 133, is **Yankee Whale Watch** (☎ 800/WHALING or 508/283-0313; www.yankee-fleet. com/whale.htm).

Beauport (Sleeper-McCann House)

Interior designer Henry Davis Sleeper adorned his "fantasy house" with vast collections of American and European art and antiques. From 1907 to 1934, he decorated the 40 rooms, 26 of which are covered on the entertaining tour, to illustrate literary and historical themes. Note that the house, operated by the Society for the Preservation of New England Antiquities, is closed on summer weekends.

75 Eastern Point Blvd. ☎ *978/283-0800. www.spnea.org. Take East Main St. south to Eastern Point Blvd. (a private road), drive ½ mile to house, park on left.* **Guided tour:** *$6 adults, $5.50 seniors, $3 ages 6–12.* **Open:** *Tours on the hour mid-May–mid-Oct, Mon–Fri 10am–4pm; mid-Sept–mid-Oct daily 10am–4pm. Closed mid-Oct–mid-May and summer weekends.*

Cape Ann Historical Museum

Here you'll get an excellent introduction to Cape Ann's history and artists. An entire gallery holds extraordinary works by the American Luminist painter Fitz Hugh Lane, a Gloucester native. Other galleries feature contemporary works, and the maritime and fisheries galleries contain fascinating exhibits on the fishing industry, ship models, and historic photographs and models of the Gloucester waterfront. The Captain Elias Davis House (1804), decorated and furnished in Federal style, is part of the museum.

27 Pleasant St. ☎ **978/283-0455.** *Follow Main St. west through downtown and turn right onto Pleasant St.; the museum is 1 block up on right. Metered parking available on street or in lot across street.* **Admission:** *$4 adults, $3.50 seniors, $2.50 students, free for children under 6.* **Open:** *Tues–Sat 10am–5pm. Closed Feb.*

Snacking & Sleeping

You've come all this way; you might as well do things right and eat at the celebrated **Woodman's of Essex** (see "A Tasty Detour en Route to Cape Ann," above). If you can't manage it, a congenial alternative is the **Boulevard Oceanview Restaurant,** 25 Western Ave., on Stacy Boulevard (☎ **978/281-2949**). It serves inexpensive sandwiches and terrific moderately priced Portuguese specialties and seafood in a dinerlike atmosphere. Reservations are recommended at dinner in the summer.

The **Best Western Bass Rocks Ocean Inn,** 107 Atlantic Rd. (☎ **800/528-1234** or 978/283-7600), across the street from the ocean, is open from late April to October. Doubles, all with water views, start at $105 in the spring and top out at $170 in the summer, and rates include continental breakfast.

Exploring Rockport

Stop by the Chamber of Commerce or its information booth and pick up a walking-tour map. There's no big museum or other must-see tourist attraction, so it's easy to forget that there's more to Rockport than knickknack shopping. You just have to look.

But first you need some postcards and key chains. **Bearskin Neck,** named after an unfortunate ursine visitor that drowned and washed ashore in 1800, has perhaps the highest concentration of gift shops anywhere. You'll find dozens of little shops carrying clothes, gifts, toys, inexpensive novelties, and expensive handmade crafts and paintings.

More than two dozen art galleries display the works of local and nationally known artists. The **Rockport Art Association,** 12 Main St. (☎ **978/546-6604**), open daily year-round, sponsors major exhibitions and special shows throughout the year.

To get a sense of the power of the sea, take Route 127 north of town to the very tip of Cape Ann. **Halibut Point State Park** (☎ **978/546-2997**) has a staffed visitor center, walking trails, tidal pools, and water-filled quarries (swimming is absolutely forbidden). Guided tours (for $2.50 per person) are available on Saturday mornings in the summer, and this is a great place just to wander around and admire the scenery. On a clear day, you can see Maine.

Tourist Traps

The most famous example of what to see in Rockport has something of an "Emperor's New Clothes" aura—it's a wooden fish warehouse on the town wharf. The barn-red shack (often erroneously rendered in bright red), known as **Motif No. 1,** is the most frequently painted object in a town filled with lovely buildings and surrounded by rocky coastline. You may find yourself initiating or overhearing conversations about what the big deal is. If you figure it out, speak up.

Snacking & Sleeping

One more reason to visit **Woodman's of Essex** (see "A Tasty Detour en Route to Cape Ann," above): Rockport is a dry town. Its best restaurant is the **Greenery,** 15 Dock Sq. (☎ 978/546-9593), open mid-April to October. Rather than exploiting its great location, at the head of Bearskin Neck, it offers high quality at moderate prices. Reservations are recommended at dinner, and there's a take-out counter. On Bearskin Neck, the **Portside Chowder House** (☎ 978/546-7045) serves delicious fresh chowder by the cup, pint, and quart.

Rockport overflows with B&Bs—the Chamber of Commerce publishes a pamphlet that lists many of them. The **Inn on Cove Hill,** 37 Mt. Pleasant St., Route 127A (☎ 888/546-2701 or 978/546-2701; www.cape-ann.com/covehill), has just 11 rooms. Its moderate prices—$68 to $115 for a double with private bathroom, $50 for one of the two rooms with a shared bathroom—include continental breakfast. The inn accepts children 12 and older, and is closed from November to mid-April.

Exploring Plymouth

Kids The logical place to begin (good luck talking children out of it) is where the Pilgrims first set foot—at **Plymouth Rock.** The rock, accepted as the landing place of the *Mayflower* passengers, was originally 15 feet long and 3 feet wide. It was moved several times before assuming its present permanent position. It's not much to look at, but the accompanying descriptions are interesting, and the sense of history is curiously impressive.

Plymouth Rock Trolley, 22 Main St. (☎ 508/747-3419), offers a narrated tour and unlimited reboarding privileges daily Memorial Day to October and weekends through Thanksgiving. It's a good idea if young children are along. Tickets are $7 for adults and $3 for ages 3 to 12. Trolley markers indicate the stops, which are served every 20 minutes.

To put yourself in the Pilgrims' footsteps, take a **Colonial Lantern Tour** offered by New World Tours, 98 Water St. (☎ **800/698-5636** or 508/747-4161). Participants carry pierced-tin lanterns on a 90-minute walking tour of the original settlement under the direction of a knowledgeable guide. Tours run nightly, late March through Thanksgiving. The standard history tour leaves the New World office at 7:30pm; the "Legends and Lore" tour leaves from the lobby of the John Carver Inn, 25 Summer St., at 9pm. Tickets are $9 for adults, $7 for children.

Kids Mayflower II

Berthed a few steps from Plymouth Rock, *Mayflower II* is a full-scale reproduction of the type of ship that brought the Pilgrims from England to Plymouth in 1620. Even at full scale, the 106½-foot vessel, constructed in England from 1955 to 1957, is remarkably small. In 1997, 2 to 3 years of extensive reconstruction and renovation work began. The exhibit incorporates workers' explanations and interpretations of their efforts. (Ordinarily, costumed guides provide first-person narratives about the vessel and voyage.)

State Pier. ☎ *508/746-1622. www.plimoth.org/mayflowe.htm.* **Admission:** *$5.75 adults, $3.75 children 6–12, free for children under 6. Mayflower II and Plimoth Plantation admission $18.50 adults, $16.50 seniors, $11 children 6–12, free for children under 6.* **Open:** *Apr–Nov daily 9am–5pm.*

Kids Plymouth National Wax Museum

The galleries here hold more than 180 life-size figures, and dramatic sound tracks tell the stories. They illustrate the Pilgrims' move to Holland to escape persecution in England, the harrowing trip to the New World, the first Thanksgiving, and even the tale of Myles Standish, Priscilla Mullins, and John Alden. This museum is a must if children are in your party, and adults will enjoy it, too.

16 Carver St. ☎ *508/746-6468. From Plymouth Rock, turn around and walk up the hill or the steps.* **Admission:** *$5.50 adults, $5 seniors, $2.25 ages 5–12, free for children under 5.* **Open:** *Mar–June and Sept–Nov, daily 9am–5pm; July–Aug, daily 9am–9pm. Closed Dec–Feb.*

Pilgrim Hall Museum

Here you'll get a sense of the day-to-day lives of Plymouth's first white residents through many original possessions of the early Pilgrims and their descendants. Displays include an uncomfortable chair that belonged to William Brewster (alongside a modern-day model—that's how you can tell it's uncomfortable), one of Myles Standish's swords, and Governor Bradford's Bible.

75 Court St. ☎ *508/746-1620. www.pilgrimhall.org. From Plymouth Rock, walk north on Water St. and up the hill on Chilton St.* **Admission:** *$5 adults, $4.50 seniors and AAA members, $3 children.* **Open:** *Feb–Dec daily 9:30am–4:30pm. Closed Jan.*

⭐Kids⭐ Plimoth Plantation

Allow at least half a day to explore this re-creation of the 1627 Pilgrim village, which both children and adults will find interesting. The "Pilgrims" are actors who assume the personalities of members of the original community and take part in typical activities, using only the tools and cookware available at the time. Wear comfortable shoes, because you'll be walking all over, and the plantation isn't paved.

Route 3. ☎ *508/746-1622. www.plimoth.org. From Route 3, take Exit 4, "Plimoth Plantation Highway."* **Admission:** *$15 adults, $9 children 6–12, free for children under 6. Plimoth Plantation and Mayflower II admission $18.50 adults, $16.50 seniors, $11 ages 6–17, free for children under 6.* **Open:** *Apr–Nov daily 9am–5pm. Closed Dec–March.*

⭐Kids⭐ Cranberry World

One of southeastern Massachusetts's claims to fame is the cranberry, the focus of Ocean Spray's interesting visitor center. Displays include outdoor demonstration bogs, antique harvesting tools, a scale model of a cranberry farm, and interactive exhibits.

225 Water St. ☎ *508/747-2350. From Plymouth Rock, walk north for 10 minutes right along the waterfront.* **Admission:** *Free.* **Open:** *May–Nov daily 9:30am–5pm. Guided tours available; call for reservations. Closed Dec–Apr.*

Snacking & Sleeping

On Town Wharf, off Water Street, the **Lobster Hut** (☎ **508/746-2270**) is an inexpensive self-service seafood restaurant with a great view and excellent "rolls" (hot dog buns with your choice of filling). Beer and wine are served, but only with meals. The moderately priced **Run of the Mill Tavern** (☎ **508/830-1262**) is near the water wheel at Jenney Grist Mill Village in Town Brook Park off Summer Street. It serves good bar fare and seafood in an attractive setting; the clam chowder is fantastic. Reservations are recommended at dinner.

Destination Plymouth's **Historic Value Vacation Package** program offers 3- and 4-night packages (2 nights in April, May, and November) that include a good deal on a room and free admission to a variety of attractions. Prices start at $100 per person, double occupancy. One participating hotel is the **John Carver Inn**, 25 Summer St. (☎ **800/274-1620** or 508/746-7100). It offers comfortable, modern accommodations, a large outdoor pool, and all the amenities, including room service. Doubles go for $99 to $179 in the summer and fall, less in the off-season.

Exploring Sandwich

You might never again hear the word *quaint* used this often (or this accurately). As you wander along Main Street near River Street and the 1640 grist mill, the centuries fall away—especially if you can tune out the whoosh of passing traffic. The town is at one end of the 7-mile Cape Cod Canal, which has a paved pedestrian and bike path. The terrain is flat, and the view and the variety of shipping are great. There's parking off Route 6A, north of the center of town.

🎯Kids Heritage Plantation

The plantation's 76 gorgeously landscaped and planted acres are worth a visit all by themselves. But wait—the buildings (one is a round stone barn) hold displays that include early American art, antique autos, military artifacts, and, best of all, a 1912 carousel with hand-carved animals in addition to horses. Allow at least 2 hours.

Grove and Pine sts., off Route 130, southwest of town center. ☎ ***508/888-3300.*** **Admission:** *$9 adults, $7 seniors, $4.50 children 6–18, free for children under 6.* **Open:** *Mid-May–Oct daily 10am–5pm; last admission at 4:15pm. Closed Nov–mid-May.*

Sandwich Glass Museum

Fans of history as well as crafts will revel in this museum, especially when sunlight floods through the colored-glass displays in front of the windows. Sandwich was a center of glass manufacturing in the 19th century, and the displays use rare authentic local products to illustrate the rise and fall of the industry.

129 Main St., in center of town. ☎ ***508/888-0251.*** **Admission:** *$3.50 adults, $1 children 6–12, free for children under 6.* **Open:** *Daily Apr–Oct 9:30am–4:30pm; Feb–Mar and Nov–Dec 9:30am–4pm. Closed Jan, Thanksgiving, Dec 25.*

🎯Kids Yesteryear's Doll & Miniature Museum

Doll collectors will want to head straight here and not leave, but nondevotees will probably find the catch-as-catch-can exhibit style somewhat vexing. If you're in the spirit, hundreds of dolls from various eras and countries arranged in apparently random order make this a great place for a multigenerational game of "Hey, remember this?"

Play Ball!

The 10-team **Cape Cod Baseball League** (usually just called the Cape League) attracts the best amateur players from around the country. They play from late June to early August, and when they're not playing or practicing, they're living with local families and holding down part-time jobs. Admission is free; you make a donation when the host team passes the hat. The Chatham A's play at Veterans Field, on Depot Street; check the local or Boston papers for schedules.

Main and River sts. ☎ *508/888-1711.* **Admission:** *$3 adults, $2.50 seniors, $1.50 children under 13.* **Open:** *Mid-May–Oct Mon–Sat 10am–4pm. Closed Nov–mid-May.*

Snacking & Sleeping

If you can excuse the goofy name, the **Dan'l Webster Inn,** 149 Main St., is a good choice for bed (☎ **800/444-3566** or 508/888-3622) and board (☎ **508/888-3623**). The chef grows his own fish, so to speak—aquacultured striped bass is a specialty—and the moderate-to-expensive fare draws locals as well as visitors. Guest rooms are good-sized, and there's an outdoor pool. Doubles in the summer and fall run $139 to $209; the plush suites ($209 to $350) are in nearby houses.

Exploring Chatham

Take off your watch and open your eyes as you wander around the loveliest town on the Cape (as you might imagine, a highly competitive category). Main Street is one of the area's best **shopping** destinations, with a good mix of merchandise and prices. On Friday in July and August at 8pm, there are **free band concerts** (☎ **508/945-5199**) in Kate Gould Park, off Main Street. Bring a blanket in the afternoon to stake out your patch of grass.

In the car, follow Main Street through the center of town; where it ends, turn right and follow Shore Road till it ends in a short-term parking lot. This is **Chatham Light,** built in 1878 and surrounded by breathtaking scenery. In the other direction on Shore Road, you'll come to the **Chatham Fish Pier,** which has a visitors' gallery where you can watch the fleet unloading its catch in the mid- to late afternoon, depending on the tide.

Snacking & Sleeping

The **Chatham Squire,** 487 Main St. (☎ **508/945-0945**), is in its fourth decade as a classic local hangout. There's pretty good bar food before the live music gets going, or you can stop in for a beer. The **Impudent Oyster,** 15 Chatham Bars Ave., off Main Street (☎ **508/945-3545**), serves adventurous international seafood preparations in the land of fried clams. It's moderate to expensive, and reservations are recommended at dinner.

Chatham's accommodations tend to be pricey—there are even two sprawling resorts. A good break and a good value is the **Seafarer of Chatham,** 2079 Route 28, at Main Street and Ridgevale Road (☎ **800/786-2772** or 508/ 432-1739). It's a 20-room motel, where doubles top out at $145 at the height of summer.

Exploring Provincetown

Even if you're just in town for a few hours, you'll have time to wander around and soak up the scenery and atmosphere that make "P-town" such a popular destination. If you're feeling energetic, snag a map at the Chamber of Commerce and head in any direction to enjoy the waterfront vistas.

Commercial Street is a famous shopping destination not just for the variety of shops but for the phenomenal people-watching. On busy weekend afternoons, when Midwestern grandparents mingle with aspiring drag queens, it's easy to forget that you're a stone's throw from excellent gift shops, kid-friendly toy and candy stores, and world-class art galleries. The best way to get a sense of the local art scene—besides just wandering the streets—is to stop in at the **Provincetown Art Association & Museum,** 460 Commercial St. (☎ **508/487-1750**). It's open daily from Memorial Day to October (call for off-season hours), and the suggested donation is $3.

⭐Kids Pilgrim Monument & Provincetown Museum

The landmark tower is impossible to miss, and you won't want to skip it. After using stairs and ramps to reach the top of the 252-foot monument, you're rewarded with a panoramic view that includes Boston when the skies are clear. On the lower level, the quirky museum contains *Mayflower* artifacts, model ships, and arts memorabilia.

High Pole Hill, Winslow St. off Route 6. ☎ ***800/247-1620*** *or 508/487-1310.* ***Admission:*** *$5 adults, $3 children 4–12, free for children under 4.* ***Open:*** *Daily July–Aug 9am–7pm (last admission at 6:15pm), Sept–Nov and Apr–June 9am–5pm (last admission at 4:15). Closed Dec–March.*

Snacking & Sleeping

The **Provincetown Portuguese Bakery,** 299 Commercial St. (☎ **508/ 487-1803**), is *the* place to go for pastries, meat pies, and sweet bread. Take your delicacies outside for an alfresco snack. It's open April to October. For a casual meal with a harbor view, **Bubala's by the Bay,** 183 Commercial St. (☎ **508/487-0773**), is a good moderately priced choice. The only problem might be making up your mind—the menu runs from waffles to mussels.

If you've decided to stay overnight, options cover the whole scale—gay, straight, family, single, from basic cot to over-the-top pampering. You'll soon be awash in brochures and suggestions. A reliable if unadventurous choice is the **Holiday Inn,** 698 Commercial St., in the east end of town (☎ **800/ 422-4224** or 508/487-1711). It's a 78-room motel with an outdoor pool. Doubles in the summer go for about $150, and it's closed from November to April.

Boston A to Z:
Facts at Your Fingertips

American Automobile Association (AAA)   Road service ☎ **800/222-4357;** other services ☎ **800/222-8252.** The Boston office is in the Financial District at 125 High St., off Pearl Street.

Ambulance   Dial ☎ **911.**

American Express   The main local office is at 1 Court St. (☎ **617/723-8400**), close to the Government Center and State Street T stops. It's open weekdays from 8:30am to 5:30pm. The Cambridge office, just off Harvard Square at 39 John F. Kennedy St. (☎ **617/661-0005**), is open weekdays from 9am to 5pm and Saturday from 11am to 3pm.

Area Code   For Boston and the immediate suburbs, it's **617;** for other nearby suburbs, **781, 508,** or **978.**

Baby-Sitters   Many hotels maintain lists of reliable sitters; check at the front desk or with the concierge. See chapter 1 for information about the agency **Parents in a Pinch** (☎ **617/739-KIDS**).

Camera Repair   Try **Bromfield Camera & Video,** 10 Bromfield St. (☎ **800/723-2628** or 617/426-5230), near Downtown Crossing, or the **Camera Center,** 107 State St. (☎ **800/924-6899** or 617/227-7255), in the Financial District.

Dentists   The desk staff or concierge at your hotel might be able to provide the name of a dentist. The **Metropolitan District Dental Society** (☎ **508/651-3521**) can point you toward a member of the Massachusetts Dental Society.

Doctors   Check with your hotel desk staff or concierge. Or try a service such as the **Beth Israel Deaconess Health Information Line** (☎ **617/667-5356**), **Brigham and Women's Hospital Physician Referral Service** (☎ **800/294-9999**), **Massachusetts General Hospital Physician Referral Service** (☎ **800/711-4-MGH**), or **New England Medical Center Physician Referral Service** (☎ **617/636-9700**).

Emergencies   Call ☎ **911** for fire, ambulance, or the Boston, Brookline, or Cambridge police. This is a free call from pay phones.

Hospitals   The hospitals closest to downtown Boston are **Massachusetts General Hospital,** 55 Fruit St. (☎ **617/726-2000,** or 617/726-4100 for children's emergency services), and **New England Medical Center,** 750 Washington St. (☎ **617/636-5000,** or 617/636-5566 for emergency services). At the Harvard Medical Area on the Boston-Brookline border are, among others, **Beth Israel Deaconess Medical Center,** 330 Brookline Ave. (☎ **617/667-7000**); **Brigham and Women's Hospital,** 75 Francis St. (☎ **617/732-5500**); and **Children's Hospital,** 300 Longwood Ave. (☎ **617/ 355-6000,** or 617/355-6611 for emergency services). In Cambridge are **Mount Auburn Hospital,** 330 Mount Auburn St. (☎ **617/492-3500,** or 617/499-5025 for emergency services), and **Cambridge Hospital,** 1493 Cambridge St. (☎ **617/498-1000**).

Hot Lines   **AIDS Hotline** (☎ **800/235-2331** or 617/536-7733), **Poison Control Center** (☎ **617/232-2120**), **Rape Crisis** (☎ **617/492-7273**), **Samaritans Suicide Prevention** (☎ **617/247-0220**), **Samariteens** (☎ **800/252-8336** or 617/247-8050).

Information   For the Greater Boston Convention & Visitors Bureau, call ☎ **800/SEE-BOSTON** or 617/536-4100. For telephone directcry assistance, dial ☎ **411.**

Liquor Laws   The legal drinking age is 21. In many bars and clubs, particularly near college campuses, you might be asked for ID if you appear to be under 30 or so. At sporting events, everyone buying alcohol is asked to show ID. Alcohol is sold in liquor stores and a few supermarkets and convenience stores. Liquor stores (and the liquor sections of supermarkets) are closed on Sunday, but alcohol may be served in restaurants and bars. Some suburban towns, notably Rockport, are "dry."

Maps   You can pick up a map at any visitor information center (see "Face Time: Getting Information in Person," in chapter 7), at most hotels, and from the clerks in most T token booths.

Newspapers/Magazines   The *Boston Globe* and *Boston Herald* are published daily. The weekly *Boston Phoenix* (available on newsstands) and biweekly *Improper Bostonian* (free from newspaper boxes), carry arts coverage and entertainment and restaurant listings. *Boston* magazine is a lifestyle-oriented monthly.

Pharmacies (Late-Night)   The pharmacy at the **CVS** in the Porter Square Shopping Center, off Mass. Ave. in Cambridge (☎ **617/876-5519**), is open 24 hours, 7 days a week. The pharmacy at the **CVS** at 155–157 Charles St. in Boston (☎ **617/523-1028**), next to the Charles T stop, is open until midnight. Some emergency rooms can fill your prescription at the hospital's pharmacy.

Police   Call ☎ **911** for emergencies.

Rest Rooms   The visitor center at 15 State St. has a public rest room, as do most tourist attractions, hotels, department stores, and public buildings. If you're walking the Freedom Trail, especially with children, be sure to use the rest room before venturing into the North End, which has no public facilities. There are rest rooms at the CambridgeSide Galleria, Copley Place, Prudential Center, and Quincy Market shopping areas. One of the few public rest rooms in Harvard Square is in the Harvard Coop.

Safety   On the whole, Boston is a safe city for walking. As in any large city, stay out of parks (including the Esplanade) at night unless you're in a crowd. In general, trust your instincts—a dark, deserted street is probably deserted for a reason. Specific areas to avoid at night include Boylston Street between Tremont and Washington streets, and Tremont Street from Stuart to Boylston streets. And watch your step anywhere near the Big Dig (that is, most of downtown), where walking surfaces can be uneven. Public transportation in the areas you're likely to visit is busy and safe, but service stops between 12:30 and 1am.

Taxes   The sales tax is 5%. It doesn't apply to food, prescription drugs, newspapers, or clothing costing less than $175. The lodging tax is 12.45% in Boston and Cambridge; the state meal tax (which also applies to take-out food) is 5%.

Taxis   To call ahead in Boston, try the **Independent Taxi Operators Association,** or ITOA (☎ **617/426-8700**); **Boston Cab** (☎ **617/536-5010**); **Town Taxi** (☎ **617/536-5000**); or **Checker Taxi** (☎ **617/536-7000**). In Cambridge, call **Ambassador Brattle** (☎ **617/492-1100**) or **Yellow Cab** (☎ **617/547-3000**). For more information, see "All Hail: Getting a Taxi," in chapter 8.

Time Zone   Boston is in the Eastern time zone. Daylight saving time begins on the first Sunday in April and ends on the last Sunday in October.

Transit Information   The **MBTA** (☎ **617/222-3200**; www.mbta.com) runs the subways and local buses. The **Massachusetts Port Authority** (☎ **800/23LOGAN**; www.massport.com) coordinates public transportation to and from the airport.

Weather   Call ☎ **617/936-1234** for forecasts.

Index

Page numbers in *italics* refer to maps.

282

DATE DUE